Other books by David Yeadon

NEW YORK NIGHTS
SECLUDED ISLANDS OF THE ATLANTIC COAST
FREE NEW YORK
BACKROAD JOURNEYS OF SOUTHERN EUROPE
HIDDEN CORNERS OF BRITAIN
BACKROAD JOURNEYS OF THE WEST COAST STATES
WHEN THE EARTH WAS YOUNG
HIDDEN CORNERS OF NEW ENGLAND
HIDDEN CORNERS OF THE MID-ATLANTIC STATES
SUMPTUOUS INDULGENCE ON A SHOESTRING
NEW YORK BOOK OF BARS, PUBS AND TAVERNS
WINE TASTING IN CALIFORNIA
SMALL TOWNS OF CALIFORNIA
HIDDEN RESTAURANTS OF CALIFORNIA

NEW YORK'S

NOOKS AND CRANNIES

NEW YORK'S

NOOKS AND CRANNIES

*Unusual Walking Tours
in All Five Boroughs*

Written and Illustrated by
DAVID YEADON

CHARLES SCRIBNER'S SONS   *New York*

Library of Congress Cataloging-in-Publication Data

Yeadon, David.
New York's nooks and crannies.

Rev. ed. of: Nooks and crannies, c1979.
Includes index.
1. New York (N.Y.)—Description—1981-   —Tours.
2. Walking—New York (N.Y.)—Guide-books. I. Yeadon, David.
Nooks and crannies. II. Title.
F128.18.Y4   1986   917.47'10443   86-6732
ISBN 0-684-18610-1

Published simultaneously in Canada
by Collier Macmillan Canada, Inc.

Composition by Haddon Craftsmen, Scranton, Pennsylvania

Manufactured by Fairfield Graphics, Fairfield, Pennsylvania

Designed by Susan Lu

Revised Edition

For my wife,
ANNE

Contents

List of Illustrations

Introduction

There was a time when I thought I knew New York City. I'd visited all the main attractions and dozens of other lesser-known museums, parks, and historic niches described in the better guidebooks. I'd written about the city, sketched it, photographed it, and used up at least a dozen pairs of shoes on its sidewalks. Yet, as I was soon to learn, I hardly knew the city at all.

One summer morning on the Upper West Side a friend happened to show me Pomander Walk, a charming little alley of Tudor-style cottages graced with privet hedges and tiny lamp posts. I was suddenly in England. The din and bustle of Broadway was left outside the iron gates; inside it was as cozy as a Somerset village. Someone was sitting on a doorstep reading a newspaper and drinking tea, sparrows chirped among the window boxes brimming with geraniums, and a lady with a feather duster (I hadn't seen a feather duster since my last visit to Yorkshire) peered at me through an upstairs window framed by bright blue shutters. I smiled and, wonder of wonders, she smiled back.

So began my rediscovery of the city. Soon, thanks to advice from friends and their friends, I accumulated a tantalizing list of riverside walks, architectural oddities, markets, strange museums, forgotten parks (even precise directions to an unspoiled river gorge), a farmhouse in the heart of the city, a rooftop jungle, a bank where concert pianists gave lunchtime renditions of Chopin, the most authentic (and least-known) Italian neighborhood in the five boroughs, and a Maine-flavored fishing village easily reached by subway.

Nook-and-cranny exploration began to absorb most of my weekends, then a good portion of my weeks. Projects stalled and faltered as I scampered off, sketchbook in hand, to visit Dead Horse Bay, a 1694 Quaker meetinghouse in Flushing, exotic gingerbread mansions in Bay Ridge, the most ornate cemetery entrance and gatehouse in the country (just a short stroll from Prospect Park), an unspoiled ravine complete with waterfalls and deep pools, a silent hemlock forest in the midst of turbulent urbanity, Aunt Len's Doll and Toy collection in northern Manhattan, a famous mystics museum, and a row of Greek "temples" along the waterfront on Staten Island.

I found a place to rent a horse in the heart of Manhattan, went deep-sea fishing with an ex-naval captain, listened to Reverend Ike's "gospel of green power" at the most sumptuous theater in the city, strolled the conservatory gardens in Central Park (one of its lesser-known attractions), watched the auctions at Sotheby Parke-Bernet, and relaxed on the green of a typical English village in the heart of Queens.

And that was merely the beginning.

Here I am, eight years later, still in love with the city, still seeking out its nooks and crannies, and still trying to keep up with the amazing rate of change and revival all over the five boroughs.

It seems hard to believe that a few years back New York was being written off with somber certainty by sociologists, economists, city planners, politicians, and a host of other noted doomsayers. Even a President joined the fray (remember Ford's "get lost" quote in banner headlines?).

And look at the old place now! Manhattan is, once again, a national and international nexus; focus of information, media, financial, and cultural activities; favorite of the baby-boom generation in their "yuppie" guises; a white-collar whirl of computer-users and communication executives; a phenomenon of almost overnight rejuvenation, spurred on by the sheer momentum and in-crowd glitz of its new attractions and possibilities. A Renaissance is occurring in almost every neighborhood (including several areas once considered by the experts to be beyond hope). New museums, new cultural attractions, hundreds of new restaurants and wateringholes are popping up, while cloud-clutching towers, new parks, and vast new opportunities for the pursuit of an ever-more tangible "American Dream" are being realized. True, there are inequities to be resolved and living conditions to be improved for thousands of disadvantaged citizens, but the attitude is right for such reforms; the melting pot bubbles with renewed vigor, the Big Apple bulges with new energy and excitement and promises even greater glories in the immediate future.

It's taken a long time—far longer than I expected—to put this book together. The problem was knowing where and when to stop. Even now my files are packed with unused clippings, photographs, hand-scribbled notes, and messages from friends beginning "I've just found this wonderful . . ." But publishers get a little nervous about thousand-page books and authors occasionally need a rest. So, readers should regard the book's 500-plus "unusual-things-to-see-and-places-to-go" as not necessarily all-encompassing, but a significant introduction to a lesser-known New York. The book should be used as a starting point for fresh discoveries and even more varied walking tours. The Mini-Tours section particularly is designed to encourage users to plan their own itineraries and routes. Newcomers will find opportunities to leave the tourist crowds and the trinket stands behind; long-time residents will rediscover their city and experience the thrill of exploring one of the most exciting and kaleidoscopic urban environments in the world.

New York, New York—you're still the greatest!

WALKING TOURS

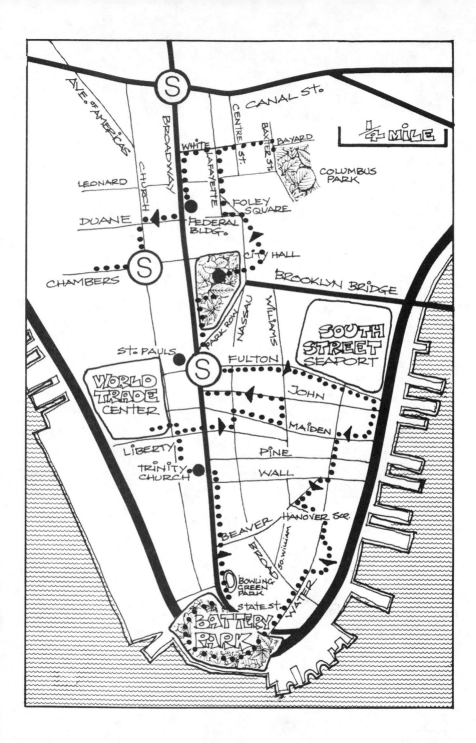

1 | Downtown

There's much more to downtown than ferry trips to the Statue of Liberty and city-views from the top of the World Trade Center. This walk reveals many of the area's lesser-known delights and surprises. Enjoy!

Peering into the canyons of downtown, one feels on the edge of a mythical city—a Dürer-like creation of towers, turrets, pinnacles, battlements, Gothic traceries, Romanesque arches, flying buttresses, and cloud-whipped eyries. Dark passages pierce the lower gloom of the crevasses while high up, hundreds of feet above the insectlike scurryings of the sidewalk crowds, the sun burnishes brilliant gold spires and highlights the grotesque gargoyles, the godlike statues of toga-clad damsels and bearded, sword-wielding men of Herculean proportions. (That some of the most exotic towers and spires are mere water tanks in disguise in no way detracts from their romantic appearance.)

But this downtown possesses other moods, other images. Four

☞ **DIRECTIONS**
Subway: *Start:* IRT 4, 5 to Fulton Street/Broadway or IND A or CC to Fulton Street/Nassau Street
Bus: *Start:* M1, M6
Return: IRT 1, 2, 3 from Chambers Street/West Broadway
Return: M1, M6

A.M. on a cool spring morning, for example, is the best time to visit the South Street Seaport area at the east end of Fulton Street. The fish market is a hullaballoo of roaring trucks, bawling merchants, hook-wielding hands tugging hundred-pound tuna across the slippery cobbles, and workers downing their beers and boiler-makers on early-morning breaks.

Then there are the quiet places—little-known parks, narrow alleys with the flavor of Amsterdam, secluded museums, and silent churches smelling of incense and redolent with history. Downtown is all this and much more, as we'll discover on this leisurely stroll.

We begin at South Street. Arrive just after breakfast on a weekday morning, say around 9:30 A.M., and beat the tourist crowds to the Seaport restoration. If this is your first time here, pick up some of the descriptive literature and enjoy this worn remnant of New York's maritime history. It's a wonderful "museum-without-walls" featuring exhibitions on all aspects of waterfront development, recreations of nineteenth-century stores, such as the printing office of Bowne and Co., on Water Street, and screenings of the "Seaport Experience" multimedia pop-history (call 669–9424 for details). Tour the Fulton Street Fish Market, where the day's catch is displayed, and explore the old ships *Peking* (1911) and *Wavertree* (1885). Take a ride on the museum's new sidewheeler, the *Andrew Fletcher,* and attend a live jazz concert free of charge along the waterfront deck during the summer months. All this plus the Fulton Street market and Pier 17—both multilevel extravaganzas of seafood restaurants, specialty stores, food from around the world served in scores of snack bars, and a mecca for people-watching. And finally, there is an array of restaurants and bars tucked in and around the old restaurant streets—North Star (famous for British ale and snacks), the Bridge Café, Jeremy's Ale House, Carmine's, Fulton's Steamer, Sweet's, Sloppy Louie's, and the Paris Bar, all serving the freshest fish and seafood.

Beyond the Fulton Market at 127 John Street is the architect Emery Roth's "fun tower," a relatively standard glass-faced office block transformed into a riot of color and activity by the addition of neon tunnels, brightly painted seats and benches, fountains, swathes of canvas awnings, odd bits and pieces of sculpture, and the largest digital clock in the world. Even the utilities level (about halfway up the building) is a carnival-like mélange of blue, red, and yellow pipes, valves, and boilers—altogether a wonderfully fresh creation.

A few minutes' walk finds us at South William Street (Beaver and William streets), an area in total contrast to the Fulton Street surroundings. Here we enter a tiny enclave of delicately detailed stores and restaurants with a distinctly mid-nineteenth-century flavor. Before the emergence of the great skyscrapers, much of downtown looked like this. Dutch-style trimmings were popular, and the meandering streets still followed the line of New Amsterdam cow paths. The mood prevails as we wander into Hanover Square itself, a pleasant breathing space with a small park and the finely proportioned India House. Originally founded as the Hanover Bank, it later became the headquarters of the New York Cotton Exchange and today contains one of the best-known businessmen's clubs in lower Manhattan.

Here in the square (the 1690s home base of Captain Kidd, the privateer-turned-pirate), one can sense the affluence of the "new" downtown. All around are the cloud-clawing towers of the nation's largest banks and financial corporations, their curtain-walls soaring high above the imaginative promenades and plazas, sculptures and gardens. Take time to explore the niches. Follow signs up and down the escalators to underground shopping areas, raised decks overlooking the East River, picnic areas where office workers lunch in a cacophony of bass-heavy radios, and Jeanette Park, a "hard" plaza of outstanding design that is a hub of activity during the summer. A little farther back, up Front Street at Maiden Lane, take a look at one of downtown's newest atriums in the Continental Center—an imaginative picnic space known for lunchtime concerts and theatrical performances.

Across from Jeanette Park is the ever-popular Fraunces Tavern, which somehow manages to contain behind its refined neo-Georgian façade (a "conjectural restoration") a popular restaurant, an invariably crowded bar, and an extensive museum dedicated primarily to the commemoration of George Washington's famous farewell to his officers on December 4, 1783, in the Long Room. (Open Monday–

Friday 10 A.M.–4 P.M. Free. Call 425-1778 for details on the many lectures, concerts, and special events that are scheduled.) Other museum displays include the Flag Room, collections of eighteenth-century dinnerware and crystal, clocks, prints, portraits, and Revolutionary War memorabilia. Although the museum can become a little overcrowded, it's a highlight of most downtown walking tours and is well worth the visit.

The lesser-known Shrine of Saint Elizabeth Seton is located in the last of a once-refined row of Federal-style townhouses where Water Street ends at Battery Park. The eastern wing of the building, below the raised dormers, is a 1793 structure and the remainder of the building, with its odd combination of bowed façade, oval side windows, and delicate columns (which are sections of masts from old sailing ships topped with Ionic capitals), is an 1806 addition attributed to City Hall architect John McComb, Jr. Inside, masses are celebrated regularly in the oval chapel. It's a pleasant place to rest; the silence and the pastel-shaded walls and pews offer welcome respite from the racket outside.

Battery Park, across from the shrine, is always full of life during the summer. Tourists throng its pathways waiting for the boats to take them on the Statue of Liberty/Ellis Island trips. Bongo drummers and promising jazz musicians blast-boom the afternoon away while lithe-limbed girls ogle and giggle, and bronzed boys jog along the Admiral Dewey promenade past the Good Humor carts and the "I Love New York" stickers. Around Castle Clinton (the smoothed remnants of a yet-to-be-used fortress, built 1807–11) are a plethora of monuments to Wireless Operators, the Walloon Settlers, John Ericsson (builder of the *Monitor,* America's first iron warship), the Salvation Army, Giovanni da Verrazano, and Emma Lazarus, who helped raise funds for the erection of the Statue of Liberty across the bay with her immortal words, "Give me your tired, your poor/ Your huddled masses yearning to breathe free. . . ."

My favorite niche here is Marine Company No. 1 headquarters on Pier A—a raggle-taggle green-and-white clapboard-and-stucco structure on a lopsided pier, looking like a displaced New England sardine factory. The clocktower at the pierhead, however, adds a touch of elegance and peals ship's bells at half-hour intervals throughout the day in memory of World War I victims.

If the park's a little too hectic (and it can hardly be described as either a nook or a cranny) stroll north up State Street past Cass Gilbert's United States Custom House (one of the most splendid examples of Beaux-Arts architecture in the country and regrettably closed for renovation at the time of writing) to the recently restored Bowling Green Park. Manhattan's first official park is surrounded by its original 1771 fence and is, if the lunchtime crowds are any gauge, the city's most-frequented space. It was here on July 9, 1776, a few hours after the Declaration of Independence arrived in the city from Philadelphia, that a rioting crowd of citizens and militia destroyed the statue of George III, which for years had gazed in somber dignity over the comings and goings of the colonial populace.

During the summer the park is one of downtown's many showcases for budding singers, musicians, mime artists, and magicians all of whom attract enthusiastic crowds and give this hard-nosed nexus of wealth and greed, a kinder, more human face. Other favored spots include Trinity Church, the Seaport, Chase Manhattan Plaza (all around Dubuffet's delightful "Forest" sculpture), the new East River plazas, and the area along the vehicle-free Nassau Street precinct.

A short distance farther north look for the entrance to a post office on the west side of Broadway. The restrained gray façade of the old Cunard building, which now houses the post office, conceals one of the most ornate entrances to any commercial structure in the world. The richly decorated vestibule with its profusion of terracotta and tiled arches, its bas-reliefs of sea nymphs, dolphins, and chubby children of Neptune is a modest preparation for the overwhelming opulence of the Great Hall itself. Step inside and look up at the main dome and the richly decorated half-domes (effective spotlighting here could transform this space). Magnificent frescoes by Ezra Winter roaring with the fury of the ocean depict the Viking vessel of Leif Ericson, Columbus's galleon, and the sturdy ships of John Cabot and Sir Francis Drake, all surging through turbulent

Bowling Green Park

seas to the New World. Subterranean gods and goddesses cavort across the ceiling and walls with mermaids and sea creatures in a riot of line and form that is almost audible. Barry Faulkner's finely executed world maps on the side walls provide rare segments of visual relief. And somehow, in the middle of all this, postal workers and their customers conduct transactions while oblivious to their surroundings. Even in the vestibule more people seem to be attracted by the tiny Philatelic Exhibition Center, with its displays of special U.S. commemorative stamps, than by the bewitchingly naked nymphs floating above their heads. (Someday I would like to make my own addition to New York's displays of graffiti with the simple phrase "LOOK UP" tastefully stenciled on sidewalks and curbs at salient points around the city. There's a vast realm of riches housed above the six-foot level, as every nook-and-cranny explorer knows.)

Continuing north on Broadway, stroll into the Art Deco-flavored Irving Trust Company Building at the junction of Broadway and Wall Street and enjoy its rich gold-and-crimson mosaic interior. Then next door, at the Bank of Tokyo, look high up (once again) at the building's Broadway façade and notice the huge flowing statues decorating the upper floors. The strict rhythm of the façade makes them almost come alive, seeming to float effortlessly in front of the building.

If you've never taken one of the more traditional tours of the downtown area you may, at this point, wish to stroll east on Wall Street to the New York Stock Exchange and the adjacent Federal Hall National Memorial (Open Monday–Friday 9 A.M.–5 P.M.) where, on April 30, 1789, George Washington took the oath of office as first President of the United States. Both of these attractions showcase extensive exhibits and provide descriptive literature. During the summer, in particular, be prepared for the throngs of tourists that make it difficult to appreciate all that's offered, although the Colonial Folk Music Concerts, from midday to 4 P.M., are worth the crush.

So much has been written about Trinity Church that it is unnecessary to repeat its long and fascinating history here. (If you'd like more information, pick up one of the pamphlets inside the church or a copy of the "Heritage Trail Walking Tour of Downtown.") Suffice it to mention that this 1846 Richard Upjohn creation is the third church to occupy the site and that the burial ground contains such notables as Alexander Hamilton and Robert Fulton. There's also a small museum here of church artifacts and papers (Open Monday–Friday 9 A.M.–3:45 P.M.; Saturday 10 A.M.–3:45 P.M.; Sunday 1–3:45 P.M. Free). The church provides a wonderful setting for lunchtime relaxation and occasional concerts, and a convenient link between Broadway and Church Street (Trinity Place).

Stroll down the back steps to the American Stock Exchange across the street (closed to the public until further notice). What originated as a curbside marketplace (there's an amusing life-size portrayal of some early stockbrokers in action at the top of the escalator) is now an immense trading hall with room for more than 1,000 people. Some sit quietly in tiered booths around the edge of the room, while others run rampant across the trading floor screaming and gesticulating with all the fervor of distraught Yankee fans.

Exchange-watching can be a fascinating pastime, and if you'd like to see the real action, continue north on Church Street to 4 World Trade Center and the relatively little-known Commodities Exchange Center (floors 8 and 9, Open Monday–Friday 9 A.M.–3 P.M.). Here one emerges from the elevator into an environment of stainless-steel trim, gray and maroon carpets, recessed lighting, and futuristic booths, while in the distance you hear the din and bellowing. From the eighth floor you can look directly into the exchange. Plush carpets are covered in the traditional confetti of order slips, and around the walls figures flash on large boards marked as silver, gold, palladium, platinum, zinc, cotton, cocoa, sugar, coffee, potatoes, and beef. The ninth floor visitors' gallery provides more information about the commodities and the action itself.

Assuming you avoid a time-consuming diversion into the new Battery City, our route continues east on Liberty Street, past Isamu Noguchi's famous sculpture of "a teetering vermillion cube gored by a cylindrical punch" (an ironic but accurate description by architect Elliot Willensky) at the base of Marine Midland's black tower. And as long as we're dabbling in pecuniary matters, where better to go next than the massive palacelike Federal Reserve Bank of New

York at Nassau and Liberty streets, where at the end of a one-hour tour you'll see more actual money in gold form than in any other place in the world. After all the paper-pushing in the exchanges, where "real" money never changes hands, it's a relief to know that here at least is a tangible foundation for the nation's currency. Unfortunately though, one can't just walk in off the street and take a tour. You must write or call (791-6130) at least a week in advance and indicate your preference for day and hour of visit (tours are Monday–Friday 10 A.M., 11 A.M., 1 P.M., and 2 P.M.). But if you have the slightest interest in the subject, it's worth taking the trouble to make advance arrangements.

Across from the Home Insurance Company stroll through the imaginative galleria at 100 William Street, lined with shops, to John Street (one wishes downtown had more such arcaded streets) and then head west toward Broadway, passing the diminutive John Street United Methodist Church. This is the site of the first Methodist church in America, erected in 1768, and the current 1841 structure is the third house of worship to be built here. Usually the doors are open, so walk inside and enjoy its simple intimacy. On Wednesdays they offer half-hour lunchtime concerts and performances from 12:10 P.M.

For an unusual sequence of contrasts after this modest structure, enter the columned halls of the old American Telephone and Telegraph Building at John Street and Broadway, an impressive reminder of the immense wealth and power of America's corporate lynchpins. Then pause to look at the interior of St. Paul's Chapel immediately to the north (there are also occasional noonday concerts here). In a sumptuous setting of a gilded pulpit, Waterford crystal chandeliers, and a pink, blue, and cream decor, one can see George Washington's pew in the north aisle and the pew of the first governor of New York, George Clinton, in the opposite aisle. If the sweet richness of the interior begins to pall, stroll in the simple churchyard that contains an unusual range of winged Death-Head gravestones before moving north to the Woolworth Building, fourth in this unusual sequence of interior spaces. Take a deep breath and enter a monument to one of the nation's most renowned capitalist entrepreneurs, a "cathedral of commerce," and one of the most exotic Gothic-Revival structures ever built. On the outside, Cass Gilbert, the architect, used almost every element and nuance of the Gothic era—spires, turrets, flying buttresses, gargoyles, and endless variations on the pointed arch.

Inside, under a vaulted ceiling of floral motifs in glass mosaics and gold-leaf-covered wrought-iron cornices, one can stroll through bronzed hallways faced in marble from the Isle of Skyros, admire the ornate elevator doors, and even chuckle (quietly of course) at the caricature sculptures of Cass Gilbert holding a model of his creation, Louis Horowitz the builder, and F. W. Woolworth himself nickel-and-diming it in the niches. Miller's Restaurant hides away in the arched catacombs while secretaries peer through palatial windows into the inner courtyard surrounding the main staircase and visitors stand wide-eyed on the polished terrazzo floors. Those who would like more information on the building itself and its founder (Woolworth paid fifteen million dollars in cash for the structure and for seventeen years—from 1913 to 1930—could claim the headquarters of his vast empire as the world's tallest building) should ask one of the guards for a pamphlet.

It's time for a rest, so stroll across to City Hall Park and select a bench for a few minutes. Look at the buildings surrounding this welcome swathe of grass and shade. Park Row, once appropriately known as "Newspaper Row," contained from the mid-nineteenth century to the early years of the twentieth century most of the city's newspaper offices. Their names evoke strong memories for older journalists—the *New York World,* the *Sun,* the *Tribune,* the *Mail and Express,* the *Recorder,* the *Evening Post,* the *New York American,* and at least a dozen more. In the park itself, statues of Horace Greeley and Benjamin Franklin are the last tangible remnants of what used to be one of the most hectic corners in town.

The newspaper offices overlooked City Hall and witnessed all the comings and goings of the "Boss" Tweed era, where graft was often openly flaunted as the big wheelers and dealers jostled for position and power. The famous Tweed courthouse, immediately behind City Hall, took almost ten years to build and cost the city more than ten million dollars, most of which ended up in the pockets of Tweed and his Tammany clique. City Hall itself, though, reflects a rather more decorous period of civic growth. It was completed in a combined Georgian/French-Renaissance style ("petit palais" is an oft-used phrase to describe its regal character) in 1812 and is generally regarded as one of New York's finest architectural treasures (Open to the public Monday–Friday 10 A.M.–4 P.M. Free).

Stroll through the City Hall lobby housing Jean Antoine Houdon's life-size statue of George Washington, and ascend the curved stairway of the rotunda. This light and delicate space was an essential element of the original design and is said to be based upon a similar feature at Wardour House in Wiltshire, England. The dome, like much of the exterior of the building, is a reconstruction. In fact it's rather amazing that anything is left of the original structure. Fires, neglect, and the annoying tendency of Massachusetts marble (originally used for the south façade) to erode rapidly, have necessitated extensive and repeated restorations since the late 1800s.

The Governor's Room is the primary area open to the public and contains mainly city-commissioned portraits by John Trumbull of such notables as George Washington, George Clinton, Alexander Hamilton, and Governor Peter Stuyvesant. Across the rotunda is the Council Chamber, which is usually also open to the public.

Outside again, across Centre Street we pass under the ornate tower of the Municipal Building, topped by Adolph Weinman's golden statue of "Civic Duty," into Police Plaza, one of the few and certainly one of the most attractive pedestrian spaces in the city. The contemporary salmon-colored building directly ahead (past Rosenthal's sculpture of interlocking steel circles) is the Police Headquarters Building, where tours are available (call 374-3804 for details), and slightly to the south is a window, the last remnant of the Rhinelander Sugar House, which contained as many as a thousand American prisoners during the Revolutionary War.

As the paved walk curves around toward Foley Square note St. Andrew's Church (without doubt one of the darkest churches in the city), where special services used to be held for printers working along Newspaper Row at 2:30 in the morning.

The irregular-shaped Foley Square is certainly one of the city's more unusual civic spaces and a favorite haunt of court-watchers who flock daily to watch the legal machinations in the Family

Court, the County Court House, and the U.S. Court House. My favorite distraction here is an incredibly ornate architectural gem at the north end of this cluster of courts. Napoleon Le Brun's chateau-style fire station for Engine Company 31, although no longer in use, is one of downtown's most exquisite buildings (Lafayette and White streets) and the type of subject I most enjoy sketching. For another diversion in this area, stroll east on White Street to Columbus Park at Bayard and Baxter streets for a glimpse of a more relaxed corner of Chinatown. It's a part of the neighborhood most visitors miss.

Then it's west on Leonard Street to Broadway and the Institute for Art and Urban Resources' Clocktower gallery. Take the elevator to the twelfth floor and then walk the remaining flight to a rather bedraggled but certainly active complex of studio space and galleries where the works of lesser-known "pioneer" artists are shown in a series of exhibitions from September through May. Brendan Gill has been an active supporter of the Institute since its creation and claims that the Clocktower and PSI (Project Studios One) in Long Island City, Queens, provide two of the most valuable centers in the city for artist interaction in a noncommercial atmosphere (Open Thursday–Saturday 12 P.M.–6 P.M., September–May; 233-1096. Free).

South on Broadway to Duane Street we pass the Federal Building, which, surprisingly, often has interesting displays open to the public as well as a marvelous bookstore (Open Monday–Friday 9 A.M.–5 P.M.) full of obscure government pamphlets and books on such varied topics as pickle and relish making, the rings of Saturn, how to breed your own Angus cattle, Mariner explorations of Mars, how to start your own car wash, how to rid your home of bats, advice on infant care, barbecue-cooking techniques, and bee-raising (25,000 titles in all). If you've never browsed through one of these places, allow yourself quite a bit of time.

At Duane Street, just west of Broadway, we discover the Fire Department Museum, one of the city's lesser-known official attractions. (Open Monday–Friday 9 A.M.–4 P.M. Free.) A large collection of old engines (incredibly ornate affairs complete with finely painted trim) occupies three floors of an old firehouse, along with pumpers, trophies, photographs, helmets, trumpets, and all the par-

Engine Company No. 31 Firehouse

Old Fire Engine

aphernalia of firehouse tradition during the nineteenth and early twentieth centuries. The Model-T Ford chief's car (circa 1920) is still in good working order and is often seen in city parades, but the most popular attractions are the early red engines with their endless array of brass trimmings and crenellated boiler chimneys—virtual caricatures of themselves.

As chance would have it, self-caricaturization was one of the criticisms leveled against the South Street Seaport redevelopment plans of the Rouse Company (famous for their Boston and Baltimore redevelopment projects). Commercial it is, but I like it a lot and find it an ideal diversion from the constant search for nooks and crannies. So why not return to where we began and enjoy a few happy-hour indulgences among the old clippers and clam bars?

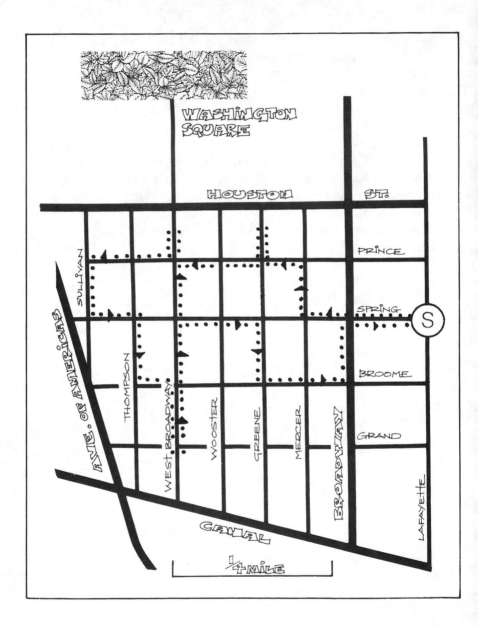

2 | SoHo

It all began a little over fifteen years ago when a handful of artists found illegal homes in old lofts and workshops in the dingy, dark streets south of Houston Street. Today SoHo is known as "New York's Monmartre," or "Gallery-Ghetto," and its face is changing so rapidly that what occurred yesterday may be out of date today.

In the early morning the streets are silent. The paint-flaked pillars of the cast-iron façades glow in a fresh light. Bits of cardboard boxes and shards of brightly colored cloth litter the sidewalks and the cobbled streets. There's a faint rumble of traffic along Canal Street to the south but here, deep in SoHo, nothing moves. It's cat-quiet in the canyons.

By midafternoon the neighborhood is transformed. Machines pound and churn in a thousand print shops, cloth-cutting outlets, rag converters, window-shade manufacturers, corrugated-box makers, and twine jobbers. Open doors give glimpses of cavernous sweatshops where workers hunch over long tables in the half-light or wrestle with pallets piled high with paper and boxes. Everybody shouts. The streets become thrombosisized veins, clotted with Mack trucks and delivery vans. Horn-honking is a popular pastime; that

☞ **DIRECTIONS**
Subway: IRT 6 to Spring Street and Lafayette Street
Bus: M1, M2, M3, M5, M6 (north/south), M12, M21 (east/west)

and bawling out the guy in front and the world in general. "Hey you, buster, get that thing outta here. Look at that guy, willya. Jus' look at that."

A door smothered in cheap-print flyers bursts open and smashes against a pile of boxes brimming with leather remnants. A short man, beer-bellied and sweating, emerges and sits on the broken iron steps lighting a cigar. He watches the street with vacant eyes and then slowly raises his head to look at the blue sky high above the crenelated cornices of the ten-story warehouses and workshops. A young girl in a long peasant-print skirt walks slowly past carrying a plastic bag full of bits of cut cloth and hessian. Two artists follow, one at either end of a ten-foot-wide canvas. They have the same dedicated, serious expressions on their faces as they slowly maneuver the painting down the street. It's a classically simple creation, single strands of wormlike white paint seemingly squeezed directly from a tube onto a light blue background. The fat man on the steps watches them for a moment and then turns his head toward the gloomy workshop beyond the door.

"Hey, Al." Al dutifully appears, a little man, very thin, rubbing his hands on an oily rag. The fat man gestures with his head toward the artists now negotiating a rather difficult section of cobbled street around the rear end of a Mack truck that effectively blocks the sidewalk. A confrontation seems inevitable. The two men are moving alongside the truck, the driver is just about to open the door. He hasn't seen them, they are oblivious to him. Any moment the canvas will be sent flying. The fat man saves the day, bawling across the street to the two artists, "Hold it—hey, you two, hold it!" They stop immediately. The truck door swings open, missing the canvas by less than a foot. The driver climbs down and stares in bewilderment as the startled artists scurry around the trucks to regain the comparative safety of the sidewalk. The masterpiece is saved. The driver, the fat man, and Al stare after them as they disappear through a tall gallery doorway.

"Jesus!" mutters the fat man and saunters back into the dark workshop. Al follows, slamming the poster-smothered door behind him.

SoHo is a crazy kind of place.

A few years back the twenty or so blocks in the area *so*uth of *Ho*uston Street (hence SoHo) were ripe for the wrecker's ball. A 1962 study by the City Club of New York called the area "the wastelands of New York city" and concluded there were "no buildings worth saving." The central part of the district around Spring, Broome, and Greene streets was labeled "commercial slum no. 1." The Fire Department was even more adamant and pointed out that "Hell's Hundred Acres" was one of the most dangerous working environments in the city. A loft fire at 633 Broadway in March 1958 killed twenty-four people and the newspapers exposed the woefully inadequate code-enforcement in the area. One beleaguered city official claimed, "The only way to enforce the codes is to pull all the bloody blocks down!" No one really paid much attention to these remarks until the proposal was made to plow the Lower Manhattan Expressway straight through the heart of the district. Actually, the concept had been on the map for more than twenty years but had gone unnoticed. New York, after all, is known for its pipe dreams and Robert Moses-inspired idiosyncrasies that never leave the bottom drawer of the planner's office.

But suddenly the project came alive, along with ambitious ideas for swathes of sunken pavement, overpasses, intersections, and lots and lots of lovely traffic—an engineer's dream. The outcry was instantaneous and unified. Led by architectural professors, media notables, and the city's cultural clique, citizens of Manhattan "discovered" SoHo. They were told of its outstanding nucleus of cast-iron structures—the finest in the country—huddled along the dark streets north of Chinatown. Nikolaus Pevsner, the noted architectural historian, described it as "a veritable museum of cast iron architecture." TV documentaries discussed its fascinating history, first as an elite residential area developed by John Jacob Astor and other perceptive entrepreneurs in the early 1800s, then as the city's elaborately exotic red-light district around 1850, followed by the cast-iron era of the later 1800s when the tight blocks became the base for the world's largest silk manufacturers, lace makers, garment cutters, and dry-goods distributors, and Broadway flourished with its ornate hotels and department stores. Architectural scholars had a field day analyzing the range of styles and influences in the

ornate cast-iron façades of the warehouses and cramped factories—
Italianate, neo-Grec, Victorian Gothic, Second French Empire,
Renaissance, and a score of other hybrid combinations.

Students with measuring tapes, cameras, and drawing boards
rushed out to record the intricate details of this "magnificent repository of American ingenuity and craftsmanship." Descriptive texts
eloquently rhapsodized about architraves, caryatids, spandrels,
quoins, pilasters, modillions, capitals, and cornices. Experts discussed the comparative merits of "the cast-iron architects"—Henry
Fernbach, Isaac Duckworth, Griffith Thomas, Jonathan Snook,
Robert Mook, Jarvis Morgan Slade, and even debated the individual
characteristics and quirks of the casting companies.

SoHo was "in" and the expressway was "out," as was a later
proposal for a vast sports complex and other city-inspired projects
considered detrimental to the preservation of the area. SoHo rose
from abysmal anonymity to historic district status in less than four
years.

Prior to the uproar, painters, sculptors, writers, and others seeking inexpensive, spacious living areas had slowly filtered down from
the more affluent neighborhoods to the north and settled quietly in
empty lofts above the warehouses and workshops. Though they
lived illegally in this nonresidential area, the city usually turned a
blind eye to this minor transgression. After the spotlight became
focused on SoHo, however, the surge of "loft dwellers" increased
dramatically and the inevitable confrontation with building inspec-
tors and fire marshals was avoided only by formal legalization of loft
living in 1970. At that time there were less than a thousand studios
in SoHo. Today the number has increased to six thousand and
continues to grow rapidly. Loft living has become popular not only
with the macro-canvas artists but with lawyers, doctors, and Dry
Dock Country people attracted by big spaces in a bohemian atmosphere and the increasingly chic image of the neighborhood.

The original pioneers of SoHo are concerned. "Keep it Dirty,"
says a spray-painted sign across a splintered doorway. "This hap-
pens every time," Alex Matheson, a SoHo artist, told me as we sat
on a rusty loading bay on Greene Street. "We find a low-rent area,
go in quietly and fix it up a bit—just enough to make it livable. Then

someone opens up a gallery or a restaurant—whatever. Then the fur-coaters come and a few decide to stay and there's a piece in *New York* magazine, and then the whole cycle begins—more galleries and restaurants, rents up, old tenants forced out, new tenants in. A few make it big—y'know you get a little clique of artists and buyers and critics and gallery owners all together and some win out—but most have to move somewhere else. There's other SoHos all over town—under the Brooklyn Bridge near the Watch Tower, across in Long Island City, over in Hoboken. Maybe there's nothing you can do about it. You get pissed off though, always having to move."

Alex's complaint can be heard over and over again in SoHo. Marginal businesses are being forced out to increase loft space; fancy bars, restaurants, and art galleries are being opened up to cater to wealthier residents and the "Saturday crowd." Another artist, Glenn Paulsen, admitted that if it weren't for the abundance of raw materials for his art he'd have left long ago. "I can't really afford it. I've had to sublet part of my loft. But I need those remnants (scores of boxes are left out on the streets filled with cloth, leather, and metal remnants—throwouts from the sweatshops). I build these creatures"—he pointed to a gallery full of life-size carnival creatures that moved and played cymbals, drums, and gongs at the pull of a string—"they're ninety percent street junk and this is the best street-junk area in town."

SoHo is alive with ideas. Sit in the coffeehouses, the bars, or stroll the galleries; listen to the artists, the people who live here; read the billboards and the signs pinned on notice boards. Ideas are created as rapidly as the silk hats and feathered frills that streamed from the somber sweatshops at the turn of the century. Exhibitions, seminars, workshops, video experiments, theater, mime, music, jazz, film, photography, neon sculpture, you name it, somewhere in Soho someone will be working on it—conceiving it, twisting it, shaping it, testing it, turning it inside out, tying it in knots, defending it, rejecting it. It's a great stewpot of creativity.

Let's begin our exploration of this rapidly evolving neighborhood by strolling westward along Spring Street from the subway at Lafayette. Pause briefly at Broadway and admire the remarkable range of architectural styles and materials. Cast-iron, brick, stone, and a few scattered contemporary structures adorn both sides of this imposing thoroughfare. In 1854 *Putnam's Monthly* magazine gushed that Broadway was "altogether the most showy, the most crowded, and the richest thoroughfare in America . . . the most famous street in the United States." The imposing private homes had rapidly given way to the great emporiums of wealth—Arnold Constable, Wanamaker's, Lord and Taylor, and Tiffany. Hotels, music halls, theaters, and beer gardens proliferated. The last remnants of the famous St. Nicholas Hotel, center of the city's social whirl, are at 521–23. The statistics were staggering. Built at a cost of two million dollars in 1853, the hotel boasted a 275-foot frontage on Broadway, 600 rooms for more than 1,000 guests, a staff of 400, 2 miles of halls, 30 miles of piping, and the most expensive—some said the most vulgar—furniture manufactured in America.

Nearby, the great six-story Niblo's Hotel, built on the site of Niblo's Garden (a landscaped series of promenades for theatergoers in the area), was joined by other equally magnificent monoliths—the Collamore, Metropolitan, American, and Prescott. The cobbled side streets leading off into SoHo contained the ladies' boarding houses, which catered to every whim and taste of a discerning clientele. Such interesting hostels as Miss Lizzie Wright's "French Belles," Miss Hathaway's prim and proper "fair Quakeresses," and Madame Kanth's house of "Germanic Order" have long since disappeared.

American Youth Hostels Inc., at 75 Spring Street, is a refreshing oasis of a different variety. The windows brim with hiking equipment, books on walking and climbing, and maps of America's little-known wilderness regions. Pristine photographs of the Sierra and Cascade ranges contrast all too vividly with the shadowed streets outside, and devotees of the outdoor life quietly compare hiking routes and equipment while traffic snarls by a few feet away. A notice board near the door posts small index cards—"Companion needed for Australian and New Zealand hike," "For the best prices to Nepal and Bhutan, call. . . ." Nearby shelves are stocked with guidebooks seldom found in the major bookstores—"Biking the

World," "Shoestring Guide to Southeast Asia," "The Insiders Guide to Thailand."

Just down the street is an institution offering other means of liberation from the city, the New York Open Center, providing a seemingly infinite array of consciousness-raising workshops, courses, journeys, and concerts. Their brochure sums it all up: "We are a center for holistic learning committed to the unity of all life and the wholeness of the individual. We aim to provide an oasis for nonsectarian spiritual nourishment in the heart of the city. And we are both haven and springboard for individuals and ideas with the potential to transform culture and society. . . . There is an enormous community of people here deeply immersed in a holistic worldview . . . a village is springing up around the oasis." Their range of workshops reflects this holistic worldview—"Tibetan Psychothera- peutic Techniques," "The Zen of Seeing," "Your Personal Image and Beyond," "Shambhala Training," and even "Attuning to the Essence of House Plants."

Mercer Street, otherwise known as "Scavenger's Row," is one of the best remnant-hunting streets in SoHo. Every weekday brings a constant flow of scrap connoisseurs sifting and sorting through the boxes and piles of cloth cutouts, metal strips, cardboard tubes, leather clippings, and the occasional odd bits and pieces of wood. It's a dignified procedure. At one point I watched three residents, all very artistic looking, standing patiently in line with their plastic bags waiting for a fourth member of the group to complete his selection of leather remnants from a huge cardboard box on the sidewalk. When he'd finished he smiled at the next one in line, who promptly moved into position and half disappeared into the box in search of his desired quota—and so on. "There's always plenty for everyone," the last artist in the line told me. "I use this stuff in collage work primarily. If I don't find what I need tonight, there'll be more at lunchtime tomorrow. I'll just get here earlier."

To many residents Fanelli's Café at Prince and Mercer is true SoHo. Here the warehousemen, sweatshop workers, local business- men, artists, and writers gather against the ornate bar and in the tiny dining room to enjoy the cold ale and generous "workingmen's specials" of roast beef, ravioli, corned beef, and spare ribs on tables covered with crisp white tablecloths. The decor is bar-basic. Aged, yellowed photographs of old boxing champions are reminders of the days when the place was a popular center for the city's fight crowd. Mike Fanelli has seen every kind of patron in his corner tavern with the erratic neon sign. I asked him how SoHo had changed in the last decade. "I still get my regulars. Some guys' been coming here since repeal, some before that. But there's more of your fur-coaters nowadays, 'specially Saturdays. That used to be a real dead day. Now you should see it."

He's right. Saturday is promenade day. The streets, particularly West Broadway, are filled with visitors from other parts of the city and out-of-towners who come for a little gallery-hopping and pub-crawling. Personally, I don't care for Saturdays in SoHo, but the gallery owners and restauranteurs love it. "Oh, most of them come just to browse and giggle," a woman gallery clerk told me, "but the darlings talk—they go home and they talk and the next week they'll bring their friends down. Eventually they buy something. You can get hooked on this place." It's true. West of Fanelli's the galleries start to proliferate. In a five-block area I counted twenty-three, and more are opening all the time. And the shows are often brilliantly produced. The wide, white spaces with an occasional Corinthian-top cast-iron pillar provide abundant space for the huge canvases, sculptures, and "constructions." Visitors are often invited to participate directly in the art forms by walk-throughs, climb-ups, push buttons, rope-pulling, and in one unusual exhibition of "stuffed shapes," punching and kicking. The clubby atmosphere of some of the Madison Avenue galleries is replaced here by a brilliant airiness, a sense of experiment for experiment's sake, and, best of all, a sense of humor both in the displays and the artworks themselves.

A brief diversion north on Greene Street will encompass, at last count, seven galleries and the Aesthetic Realism Foundation, which boldly propounds the teachings of Eli Siegel ("art is the oneness of opposites") and exhibits prints of masterworks that supposedly confirm his principles.

Watch out for Richard Haas's wall painting at 112–114 Prince Street just west of Greene. Look carefully. At first it appears to be the side elevation of the neo-Grec frontage complete with ornate cast-iron detailing, window blinds, plants, and a cat—then suddenly you realize (actually the peeling surface helps a little) that it's a trompe l'oeil creation, a magnificent three-dimensional illusion on a flat surface.

Farther west on Prince Street, the Dean & Deluca store is all too real, a wonderful potpourri of gourmet foods and cookware with such obscure creations as portable solar cookers and a Raclette oven for creating those redolent browned-cheese concoctions supposedly so popular with European mountaineers. Sausages and hams dangle on ropes or nestle together comfortably in their display cases. Cheeses, over 180 different varieties, beam up at the goggle-eyed customers. Pickles, salads, pâtés, pasta-makers, and a thousand more pots, pans, and paraphernalia await the jaded cook. Appropriate adjuncts to this fairly recent arrival in SoHo are Donald Sack's, locally renowned for its crisp, fresh sandwiches, Wholefoods in SoHo, with one of the widest selections of beans and oils in Manhattan, and two of the neighborhood's better-known restaurants—the Greene Street Café and the SoHo Kitchen and Bar. Although the latter two are both owned by Tony Goldman, the contrast could not be more marked. Greene Street Café is the expensive epitome of elegance (another SoHo transformation—it used to be a garage), complete with gentle jazz, whereas SoHo Kitchen is one of those noisy in-places serving inexpensive pizzas, pastas, and grills to a high-style, young clientele. They do, however, share one common characteristic—an excellent wine cellar and an innovative policy of tastings, which at SoHo Kitchen is presented in the form of "flights" —"1½-ounce servings of eight wines in a single category." There's your basic budget flight of eight Chenin Blancs for $10.50 up to a top-flight tasting of Bordeaux wines for $29.50. A most diverting way to pass an evening.

Food Restaurant, on the corner of Prince and Wooster, is one of the old-school SoHo eateries, offering generous portions of wholesome snacks—black bean burritos, chicken baked with tarragon, tomato and zucchini pizza, huge chocolate chip cookies, and great slabs of carrot cake. Equally down-home and earthy (don't mind the pun) in a different sort of way is the Dia Art Foundation's unusual

New York Earth Room exhibit at 141 Wooster Street, where a three-foot-deep layer of soil covers an entire gallery floor (Open Wednesday–Friday 12–4 P.M.; Saturday 12–6 P.M.). And if all that earth fails to impress, see what artists can do with an earth- or at least sand-based product at Gallery Nilsson, directly opposite Dia, with its displays of glass and crystal creations.

And then there's West Broadway, the spine of SoHo, where everyone comes to see and be seen, to discover what's hot and what's not, to be near the cutting edge of art and fashion, and to while away the hours in Central Falls and i tre merli, a swank wine bar. Some of the more established galleries are still here—Nancy Hoffman, Circle, Vorpal, Leo Castelli, O.K. Harris, Jordan Volpe—but boutiques have taken over in the last few years along with Robert Lee Morris's spectacular jewelry outlets, and the gloriously extravagant Gallery of Wearable Art at Houston Street. There are refreshing surprises, also, in the form of Rizzoli's delightful narrow-frontage bookstore, Harriet Love's Vintage clothing, DAPY's wonderful extravaganza of crazy clocks, radios, cocktail accoutrements (and just about anything else with double-entendre potential) and—of course—Think Big's rendering of everyday objects as giant-sized sculptures!

Continuing west on Prince Street, past Alex Streeter's tiny jewelry store at 152, we enter a more restrained section of SoHo. The Vesuvio Bakery, and, farther down, Raoul's Bar, mark the eastern fringe of an old Italian neighborhood that once dominated the southern part of Greenwich Village. The street clubs are still here—Fanelli's Republicans and the Sullivan Knights. North on Sullivan Street itself there's Mario Amarino's Italian butcher shop, the Zampieri Bakery with a windowful of glazed panettone di Milano cakes (some over ten pounds), and Joe's Dairy (homemade mozzarella and latticini freschi) where Grace Campanelli and her son Anthony smoke their plump mozzarellas every day. I looked for Cardine Canevari's sausage shop, where Cardine used to make her own northern-style cotegino, lugigana, and capicolla sausages, but Grace told me the place had closed. "We lose a few but things don't change too fast around here. Maybe some more Portuguese but that's about all. Down the street? Well, that's different—it changes every day over there. It's a bit crazy—don't you think so? Crazy!"

Aldo Boya, in the park at Thompson and Spring, agrees. "You see that place on the corner there?" He pointed to the SoHo Charcuterie and Restaurant, a resplendent niche of homemade gourmet fare and elaborate prices, on the corner of Spring. "You should see the cars, 'specially 'round lunchtime. Great black limousines lining the street halfway to Vinnie's Bar—Rolls, Caddies, Lincolns, the lot. You could keep an army warm in the fur coats at that place." He paused to aim and throw. "What the hell they wanna put that there for? There's no ritzy people living 'round here."

At the corner of Thompson and Spring, just by the play area, a Portuguese crowd gathers daily for its street forum. Joe's Grocery, just north on Thompson Street next to Dominick Barbato's Pork Store, sells many hard-to-find Italian and Portuguese delicacies to a devoted clientele.

Around the corner, heading east on Broome Street, close your ears to the terrified screeches of hens about to meet their untimely demise at the Live Poultry Market. A large man in a blood-stained apron sits outside, nearly overwhelming an upright cane chair that creaks pitifully as he moves. An elderly Italian woman emerges with a white bird wrapped in newspaper, its head lolling hideously. The large man leers up at me. "Chicken?" he asks with what can only be called "a menacing grin." Across the road a group of rusty street sculptures huddle creaturelike in the middle of the road.

And immediately behind this, the new Manhattan Brewing Company attracts a constant stream of home-brewed beer lovers to its upper-level taproom and Ocean Grill Restaurant. Here the young crowd pound their feet on the sawdust-strewn floor while a German band thumps out drinking songs and hundreds of pints of Royal Amber Ale and Special Porter pour down parched throats—all this in a huge abandoned Con Edison substation that now accommodates kettles, lauter tuns, and all the bulbous copper vats and pipes associated with brewing beer.

I pause—with relief—at Kenn's Broome Street Bar, a delightful SoHo pub at the corner of Broome and West Broadway. Outside, a gilded lion's head dangles over the doorway of this diminutive structure dwarfed by the colonnaded façades of nearby loft build-

Broome Street Bar

ings. Inside, Kenn Reisdorff mingles with a very SoHo clientele and occasionally takes over the bar to administer restorative draughts of Pryor's Dark, McSorley's Ale, and Stegmaier Porter to thirsty customers. Talking is thirsty work, and the babble here never ceases. If voices wear out there are blackboards and multicolored chalk available for budding graffiti artists. Kenn boasts that his pub was once a renowned German restaurant, when the partially developed neighborhood was known as Kleindeutschland (Little Germany). Later it was owned by the seven burly Wagner brothers, Italian, not German, and all boxers. Today, along with his wife's smaller establishment, Berry's at Spring and Thompson, The Broome Street Bar is one of SoHo's most popular wateringholes.

Just south of Kenn's, past the Cupping Room (a perfect place for breakfast), are SoHo's new restaurants clustered all around West Broadway and Grand. Talk about eclectic—there's the leafy Tamu offering Indonesian dishes and a respectable rijstaffel; Cinco de Mayo's fiery Mexican cuisine; spicy Cambodian platters at Middle of the Road; even spicier Ethiopian creations at Abyssinia; some of Manhattan's best French cuisine served in La Chanterelle's spartan dining room at Grand and Greene; Brazilian dishes in the shadowy Amazonas; Chinese-American at Oh-Ho-So, and brasserie snacks and a lively crowd at La Gamelle. A genuine New York Reuben can be found at the flashy little Moondance Diner (Grand and Avenue of the Americas), or a couple of cocktails at Comedy U Grand (call 431-4022 for show details). Add a visit to the Museum of Holography (Mercer near Canal—a fascinating introduction to the world of holograms), attend experimental theater at the Performing Garage Center (Wooster near Grand, 966-3651), witness the unusual Museum of Colored Glass and Light (Wooster near Spring), or sit in on one of Chuck Levitan's performances at the gallery at Grand and West Broadway—and you have all the makings for a fascinating night out in SoHo. There's more to be found here, but I want to leave some nooks and crannies for you to discover.

If you're a photographer, the neighborhood is a playground of creative opportunities. It's best to get here in the morning when the sun is bright and fresh and the shadows most pronounced. Cast-iron-architecture devotees will find Greene Street between Spring

Queen of Greene Street

and Broome one of the most prepossessing areas, filled with revival masterpieces by Henry Fernbach and Jonathan Snook. The elaborate French Renaissance structure at 72–76 Greene Street, known locally as "the King of Greene Street," is an Isaac Duckworth creation and, in contrast to many of the others, has a pronounced three-dimensional façade topped by a magnificently ornate cornice. Another Duckworth, the blue-painted "Queen" at 28–30 Greene Street, is the best example in SoHo of the Second Empire Style and comes complete with mansard roof and ornate dormer windows.

Turning east on Broome Street we head back toward Broadway (look out for Global Village, a video media center with regular public showings). We're approaching the black Haughwout Building, the "Parthenon of Cast Iron," on the northeast corner of Broome and Broadway. It was styled by John Gaynor as a Venetian palazzo in 1856. Surprisingly, this sophisticated structure was one of the earliest cast-iron buildings in the city and the first to use Elisha Otis's steam-powered passenger elevator.

Back on Broadway we leave the cluttered streets behind—the crashings of grimy machines in dim workshops, the boxes of leather pieces, the clothes drying on fire escapes, the glimpses of elaborate loft spaces through palm-fronded windows, the long conversations at café tables, the vast white-spaced galleries, the snarled traffic, the barking of truckers, the obliviousness of artists, and the chitter of fur-coated trend-setters. At Broadway we return to the wider, brighter spaces and the long lines of austere business frontages. But the artistic spirit of SoHo can yet be found at the New Museum between Prince and West Houston (one of a handful of galleries giving prominence to neglected artists), and even at the Chase Manhattan Bank on the corner of West Houston, which resembles an art gallery far more than a financial center.

And that's it—unless of course you wish to start the fun all over again in the elegant and lively bars and restaurants along NoHo's Broadway.

But that's another story. . . .

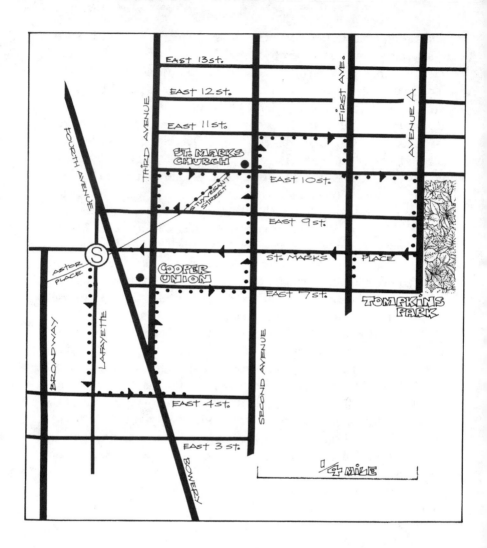

3 | The East Village

> *"Surely you're not doing the East Village?" asked a dear friend.*
> *"No one wants to walk down there. That neighborhood's gone,*
> *it's finished." And in spite of its recent phenomenal redevelop-*
> *ment by real estate moguls intent on its gentrification, such*
> *sentiments are still shared by thousands of New Yorkers who*
> *associate the district with Bowery bums, beatniks, hippies, and*
> *a patently unconventional life-style that rejects societal norms*
> *with the single-mindedness of a mainlining addict. But that's*
> *the interest of the neighborhood—the contrasts, the surprise of*
> *the unexpected, the endurance, all in the face of rampant*
> *change.*

It was during the fifties that Ginsberg, Kerouac, and LeRoi Jones established the abrasive literary tone of the East Village. St. Mark's-in-the-Bouwerie was home to the free-floating New York Poets, and budding Timothy Learys gave guru sessions on stoops to spaced-out admirers tripping away on LSD. "That was the best time," a frazzle-haired young woman told me as we stood chatting near RedBar, an avant-garde hangout on First Avenue at 7th Street. "Haight-Ashbury and here. They were the only places worth being. But it was the psychedelic sixties that really put the East Village on the map—the era of Bill Graham's Fillmore East, the Electric Circus, Ed Sanders's Peace Eye bookstore, the Phoenix, and a score of high-flying taverns and coffeehouses.

But the era faded. The Fillmore closed; Ratner's enormous ko-

☞ **DIRECTIONS**
Subway: IRT 6 to Astor Place/Fourth Avenue
Bus: M13 (east/west), M101, and M102 (north/south), M1, M2, M3, M5, M6 (north/south)

sher dairy restaurant next door, hangout of the hippiest of the hippies, vanished; and the once-glorious beatnik bookstores became thrift centers and machine-repair shops. LSD-tripping was replaced by more serious addiction to hard drugs. The neighborhood became known for vandalism, muggings, rapes, break-ins, and an occasional murder, and outsiders stayed away. Newspapers stopped reporting the crimes and landlords stopped collecting rents. Even the police were reluctant to patrol certain blocks deep in the district. "Things got about as bad as they could," an ex-city cop told me. "In the early seventies you kept away from this place. That's the way most people still see it. You mention 'East Village' and people think of drugs, murder, winos, slums, mugging—the lot. Most of them haven't been down here for years though, maybe not since the flower-power days."

But Manhattan neighborhoods have an ability to bounce back. The East Village still has its problems—some serious—but there are abundant signs of improvement. Recent restoration of finely detailed nineteenth-century townhouses on St. Marks Place, 9th Street, and along the north side of Tompkins Square has revealed new potential in the old blocks. Improvement associations abound. Sidewalks have newly planted trees, and the vandalism rate is low. Off-Broadway theaters flourish in an atmosphere of mutual support, new pub-restaurants open along the notorious Bowery, immaculate sushi restaurants appear along First Avenue and Avenue A, fancy gourmet food stores proliferate as fast as the strange varieties of mushrooms they sell to eager young newcomers, and crisp white-walled galleries come and go in the battered buildings all around the eastern end of Tompkins Square.

"The roller coaster's really rolling now," said 27-year-old graphic artist Ken Brewster, who pays $1,600 for a two-bedroom apartment near St. Marks Place and considers it a bargain. "I wanted to buy but I was six months too late—it's all getting locked up tight by real estate partnerships and the big-money boys. Even way down Avenue C—even D—you don't get a look-in." Graffiti is the dominant form of communication in the streets around Tompkins Square Park, and the retaliatory message to escalating prices and outside investment, mainly from long-time, low-income East Villagers, is clear: "Speculators out!", "Rent strike—keep it going," "This is your *dead*-line—keep out if you don't live here!"

Yet the melting pot bubbles on—green-haired punks, Madonna-clones in layers of antique clothing and bright plastic baubles, Hell's Angels in bulging leather gear and spiked wristbands, elderly Ukrainian patriots eagerly digesting and debating news from the USSR in the *Ukrainian Weekly,* and dainty yuppies sneakering the sidewalks with string-tied boxes from DeRobertis Pastry Shop and Veniero's.

We begin our walk at Astor Place near Conran's and the Astor Place Liquor Store, which features one of the largest selections of foreign wines in the city—a veritable library of labels. Astor Place was named after John Jacob Astor, who arrived in America in 1784 with less than twenty dollars in his pocket. At the time of his death in 1848 he had not only accumulated an immense fortune but had earned himself a series of notorious nicknames, not least of which was "Landlord of New York."

Following his first land purchase in 1789, a small plot of land between the Bowery and Elizabeth Street, he went on to acquire enormous holdings that assured his family a permanently promi-nent place in metropolitan society. When he died he bequeathed almost half a million dollars and land for the construction of "the finest library in the nation" on Lafayette Place. The Astor Library was designed in Italianate style and opened with great ceremony in 1854.

Today as the New York Shakespeare Festival Building, better known as Joseph Papp's Public Theatre (seven separate theaters at last count—call 598-7150 for more information), it remains the cultural nucleus of the district. The architect Giorgio Cavaglieri supervised its restoration for this purpose beginning in 1967 and one wishes his commission could have included the nearby remains of townhouses called Colonnade Row (La Grange Terrace). Here along with the Astors lived the Vanderbilts, the Delanos (FDR's grandfather), and other prominent citizens of the day. President John J. Tyler was married on the second floor of one of these magnificent colonnaded townhouses, and Washington Irving, Dickens, and Thackeray all stayed here for brief periods. When originally developed by a wealthy speculator, Seth Greer, in 1832, the row consisted of nine Greek Revival townhouses and was named La Grange Terrace after the Marquis de Lafayette's Château de la Grange just outside Paris. Plans originally called for pergolas and elaborate roof gardens but these were never realized. In fact the project has a history of constant abuse. Even before its completion, stonecutters in the city threatened to demolish the emerging structure unless the builders stopped using stone quarried and cut by Sing Sing inmates. Then early in this century John Wanamaker demolished five of the houses for a delivery-truck garage. Tasteless protruberances have been added to the roof to increase rentable floor space, the garden and its terrace are gone, and much of the refined ornamentation is missing.

Of course, it was not all opulence and tranquillity in those early years around Astor Place. On the evening of May 10, 1849, one of the bloodiest riots ever recorded in the city erupted outside the Astor Place Opera House (near 8th Street at Lafayette), where the British actor William Macready was giving his famous rendition of Macbeth. At the time there was strong resentment of the influence that England seemed to have over this nation's affairs. Poor Macready was hardly to blame, although ill-concealed bitterness between the actor and his American "rival," Edwin Forrest, had been sensationalized by the press. Throughout the play the audience hissed and booed whenever Macready appeared on stage. The climax came as Forrest shouted out the fiery line "what purgative drug will scour these English hence?" Pandemonium broke loose. The audience went wild, destroying the seats, the wall lamps, the curtains, and the great crystal chandelier. Outside were several thousand more rioters. The police were quickly outnumbered and on more than one occasion only escaped with their lives by firing point-blank into the crazed mob. The melee lasted three days, the theater was almost destroyed, and at least twenty-three people (some sources estimate thirty-one) were killed. Macready somehow escaped with his life and returned to England to be personally welcomed by Queen Victoria. He never came back to New York.

Lafayette Street south from Astor Place contains some splendid nineteenth-century structures including the Durst Building (409–411), a powerful blend of brick with cast iron, and the Romanesque-flavored De Vinne Press Building (393–99), named after the renowned author of books on the art and history of printing, Theodore De Vinne. Then abruptly, as we turn the corner onto East 4th Street, the mood changes and we find ourselves facing the diminutive Old Merchant's House, thought to be one of the last complete Greek-Revival houses in the city (Open Sunday 1–4 P.M.; 777-1089. Fee).

At one time the whole street was lined with similar structures and must have matched Washington Square North in character. Built in 1831, the Old Merchant's House was purchased in 1835 by Seabury Tredwell and remained in his family until 1933 when a distant relative, George Chapman, managed to ensure its preservation as an example of late-nineteenth-century life in the city. Everything is intact. Most of the objects—the beds, chairs, tables, paintings, clothes, and trinkets—were accumulated by the Tredwells during their century-long residence here. One feels like a guest in the home of a family of refinement. Trunks upstairs in the bedroom still contain the Tredwells' clothes and shoes. It's a captivating glimpse of yesteryear.

Then abruptly we're out on the Bowery itself, a brash, battered street full of character and history. It was named after the road built in the 1600s from the city to Peter Stuyvesant's "bouwerie," or farm, which included all land presently east of today's Bowery between 4th and 7th streets. The governor located his stone house on what is now the corner of 10th Street and Second Avenue, erected the first St. Mark's-in-the-Bouwerie Church, and encouraged the settlement of Dutch pioneers in the adjoining Bouwerie Village. After the British takeover of New Amsterdam in 1664, Stuyvesant retired permanently to his estate and following his death in 1672 was buried in the graveyard of his own church.

For almost a hundred years Bouwerie Village remained unchanged, a pleasant pastoral enclave. Even when Seth Greer was busy building his La Grange Terrace the more conservative New Yorkers considered this area still "country" and ridiculed any attempt at land development. But by the mid-1800s, as the city ex-

Old Merchant's House

panded northward, the Bowery had become a burgeoning entertainment strip of theaters, taverns, and beer gardens.

The opening of Sperry's Botanical Gardens, later Vauxhall Garden, near Astor Place was followed by the establishment in 1826 of the Bowery Theater on the site of the Bull's Head Tavern. It was here that Washington had paused to quench his thirst with Bowery Ale on Evacuation Day in 1783. Later came the Windsor Theater and for a while the finest actors of the time strolled the stages of a dozen or more opulent establishments. Then, in typical Manhattan fashion, the tide of fashionable residences continued up the island, taking with it the finer cultural facilities and leaving in its wake a flotsam and jetsam of sleazy alehouses, rotgut liquor saloons, and a plethora of gangsters, beggar-girls, card sharks, and ladies of the night. By 1898 the Bowery had ninety-nine houses of entertainment, of which only fourteen were classed as respectable by the police. Here's the reaction of a Southerner who made his first visit to the street around this time:

> These places (theater and bars) were jammed to suffocation on Sunday nights. Actresses too corrupt and dissolute to play elsewhere appear on the boards at the Bowery. Broad farces, indecent comedies, plays of highwaymen and murderers, are received with shouts by the rag-pickers, begging girls, collectors of cinders, all who can beg or steal a sixpence, fill the galleries of these corrupt places of amusement. There is not a dance hall, a free-and-easy, a concert saloon, or a vile drinking-place that presents such a view of the depravity and degradation of New York as the gallery of a Bowery theater.

By 1930 there were hardly a dozen theaters left, and most of these were devoted to burlesque and movies. The vast beer gardens that seated fifteen hundred customers at large trestle tables were gone, along with the odd mélange of characters that gave the Bowery so much of its notorious color. The street sank into a decay that has lasted for almost half a century.

Today, that aspect of decay and impoverishment remains, with its Salvation Army centers, wholesale restaurant-supply outlets, and flophouses, but there are promising signs of a commercial renaissance. New bars and restaurants are once again hectic night-life places and the funky C.B.G.B. still roars on as a punk and New Wave nexus. Legitimate theaters flourish after a long absence—La MaMa's, the Truck and Warehouse, the New York Theatre Ensemble (all on East 4th Street just past Phebe's), and the Bouwerie Lane Theater, housed in an example of exquisite cast-iron architecture in the French Second Empire style located on the corner of Bond Street and the Bowery. In those places where the details are missing, a talented artist has painted two-dimensional replicas in convincing trompe l'oeil manner.

And there are the old East Village remnants too. Just off the Bowery, up a little alley on 2nd Street near Second Avenue, is the New York Marble Cemetery, one of the few remaining active cemeteries in the city. Nearby is the New York City Marble Cemetery (52–74 East 2nd Street between First and Second avenues) with proud headstones commemorating members of the city's early premier families—the Roosevelts, Beekmans, Varicks, and Scribners.

To the north, McSorley's Old Ale House at 15 East 7th Street (near Third Avenue) is little changed since it first opened back in the 1850s, and is the neighborhood's bastion of permanence. Everyone who was anyone in New York has drunk McSorley's rich ale and eaten the chili and ham-and-cheese sandwiches. Peter Cooper's chair and mug are preserved without fanfare and the old-timers point with a grin to Brendan Behan's favorite corner near the pot-belly stove. And towering over it all like a stern but kindly father is the chocolate-colored Cooper Union Foundation Building. The view north of this famous college devoted to science and art is one of the most impressive in the East Village. Fourth Avenue continues north past the remnants of Book Row (the Strand is the only bookstore of real significance still left) and disappears into a shadowed canyon topped by a skyline of golden towers and the majestic Empire State Building.

Of course when the Cooper Union was first established, this was still a pastoral enclave of rolling fields dotted with a few select mansions. Peter Cooper himself, philanthropist, reformer, and inventor, was determined to found a center for free technical educa-

tion and for the open expression of opinions by significant spokes-
men on crucial issues of the day. (He was also curious to see if his
railroad rails, produced in his Trenton plant, could be used effectively in building construction.) In 1860, shortly after the opening,
Lincoln made his important "right makes might" address here,
which established his reputation as a powerful orator and potential
presidential candidate. Henry Ward Beecher, William Cullen Bryant, and William Lloyd Garrison also used the stage of the Great
Hall to deliver major speeches against slavery and in defense of the
Union.

Augustus Saint-Gaudens's prominent statue of Cooper (1897) in
the little triangular space south of the Union shows a stately, powerful man sitting kinglike on a high-backed chair. Saint-Gaudens was
slightly biased, of course. He, like many of America's leading artists,
had received a free education at the Union and had enormous
respect for the farsightedness of its founder. Other contemporaries,
however, described him in more familiar terms as "a kind man, full
of ideas and fun" and called him "the leprechaun."

Today the building remains an important center for education.
Free public lectures, seminars, and concerts continue to attract
large crowds to the Great Hall, and inexpensive courses are offered
in a wide variety of subjects ranging from Western Philosophy and
Graphoanalysis (handwriting analysis) to Comparative Religious
Mysticism and Assertiveness Training (call 254-6300 for details).
The Cooper Union Museum, once also housed here, is now located
at the Cooper-Hewitt Museum at 9 East 90th Street in the Andrew
Carnegie Mansion. Call 860-6868 for further information.

At Third Avenue and East 7th Street we pass into a little world
of onion domes and painted eggs, finely embroidered blouses, and
Slavic music dancing out from diminutive stores. The Bowery and
the cultural monoliths around Cooper Square and Astor Place seem
far behind. We're abruptly in the heartland of the Ukraine.

Until recently the domes and Byzantine bulges of the two Russian
Orthodox churches nestled together like a devoted married couple,
reflecting the strong traditions of the neighborhood. The old St.
George's was a dark, romantic place with glimmers of gold mosaic
piercing the gloom, but it was demolished to make room for a

parking lot. The new St. George's, white and fat, opened in April 1978, with a bright light-filled interior, and reflects the unchanging solidarity of the inhabitants of this Little Ukraine.

Taras Schumylowych, an architect and artist who worked on the plans for Independence Plaza and the Rupert Houses in downtown Manhattan, told me, "That church is the best thing that's happened to us in years. It's a reminder to others—and to us sometimes—that we're still here." Sixty-five-year-old Irene Kmetyk feels the same pride for the district. She's the local expert in "pysanky," the painted eggs you'll see in the stores throughout this part of the East Village, and she used to conduct classes in the art at the little-known Ukrainian Museum at 203 Second Avenue between 12th and 13th streets (Open Wednesday–Sunday 1–5 P.M.; 228–0110. Fee). Don't miss the museum's excellent displays of ceramics, jewelry, wood carvings, and textiles, as well as the richly decorated eggs. "Our crafts, our culture, are different. We try to keep it alive," she told me. Talk with the people as you wander down East 7th Street and north on Second Avenue. Szonksz Rusych, owner of one of the exclusively Ukrainian stores opposite St. George's, loves to chat with strangers. "We're proud of our background. We like to talk about it—or about anything else too. You get a Ukrainian started and you'll have a problem stopping him—unless you feed him!"

North on Second Avenue we pass the Ukrainian Mission, the Ukrainian Sports Club, the headquarters of the Ukrainian Liberation Front, and the Ukrainian National Home with its famous restaurant (offering such Eastern European dishes as borscht, pirogi, blintzes, goulash, and stuffed cabbage), The Kiev at 117 Second Avenue, and the Ukrainian Restaurant at Second Avenue and St. Marks Place. The Orchidia at 9th Street, a well-loved oddity professing to be the only Italian/Ukrainian restaurant in the city ("pizza, pirogi, and pilsner"), was one of the early victims of gentrification in this part of the East Village. Maria Pidhorodecky wept when she had to close the place in 1984 after 27 years. Her landlord quadrupled her rent overnight and told her to raise her prices. "I just couldn't do it," she told me. "There are fourteen tables here and I can't charge Four Seasons prices!"

In spite of the decidedly Ukrainian flavor of the neighborhood, there is a brilliant array of cuisines to sample here, from the refined and elegant French dishes at Evelyne's (87 East 4th Street) to the unique restaurant row along 6th Street between First and Second avenues with over fifteen Indian and Pakistani establishments, most notably Anar Bagh, Royal Indian (on First Avenue), and Gandhi. Add to these half a dozen excellent and inexpensive Chinese restaurants (serving mainly Szechuan and Hunan dishes), the Bink and Bink gourmet take-out (80 Second Avenue), the Second Avenue Kosher Delicatessen and Restaurant (156 Second Avenue), the Pasta Place (163 First Avenue at 10th Street), Kanpyo's excellent sushi and sashimi (85 First Avenue near 5th Street), and the famous Gem Spa (St. Marks Place and Second Avenue), which claims to be the creator and only authentic dispenser of egg creams in New York. These restaurants, coupled with a handful of top-flight gourmet food stores, bakeries, and bargain-price cheese stores (try the tiny East Village Cheese Store at 239 East 9th Street at Second Avenue), reveal the multifaceted appeal of the East Village.

At this point in the walk we're deep in the heart of what used to be the old Yiddish Rialto, a second Broadway of theaters offering productions almost exclusively to a Jewish population living in the Lower East Side. In its heyday it stretched all the way from Houston Street to 14th Street and many famous Jewish actors, including Edward G. Robinson, Paul Muni, Maurice Schwartz, and Stella Adler, pranced the boards to the delight of audiences who loved the "immigrant-makes-good" themes of many of the productions. Today they are all gone, with the exception of the Hebrew Actors' Union opposite St. George's Church on East 7th Street and the Theater for the New City, offering avant-garde poetry, music, and dance. Even the famous Café Royale at Second Avenue and 12th Street, forum for the Jewish intelligentsia and theatrical critics, has vanished. The Jewish population, in typical Manhattan fashion, "made good" and moved north. The durable Eden managed to keep going longer than the others, offering fine progressive theater, but even that has vanished now.

Fortunately there's one enclave around the church of St. Mark's-in-the-Bouwerie that reflects, in a relatively unmolested state, the earliest history of the neighborhood—long before the Bowery bums, the Jewish, Ukrainian, and Polish immigrants, and the flower people. St. Mark's Church itself, built first as a Dutch chapel in 1660 and rebuilt in 1799, was badly damaged by fire in July 1978 but has subsequently been restored to an active, action-oriented center.

The church was long renowned for being somewhat unconventional. In 1878 the remains of A. T. Stewart, millionaire founder of Wanamaker's, were removed and held for a ransom of $250,000. Two years later the body was finally relinquished after Stewart's widow had paid out $20,000. Then in the 1920s Dr. William Norman Guthrie shocked the less-enlightened members of his congregation by introducing a church ritual expressing the essential unity of all religions, which included American Indian chants, Greek folk dancing, and Eastern mantras. He also established a Body and Soul Clinic aimed at providing combined physical and spiritual treatments, a most advanced concept of healing in those days.

Later, particularly during the flower era, the church became a locus for the new wave of poets and playwrights and until the fire the Monday and Wednesday poetry readings (8 P.M.) were an integral part of neighborhood culture. In the cemetery, which still contains the bodies of Governor Peter Stuyvesant and Commodore Matthew C. Perry, the area around the graves has been paved over to enable more intensive use by nearby residents. Spend time here under the shade trees, reading the old headstones and admiring the sculpture around the portico. The two weathered Indians were the work of Solon Borglum, who spent much of his early life traveling the Sierra Madre. His statues depicting the characters and flavor of the Old West can be found in museums throughout the country, including the Metropolitan in New York City. On either side of the main door are two chunky lions, both of Florentine marble. Toom Dupuis's sculpture of Peter Stuyvesant peers somewhat indifferently over the graveyard (a gift from Queen Wilhelmina of Holland in 1915), and at the opposite side is Daniel Tompkins, governor of New York from 1807 to 1817, famous for completely abolishing slavery in the state.

Today pick up a leaflet at the church outlining the special events offered in conjunction with St. Mark's Poetry Project, Community Documentation Workshop, Danspace Project, and work-training programs for neighborhood youth. And try to visit the summer Greenmarkets here too, every Tuesday 8 A.M.–6 P.M.

To the east of the church is the delightful triangle of sixteen Italianate houses on Stuyvesant and East 10th streets. Because of the splayed angle of the street (one of the few true east-west streets in Manhattan), it's easy to miss. With the exception of the elegant Federal-style Stuyvesant-Fish House at 21 Stuyvesant Street (built by a great-grandson of the governor in 1804 as a wedding gift for his daughter), all the other townhouses were conceived and constructed as a group in 1861. Stanford White was born here, Dwight Macdonald lived nearby on East 10th Street, and W. H. Auden, who was a parishioner of St. Mark's, spent much time in one of the Stuyvesant Street houses. During the fifties this became the territory of Ginsberg, Kerouac, Mailer, Frank O'Hara, and LeRoi Jones. The local coffee shops were the focus of the "beat" culture—Mickey Ruskin's 10th Street Coffee House, Les Deux Magots on East 7th Street, and Café Le Metro. How pristine the triangle must have seemed against the kaleidoscope of the avenues and the frantic party-paced life of the times. Kerouac gives this brief description of the neighborhood in his book *The Subterraneans*:

> The wash hung over the court, actually the back courtyard of a big 20-family tenement with bay windows, the wash hung out and in the afternoon the great symphony of Italian mothers, children, fathers BeFinneganing and yelling from stepladders, smells, cats mewing, Mexicans, the music from all the radios whether bolero or Mexican or Italian tenor of spaghetti eaters or loud suddenly turned-up KPFA symphonies of Vivaldi harpsichord intellectuals performances boom blam the tremendous sound of it.

The atmosphere changes as we walk down East 11th Street, heading toward First Avenue and eventually reach Tompkins Square Park. We enter an Italian mini-neighborhood, leaving behind the pirogi and borscht for a while. The Veniero Pasticceria near First Avenue brims with trays of the most tempting sugary delights. Locals sit inside on the soda fountain chairs drinking espresso. At the far end, the great chrome-plated coffee machine gleams like an altarpiece. Next door is Russo's, famous for its homemade mozzarella and pasta, where Tony Russo can often be seen smoking his plump, round cheeses in a sidewalk brazier. Then on First Avenue there are the all-day, all-night vegetable and fruit stands, DeRobertis' Pastry Shop (ice-cream parlorlike with white tiled walls), and Lanza's, with its dimly lit dining room and oil paintings browned with age and the smoke of strong cigars. Pete's Spice Store is perfectly at home in this redolent section of the avenue.

Down East 10th Street the flavor changes again. We pass a Russian and Turkish bathhouse, or "schvitz," and the oddly styled St. Nicholas Carpatho-Russian Orthodox Church on the corner of Avenue A. Founded by the Rutherford-Stuyvesant family in 1884, it was known as St. Mark's Chapel of the Bouwerie until it became an Orthodox church in 1925. The rich interior is renowned for its beautifully tiled walls, carved beams, and stained glass.

Then we're finally at Tompkins Square Park, counter-culture center and one of the city's most active and kaleidoscopic mini-neighborhoods. Here sushi meets spaghettini, yuppie confronts yahoo, Jerseyites mingle with wild-haired junkies, and millionaire lawyers hide their Mercedes and dress down-market in their search for the next real estate killing.

On East 11th Street, behind the newly renovated townhouses bounding the northern edge of the park, is a unique experiment in innovative urban-energy alternatives. Various neighborhood groups including "Adopt a Building" (an organization encouraging the rehabilitation of abandoned apartment buildings using "sweat equity" as a prime resource), the Energy Task Force, and the 11th Street Movement cooperated in the development of solar and wind power systems to minimize fuel costs for low-income tenants. Nearby, at 12th Street between avenues A and B, another group has initiated a community garden project with promising results. "We have no vandalism problems at all," Mary Christianson, a member of the Energy Task Force, told me. "There's too much of the community invested in these projects."

Along the eastern edge of the park, around 10th Street and Avenue B, is what at first appears to be a typical example of urban decay complete with roofless buildings, graffiti-smothered walls, ominous Hell's Angels hangouts in abandoned stores, and sidewalks ankle-deep in garbage. But surprise! Closer inspection reveals a rich plethora of small art galleries, restaurants such as Life, offering poetry readings along with an eclectic menu, the Limbo Lounge's live performances in its gallery space, and Space Drama's odd assortment of fifties furniture (kidney-shaped tables and all).

Along Avenue A, on the park's western edge, is an equally surprising mélange of punk bars, gay hangouts, The Pyramid Cocktail Lounge featuring funky bands, Beulah Land's odd combination of art, cocktails, and fashion displays, and the never-changing Odessa Restaurant. Here the blintzes, pirogi, and borscht still attract the local Eastern European residents who gather at the southwestern corner of the park every day to discuss the weather and the state of the world. Scores of them, most of them in hats and dark coats, stand in tight groups gesticulating and arguing in their native tongues. Appropriately, the nearby statue of Samuel Sullivan Cox, "the letter-carrier's friend," shows a stern-bearded gentleman in a frock coat waving his finger in a grand oratorical gesture. "They're here every day," a young man told me as we watched the fiery discussions. "You think sometimes they're going to massacre each other, it gets so noisy. But then they go away and come back the next day, all smiles and handshakes."

Back on First Avenue, between 7th and 8th streets, the aroma of smoking meats wafts out over the sidewalk from E. Kurowycky and Son's butcher shop, mingling with the smell of fresh loaves from the New First Avenue Bakery. Nostalgia hangs heavy over this part of the neighborhood and, indeed, is given pride of place at Theatre 80 St. Marks on the corner of St. Marks Place and First Avenue (254-7400). Here Howard Otway presents his nightly double-billing of early movies, featuring such notables as Fred Astaire, Rita Hayworth, Rosalind Russell, Paul Robeson, Orson Welles, John Barrymore, George Raft, and other latter-day superstars. Note the handprints and signatures on the sidewalk, à la Grauman's Chinese Theatre in Hollywood. Inside an old speakeasy bar now functions as a candy counter and in the foyer there's a memorial niche to Joan

Theatre 80

Crawford. "She was a good friend" is all Howard will say about her.

St. Marks Place between First and Second avenues is a splendid indication of the renovation potential of the neighborhood. Admittedly some of the townhouse remodeling has been misguided and uninformed, as exemplified by an almost callous removal of elegant steps and wrought-iron railings. But the street has an air of new life to it, the spirit of a fresh start. There's a Polish Club here, a Montessori School, a number of refined churches that blend perfectly with the terraced townhouses, a ballet school, a group whose motto is "Aid to the Feeble, Comfort to the Aged," and a few new stores and restaurants. The neighborhood is alive with clubs and organizations, the threads that hold the web of community together.

As we complete the final leg of our walk, we pass through the heart of the East Village: St. Marks Place between Second and Third avenues is a riotous summation of all the East Village has been and possibly will be. The street blazes with color and noise. Radios blast from open apartment windows, a rooster crows from a purple fire escape, residents hang out of the windows carrying on conversations with passing friends. The bright blue building on the north side of the street was originally a well-known Polish club, the Dom, then later became the Electric Circus, and today contains a beehive of craft classes and activities. The Saint Mark's Book Store is the center of the neighborhood's counter-culture, featuring a wide selection of poetry by those New York poets who appear regularly at St. Mark's Church, a comprehensive selection of Marxist/Third World publications, books on Eastern philosophy and women's studies, and—at last count—over 420 different periodicals.

The trinket-laden window of a "Reader and Advisor" nestles among stores with such bizarre names as Manic Panic, Trash and Vaudeville, Hair Power, and Conscious Decision. People walk at an almost Californian pace and the air is rich with incense and other more illicit aromas. Two children, completely naked, romp together on the sidewalks as their smiling mother, dressed in a sarilike outfit, chats with a companion on a stoop. A young man with a beard hanging to his navel strolls along the sidewalk singing Dylan and strumming a battered guitar. An ice-cream parlor features such flavors as Panama Red and Acapulco Gold. Everywhere there's construction going on—stores being remodeled, townhouses being renovated. A few years back it seemed the area was almost beyond reclamation. Now one can see the new confidence and the new sense of purpose. There's still much to be done, but the pace of change accelerates every day.

It's a great place to explore.

4 | The West Village

Our walk will take us along some of the most restrainedly dignified streets in the city, where mellowed façades and delicately pruned shade trees reflect a way of life that is entirely nineteenth century. The village has always had its quiet corners. It's time for us to rediscover them on our walk.

Where else could a tour of the village begin but at the base of one of its best-loved landmarks, the Jefferson Market Courthouse, now a public library, at Sixth Avenue (Avenue of the Americas) and West 10th Street. Set in the delightful Jefferson Market Greening park (a hard-won creation of local residents), its architecture, both formal and frivolous, is an apt expression of village character.

It all began rather quietly in the 1790s. The verdant pre-Revolutionary estates, rolling acres of grassland, woods, and marshes that characterized this portion of the island, were gradually divided up and sold off in modest lots to craftsmen, carpenters, and sailmakers looking for a base close to the Hudson River, away from the heat and congestion of the New York docks. Then, following a series of

☞ **DIRECTIONS**
Subway: Shuttle (BMT/LL) on 14th Street and Sixth Avenue or IND AA, CC, E, A to West 4th Street/Washington Square and Sixth Avenue
Bus: M5, M6, M10 (north/south), M13 (east/west)

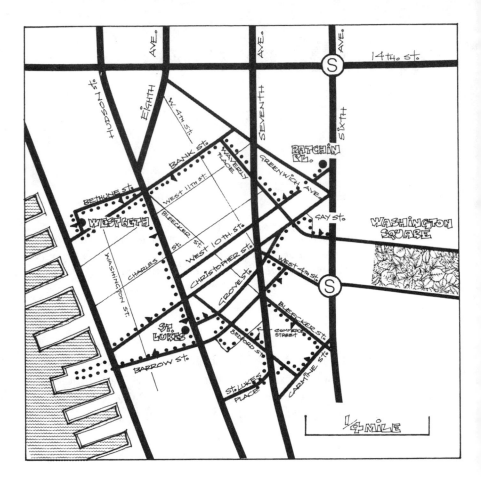

smallpox, yellow fever, and cholera epidemics that plagued the city around the turn of the century, anxious citizens fled north to the balmy, breeze-blown meadows of Greenwich. Many regarded this as a temporary expedient and the fragmented proliferation of streets reflected a lack of concern for overall community structure. Some streets merely followed previously used cowpaths. Plans for parks and open spaces—more than 170 acres of them—were conveniently bottom-drawered as the expansion continued. By 1830, however, Washington Square had been transformed from a parade ground into a fashionable residential area, and the later founding of New York University on the east side bestowed formal sanction on the village.

Then, as occurred in every part of the city, the whims of fashion and the continuing northward scramble of the population led to a series of declines in the village around the beginning of the nineteenth century. Tenements and noxious industries along the Hudson cast a pall over the more refined enclaves, whose sensitive occupants hurriedly left. Rents fell, attracting the "huddled masses" from the lower city—the Irish and Italians particularly. Similarly, writers, artists, and others of bohemian persuasion were charmed by the quaintness of the place and moved into the small apartments and mews cottages. The roster of residents reads like a Who's Who of the American arts—Twain, Poe, James, O. Henry, Greeley, Whitman, Dreiser, Millay, Bret Harte, Saint-Gaudens, Hudson River School painters, proponents of the "Ashcan School" Glackens and Sloan, and the painter Edward Hopper.

The village's position at the forefront of American culture, or anticulture, depended on the prevailing attitudes of the times. The "bohemians" became the "beatniks," while jazz and folk music flourished in a score of famous cellar clubs until the emergence of the honky-tonks, the porno palaces of the fifties, and increasingly inflated rents led to a gradual emigration of its more creative spirits to such neighborhoods as SoHo and the East Village.

Today this disjointed patchwork of fragmented streets, hidden courts, odd bars, famous clubs, tourist strips, and quiet sparrowed parks continues to reflect almost every stage of its own growth. There are still plenty of artists and writers here; not everyone has moved to SoHo. The literary bars still attract the literary types and the gay bars have their own distinct clientele. Little old ladies struggle up the steps of elegant townhouses. Coffeehouses dot almost every block. Health-food restaurants flourish. Behind the Italianate, Federal, neo-Georgian, and even "fairy-tale" façades, the village life continues. Sometimes crass, sometimes crazy—always captivating.

The key on this walk is—keep your eyes open. Immediately to the north of the Jefferson Library, for example, peep past the splendid Bishop's crook lamp post into the diminutive Patchin Place. If you walk too fast on West 10th you'll miss it. Built in the mid-1800s as inexpensive apartments for the Basque waiters at the elegant Brevoort Hotel on Fifth Avenue, this tiny court of off-white townhouses has housed many famous literateurs—John Masefield, England's brilliant poet laureate who once made a living polishing the floors of village saloons, Theodore Dreiser, Eugene O'Neill, and E. E. Cummings. A row of delicate ailanthus trees, a species indigenous to India and once thought to absorb "bad air," provides welcome shade from the sear of summer streets, and there's a little-known view of the Jefferson Library from the far end of the cul-de-sac. I paused one warm afternoon to make a sketch. An elderly lady peered at the drawing and beamed at me. "You should," she said. I looked at her questioningly. "You should draw that view. I've been looking at it for thirty years and I think it's the nicest in the village. It's right to share it." We chatted together about the city. "There's so much that's changed," she told me sadly. "I think people should be reminded there are places left like this." I finished the sketch while drinking the cup of tea she brought me.

Just around the corner on Sixth Avenue is the even more concealed Milligan Place, deep in shade behind its wrought-iron gateway. The houses you see were built in the 1850s for Samuel Milligan, who acquired the property in 1799. Eugene O'Neill spent many

Patchin Place

long hours here working with Susan Glaspell and her husband, George Cram Cook (founder of the Provincetown Playhouse), on his play *The Emperor Jones.*

Up the block, cross the road for another hidden gem on West 11th Street just east of Sixth Avenue. The tiny Second Cemetery of the Spanish and Portuguese Synagogue is all that remains of a larger plot, paved over when 11th Street was extended to join Sixth Avenue in the mid-1800s.

Back on 10th Street continue west across Greenwich Avenue to Waverly Place. The dimly lit Julius pub on the corner is one of the oldest bars in the village and a popular hangout with the gay crowd. Like most pre-Prohibition establishments, it possesses a generous repertoire of hidden-booze and sliding-panel tales. Fats Waller once gave impromptu concerts here, and later admirers, Truman Capote, Tennessee Williams, and Rudolf Nureyev, reaffirmed its reputation as one of the village's more important wateringholes. Nearby is the Three Lives and Company Books, specializing in modern fiction, art, and photography, and well-known for its free prose and poetry readings on Thursday nights (usually from 8 P.M.).

We continue up Waverly Place, across Seventh Avenue, past the well-loved Village Vanguard and the Caffe da Alfredo, to St. John's in the Village, an unusually diverse grouping of religious and community facilities. In addition to the church itself, designed by Edgar Tafel in 1974 especially for performing arts presentations (a fire destroyed the original Greek Revival "Temple"), there's a courtyard area used for theatrical and musical productions, and a charming hidden garden originally developed in the early 1900s by clergyman John Armstrong Wade as part of the St. John's Artists colony. Access to the garden is through an old "horse walk" and visitors are welcome to call at the Church Office (224 Waverly Place, 9 A.M.–5 P.M.; 243-6192) to gain entry.

Approaching the north end of Waverly Place, where it joins Bank Street, we enter the true West Village, an intimate neighborhood of narrow tree-lined streets, terraces of elegant townhouses, and tiny restaurants. The Waverly Inn offers traditional American fare in a genuinely Elizabethan-tavern atmosphere of high-back seats, fireplaces, and mellow candlelight. La Chaumière on West 4th Street is typical of the high quality and restrained dignity of the eating places in this part of the city. Down Bank Street the Hudson River sparkles between the large waterfront buildings. A young girl wheels her bicycle along the sidewalk with a loaf of crusty French bread tucked under her arm. An elderly gentleman dressed like an English squire in plus-fours, tweed jacket, and a deerstalker hat pauses on the corner to gaze at the river. Great billows of smoke from his black briar pipe swirl around his face. His silver mustache, slightly yellowed, and his ruddy cheeks stand out prominently. He whistles a short sharp note, a very gentlemanly whistle, and a frizzled Yorkshire terrier leaves his lamp post and bounds along the sidewalk to stand panting at the squire's side. The two continue slowly down the street to the river.

At Hudson Street a broad expanse of park and play area is filled with children and napping mothers. On the other side are the first restaurants and taverns of the burgeoning Hudson Strip. The nautical-flavored Ivory Seahorse, which only recently closed its doors, was the home of a sea captain during the mid-1800s. At that time the blocks down to the river were a riot of dockland activities and related antics of a more recreational nature. Houses of ill-repute flourished. Hole-in-the-wall gin palaces sent sotted sailors tumbling into the streets. Brawling and braggadocio produced a night-long bedlam in the narrow cobbled streets. "It was a hell of a place down here," Jack Herbert, one-time owner of a pub here, told me. His grandfather designed many of the liners that steamed the Great Lakes, and Jack has long been fascinated by sea life. "There were street gangs. The Hudson Dusters were the worst. Gave the penny-dreadfuls plenty of material for their lurid stories. It's pretty quiet now, though. About the only activity you'll find down by the river is at Westbeth." So if you don't mind a short detour away from the sedate streets, stroll down Bethune Street to this interesting complex of artists' studio space and living quarters housed in the old Bell Telephone Laboratories, an austere monolith near the waterfront.

Long before Westbeth was conceived, the Bell Laboratories had developed a remarkable reputation for creativity in the electronics field. The first "talking" movie, Al Jolson's *Jazz Singer,* was produced here on a sound stage that still exists within the complex. Later developments came in the form of TV experiments and transistor research. In 1967, sponsored by grants from the Kaplan Fund and the National Council on the Arts, the laboratories were refurbished to provide 383 apartments for New York artists and space for public-related activities including theaters, workshops, and the Merce Cunningham Dance Studios. Since then the complex has nurtured successes and experienced its share of disappointments, inevitable in an environment of this nature. From time to time there are ambitious plans for increasing interaction between Westbeth's inhabitants and the outside community—talk of new workshops, galleries, festivals, and more theatrical productions. "There's a real renaissance going on," a young resident raved. "There's always a bloody renaissance," muttered one of the older occupants, who'd seen it all before. Still, it's a unique experiment and worth the detour. (Call 242-5089 or 691-1426 for the latest information on exhibitions and performances.)

Back on the Hudson Strip, it's antiques, restaurants, and bars along a street that's far too wide for intimacy and far too fragmented architecturally. But there's character and fun here. Dylan Thomas thought so when he frequented the White Horse Tavern on the corner of West 11th Street and that was long before it became an adjunct of the West Village. Afternoons in the tavern are usually quiet, ticking away with the clock; fly-specked mirrors and chipped white horses (the one in the window has lost most of his natural accoutrements) give it the flavor of a true New York bar.

But evenings bring life to the street. Conversation flows faster than ale at the No Name and the Sazerac House; lovers of the sweet life indulge themselves at restaurants like Village Green, Harlequin, Finalment, and La Ripaille; leather freaks gather in studded groups in the pubs around Christopher Street, and a bunch of rollicking out-of-towners try to play a tuba dangling over the sidewalk outside an antique store. Yet a short distance off Hudson, at Charles and

Greenwich streets, is a cottage so peacefully set in its own garden that it's hard to believe you're still in the city.

The mood prevails at St. Luke's-in-the-Fields, built in the early 1800s as a county church to serve a still rural hinterland. It was here that "sixpenny loaves of wheaten bread" were distributed every Sunday to "such poor as shall appear most deserving" in accordance with the terms of a will and fund set up by John Leake in 1792. In 1890 the congregation had a larger church built way uptown at Convent Avenue and 141st Street, and this diminutive building was purchased by Trinity Church in 1892 and rededicated as a chapel of Trinity Parish. Today it's one of the most delightful places in the West Village following extensive restoration after a 1981 fire. The garden is tiny and tranquil, set behind a group of minuscule Federal-style townhouses. Bret Harte once lived at number 487, the last one on the right.

Charles Street Cottage

Grove Court

If you're here before sunset, take another brief detour west down Barrow Street to Morton Street Pier (Pier 42), a favorite summer-evening haunt of villagers. Even on the most humid days the breezes at the end of the pier are cooling as you stand overlooking the river, the great industrial plants on the Jersey side, the Statue of Liberty in the harbor, and the haze-blue hills of Staten Island beyond. Return to Hudson Street by way of Christopher Street, past the new River Hotel with its sophisticated rooftop restaurant, and the ornate St. Veronica's Roman Catholic Church. Note the elegantly massive bulk of the U.S. Federal Building at Washington Street, built in 1899. There were plans to convert it into a five-story galleria of shops and restaurants but, at last visit, the place looked sadly abandoned. These plans are currently on hold.

At Grove Street, east of Hudson, we return again to the tranquillity of the West Village, to the delicate Federal-style townhouses and the narrow, intimate streets. Pause at Grove Court, one of my favorite hidden niches. Residents in these delightfully shaded rowhouses, originally built in the mid-1800s as workers' cottages, (known locally as "Mixed Ale Alley"!), are generally tolerant of intruders quietly exploring the walled courtyard. O. Henry is said to have conceived his short story "The Last Leaf" here, and many subsequent authors, sculptors, and artists have found that this enclave provides just the right amount of seclusion from the occasionally overbearing social whirl of village life.

The odd fairy-tale structure at 102 Bedford Street (a lovely pink idiosyncrasy) was remodeled as "an inspiring home for creative artists" by philanthropist Otto Kahn in 1926 and aptly named "Twin Peaks." Adjoining the structure is the 1822 clapboard workshop of William Hyde, a sash-maker, and a diminutive "slaves' quarters" with canary-yellow shutters. This is surely the oddest collection of structures in the village. Appropriately enough, a little farther down Bedford Street, number 75½ is the "narrowest house," boasting a 9½-foot frontage (just wide enough for a horse and carriage). Edna St. Vincent Millay lived here briefly during the early 1920s.

You may not have noticed an ancient wooden doorway complete with iron grille as you walked down Bedford Street. Well, look again

Twin Peaks

at number 86, or better still, turn left at the corner of Barrow just past the community bulletin board and enter the first courtyard on your left (number 70). Walk to the far end, open the large door facing you and lo, you're entering one of the best-hidden and most notorious speakeasies in the city, the famous Chumley's. It was here, during the thirties and forties, that the literary notables of the village met to drink, talk, or do whatever literary people do in cozy places away from the hoi polloi. John Steinbeck, Ring Lardner, James Joyce, and John Dos Passos were all regulars. Look at the displays of browned book jackets along the wall. Little has changed since Joyce scribbled segments of *Ulysses* in the corner table by the far door. It's a delightful place to spend an hour or two, if you can find it!

This corner of the village is full of surprises. For example, behind Grove Court, on Barrow Street, is a diminutive courtyard of bushes and fountains surrounded by a dark, rustic, brick apartment building and, if the doorway at 34½ Barrow Street is open, stroll through the tunnel to the shaded backyard where a lovely wooden cottage sits by itself in a little garden.

The short Barrow/Commerce Street loop takes us past a most unusual duo of mansard mansions adjoining the Cherry Lane Theater and that well-loved village hangout, the Blue Mill Tavern. Popular legend has it that the mansions were built by a sea captain for his two unmarried daughters in 1831. Why not one house? Well, it appears that the daughters never spoke to each other and refused to live together, so the captain arrived at this unusual architectural compromise, leaving the garden between the houses open to encourage an eventual rapprochement. Alas, the sisters became more and more indifferent to each other and the garden was allowed to grow wild—a totally appropriate tale in this tiny fantasyland deep in the heart of the village. And, talking about fantasies, number 11 Commerce Street (near Seventh Avenue) is said to be the house in which the darling of the village literati, Washington Irving, wrote his beloved "Legend of Sleepy Hollow."

A brief detour down Seventh Avenue takes us to St. Lukes Place, a street that at first appears unprepossessing. But continue around the corner and you'll discover one of the most sedate terraces of

Italianate townhouses in the city, shaded by a row of unusual ginkgo trees. Jimmy Walker, mayor of New York during the boisterous Prohibition days, lived at number 6; Sherwood Anderson spent time here in 1922; and Theodore Dreiser put the finishing touches to *An American Tragedy* at number 16. It's a lovely backwater whose tranquillity is marred only by occasional teenage bawlings in the park across the street. But even the park has its own bit of history. Before 1890 it was a graveyard and, so 'tis claimed, the long-lost body of the Dauphin of France was buried beneath a stone with the simple if somewhat misleading inscription "Leroy" (Le Roi?).

Across Seventh Avenue, on Carmine Street, we enter the last vestiges of a once-flourishing Italian district. At the southern end, Urbino and Cent' Anni restaurants attract a well-heeled crowd, Mary's is almost a village institution famous for Italian Abruzzi cuisine served in tiny dining rooms, and at the northern end at Bleecker (across from Our Lady of Pompeii Catholic Church, where St. Francis Xavier Cabrini, the first American saint, often prayed) you'll find Caffe Lucca and the mecca of minestrone lovers, the Bleecker Luncheonette. An interesting array of neighborhood stores and restaurants line the street, many of them newcomers to the neighborhood—Mostly Magic at Bedford and Carmine with shows Tuesday–Saturday from 9 P.M., a fresh bevy of Chinese, Indian, Middle Eastern, and Spanish restaurants, and Joe Coppa's "Welcome to New York" store brimming with Big Apple memorabilia, vintage postcards, Empire State lamps, and over 100 different New York-logo T-shirts.

Up Bleecker Street toward Seventh Avenue, the redolent Italian flavor is maintained by Faicco's pork store (fat, fennel-spiced Italian sausages and smoked mozzarella), Rocco's Pastry Shop (excellent Milanese Panettone and homemade ices), Zampognaro's Gourmet Foods, Ottomanelli's meat market, John's Pizza (claimed by devotees to be the best in town), and Zito's Italian bakery.

At Barrow Street and Seventh Avenue note the imposing Greenwich House, topped by what looks like a Flemish town hall. Since 1902, when this part of the village was a melting-pot slum of Irish, Italian, and French immigrants, the Greenwich Village Improvement Society pioneered neighborhood services for medical aid, child education, improved sanitation, and cultural development. Today the spirit continues in the form of youth programs, pottery classes, music and dance schools, drug-counseling, and a nearby fund-raising thrift shop. (Call 242-4140 for details on activities, some of which are free.)

Following Barrow Street to Sheridan Square, we pass One If by Land, Two If by Sea, a lovely transformation of Aaron Burr's carriage house into a refined restaurant. The owners have many tales to tell of discovering tombstones and vaults under the basement floor during renovations, as well as a segment of tunnel that once ran all the way to the Hudson (the river was once much closer), part of the ingenious "underground railroad" used for transporting Southern slaves to freedom in New England and Canada. In contrast, Jimmy Day's, at Barrow and West 4th streets, is a boisterous tavern—as is the tiny Peculier Pub (over 200 varieties of beer sold here), and on the north side of Sheridan Square the Lion's Head attracts the literary crowd (more book jackets), in addition to a highly unlikely neighborhood bunch of "Jewish drunks, Irish lovers, and Italian intellectuals!" (according to Al Koblin, one of the owners).

The diminutive Gay Street, off Christopher Street, was originally a secluded niche for black residents, and during Prohibition, a popular speakeasy strip. Today it is once again tranquil and provides a brief respite before we emerge once again into the bustle of Sixth Avenue, our exploration of the West Village complete. If it's a warm day the street vendors will be active by the railings on the other side of the street. They're a reminder of the "other" village, the tourist village that we've studiously avoided.

Well, the culture trip is over now, so why not take a stroll on Christopher Street and Grove Street and join in the hullaballoo for a while?

5 | 14th Street— A Slice of New York

The rapid transformations that are taking place along and around this vibrant corridor are striking evidence of yet one more Manhattan renaissance. Six years ago, 14th Street was being written off, but today . . .

Fourteenth Street has long been regarded as a kind of no-man's land separating a hectic midtown from the restrained streets of the village. To the north are the frenzied anthills of the garment district, the flower district, the fur district, the diamond district. To the south, boutiques mingle with outdoor cafés, avant-garde theaters, bistros, health-food stores, and exclusive residences in a jumble of streets that form tributaries of "the valley"—a term used to describe the dense, low-rise blocks stretching southward to the canyons of downtown.

To those who pause awhile, however, 14th Street is more than just a vague demarcation line or a convenient subway interchange. It tingles with life from the early hours of dawn down in the Gan-

☞ **DIRECTIONS**

Subway: Union Square is a major interchange point, but if you intend to start at the far west end of the street, take the Eighth Avenue subway (IND A, E, AA, CC to 14th Street) or take the BMT LL shuttle from Union Square to 14th Street and Eighth Avenue

Bus: M10 or M11 (north/south), M14 (east/west)

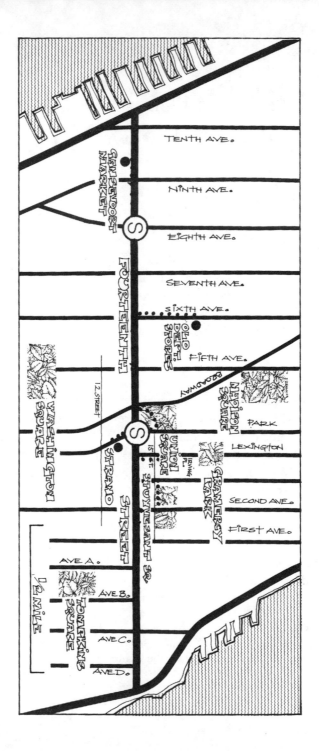

sevoort meat market to the latest hours of night around Third Avenue. During the day it booms. The street is a raucous open-air market, a bazaar, a souk. Even Macy's on Christmas Eve hardly compares with the frenzied push and tumble of the crowds as they churn between Union Square and Seventh Avenue.

It's a street of fun, of contrasts, of life. It's a street worth exploring and, more often than not, a street worth liking.

At six in the morning the stores are closed tight. Crumpled paper and cardboard boxes litter the sidewalk or rest in piles against the

Gansevoort Meat Market

steel shutters. Thick padlocks catch the dawn light as it glows over the buildings and silhouettes the chimneys of the Con Edison plant at the far eastern end of the street. An occasional bus rumbles along one of the avenues. The sound of its engine echoes against the dark walls.

Walk westward to where the street ends at Pier 56. The change is abrupt. The meat market is open and sidewalks are black with grease. Red refuse cans stamped "Inedible" brim with chunks of fat, kidneys, heads, pieces of feet, and an occasional unblinking eyeball. A steel door opens with a blast of refrigerated air and a line of carcasses emerges and hangs limply over the sidewalk, dripping a little. A truck pulls up under the canopy in a cloud of blue exhaust smoke. Men in white coats and little white hats tug at the meat with hooks. Inside are more men in white coats positioned along a wide table. Chop, chop, chop, chop. Shapeless slabs become neatly trimmed shell steaks, filets, and London broil. Someone in a white hardhat scribbles in a looseleaf folder.

Outside, a group of men are gathered around a small fire, their faces bright orange in the glow, eating thick sandwiches and drinking from a bottle in a paper bag. The market snack bar is packed, standing room only. A silver Mercedes-Benz squeezes in between two tractor trailers, and a gentleman in a tweed suit and alligator shoes tiptoes between little dark pools to a white-coated man. White coat and tweed suit disappear behind a stainless-steel door. Another slice of cold air cuts across the sidewalk.

It's only a small area, this meat market, but until lunchtime it's the busiest part of 14th Street. Scores of workers scurry and bawl around the warehouses, throwing great sides of beef, whole lambs, and pigs into the waiting trucks. The din increases throughout the morning; trucks roar away in clouds of smoke, white aprons get bloodier and bloodier, and the cans of "inedibles" crowd the sidewalks.

Then comes lunchtime. Burly porters in bloody overalls and little hats that read "Buy Beef!" churn around the bar in Howley's at 13th Street and Washington, with their beers and bowls of homemade soup. On 14th Street, right in the heart of the market, Frank's does a roaring trade in pasta, veal, and chicken lunches served on plain-set tables, packed tight on a sawdust-strewn floor. Papa George Molinari opened the place in 1912, and his son Christopher now supervises the strange transformations that occur daily beginning at 2 A.M. when Frank's opens as your basic early-morning coffee bar; then at 4 A.M. when it becomes a bustling breakfast hangout for the meat market workers, serving enormous steak platters; then at noon when a slightly more varied clientele enjoy Italian-style lunches; and finally around 7 P.M. when the place Cinderellas into a refined dinner restaurant. The bar is curtained off, tablecloths and fresh flowers appear, and some of the best (and largest) steak dinners in town are served to an elegant clientele. "It's a whole new experience in the evenings," Chris Molinari told me. "We've even got your coquilles, your escargots and, at last count, twelve different types of mushrooms. Twelve!" Frank's closes around midnight, which allows the staff about two hours to prepare for the start of the cycle all over again.

Just across Ninth Avenue is the Homestead Restaurant, another ancient institution in the area, with its brown awnings and ornate wrought-iron work. Here in the chintzy dining areas gather the meat lovers of Manhattan. They come for the filet mignon and those enormous prime-rib platters matched only by Durgin-Park pub in Boston, an equally venerable institution. It's amazing to see the same men who have been working with meat in every shape and form since the early hours of the morning launch themselves with gusto into one of those gargantuan Homestead meals.

Until recently the meat market was exclusively a place for the trade. The public rarely ventured into the area except for the "cattle rustlers" (junkies who occasionally try to run off with the odd sides of beef) and "institutional representatives" requesting handouts for a good cause—often their own stomachs. But not too long ago a couple of wholesale/retail places opened up at the east end of the market near Ninth Avenue and have attracted devotees who flock to buy (at some of the best prices in town) bulk meats, whole salamis and hams, twenty-pound cans of beans, gallon jars of ketchup, and whole cheese wheels. Items are available in smaller amounts but the price tends to be higher—so wait till you're about to throw a big barbecue and then come down here and enjoy yourself.

Between the meat market and Eighth Avenue is one of the more restrained sections of 14th Street—an enclave of churches, convents, funeral homes, and medical centers. The Eagle Tavern occasionally destroys the docility, though, with its popular Ceilidh nights of Irish folk songs and dancing, and its Monday evening "Seisiuns" when this "flourishing citadel of traditional music" becomes a hotbed of Gaelic fervor (call 924-0275 for details). The Stuyvesant Bicycle Shop nearby invites fervor of another kind from enthusiasts who come to goggle at the $2,500 Puch and Atala machines in the vast selection here. Also note the new stores and restaurants—The Integral Yoga Natural Food Store, The Tamu Indonesian Restaurant famous for its multi-platter rijstaffel, and the elegant French restaurant Quatorze—all signs of a healthy neighborhood revitalization.

Stroll farther up the street and climb the steep steps to Iglesia Católica Guadalupe, a delightful little church set in a Georgian-style row of townhouses (recently converted into apartments). The street sounds are muffled and a great fan hanging from the frescoed ceiling wafts incense into every corner. A few dark figures huddle in the pews, rosary beads clicking like watch beetles, and a short man with a face as gnarled as an olive tree kneels at each of the stations of the cross. A sign over the confessional reads: "Father Dennis—speaks Spanish, English, French, Portuguese and Dutch" (!). Two shafts of sunlight gild the baroque carvings on the altar. It's all very still and beautiful.

Back on 14th Street again, continue eastward into a section famous for its Latin/Spanish restaurants, where one can dine on great platters of bacalao (salt cod) à la Biscania, paella Valenciana, varied octopus and squid concoctions, Pepitoria de Gallina (chicken in egg and saffron sauce), and delicious tripe dishes, including one splendid creation using a filé-based sauce with chick peas. Or try some of the combination platters at one of the local Cuban-Chinese establishments—by no means the best food in town, but generous and inexpensive.

Whether you're in the mood for eating or not, don't pass by Casa Moneo, which is on both sides of the street just before Seventh Avenue. The store on the north side is the more recent and is filled with Spanish and Latin-American products—guitars, flamenco hats, great woolen shawls, records, perfumes, tapestries, and a wide selection of plaster madonnas, three-dimensional Christs in plastic-baroque frames, and garlands of rosaries. The other store is a must for lovers of make-it-yourself Spanish and Mexican cuisine. At the far end there are chilies of every type and temper, tortillas (corn and flour), or the masarina in case you have your own tortilla oven, magnificent orange chorizo sausages, real Monterey Jack cheese (a must for authentic chili rellenos), nougat, quince paste, and all the cooking equipment you'd ever need for classic Castilian dishes (and a lot of canned equivalents in case they don't work out). For real enthusiasts there are also San Miguel, Carta Blanca, Bohemia, and Portena beers, and sparkling Spanish and Argentinian ciders.

Approaching Sixth Avenue we meet the 14th Street bazaar. Stores spill out onto the sidewalks in a welter of trestle tables, up-turned drawers, and packing crates smothered in cuddly teddy bears with bright orange fur, clockwork trains clicking and hooting endlessly around circular tracks, Spanish LP's with glossy photographs of overendowed young ladies, mounds of plastic sandals, Japanese dinner sets with paisley decorations, boxes of price-slashed toothpastes, mouthwashes, and bug-killers, and even an occasional stack of galvanized scrubbing boards. Clothing stores, which from their signs always appear on the verge of bankruptcy, feature absolutely the "last and final closeout bargains" in nylon double-knits and the best $2.99 jeans in town.

In one storefront, a young salesman, very sweaty, scrubs violently on an oil-stained square of carpet: "Ladies, look at these typical household carpet stains, see how easily [puff, puff] this specially formulated cleaner, developed exclusively for this store, removes oil, soot, and grease [puff, puff] and makes your carpets like new again." A long silence as he scrubs, then a final puff as he removes the last dark specks and straightens up. He's very nervous. A small crowd of plump matrons have gathered around him and he keeps talking at the store window. Someone makes a clever remark and the crowd giggles. The poor man blushes and, still with his back to the customers, proceeds to cover the little square of carpet with an obnoxious black liquid (presumably a "mixture of typical household carpet stains"). After a hurried glance at his watch, he begins again: "Ladies, look at these typical household stains, see how easily [puff, puff] . . ."

Pause briefly at Sixth Avenue and walk northward to the Old Tenderloin District. Although there's little left of its vigorous past, you can stroll between 18th and 22nd streets and see the grandiose remnants of what used to be Manhattan's Department Store Row (part of the famous "Ladies' Mile") during the early years of this century. The most extravagant of all is the old 1896 Siegel-Cooper store between 18th and 19th streets with its triple-arch entrance and classical trimmings. Once considered "a city in itself," this edifice is rusting and paint is flaking from its great pillars. The building is currently used as a warehouse. The others, such as Altman's, Simpson-Crawford's, O'Neill's, Adams's, and Cammeyer's, have all suffered similar indignities, but if you ignore the miscellany of tiny businesses occupying their lower floors, these buildings still possess enormous charm and character. What a street this must have been in the year 1900!

But back to the 14th Street bazaar between Fifth and Sixth avenues, where the real professionals are at work in the appliance stores. The window displays are masterpieces of material abundance —brimming with televisions, cameras, stereos, VCR's, binoculars, lighters, clock radios, watches, slide projectors, tape recorders, and calculators. Show the slightest sign of really wanting something and the price soars. Wander around casually. Start by asking about things you've no intention of buying—work up to what you want slowly. Act bored and appear to be on the verge of leaving. Then, as you're walking up to the door, ask the salesman for a price on the item of your choice. (Be very uninterested.) Whatever price he quotes, turn, murmur total incredulity, and make for the door again—slowly. Invariably he'll panic. "Hey, how much you wanna pay?" Don't answer. Let him follow you. "Hey, okay, I'll make a deal . . ." At that point, pause. Go back and take another look. Twiddle knobs, push buttons or whatever, but let him do the talking. Start to look skeptical. Whatever price he suggests, offer him half. (It's always best to find out beforehand what the item sells for at more reputable stores.) At this point you might lose him, but it's unlikely. If he stays, you can relax a little. Bargain as long as you want. Start to finger your wallet (but don't open it). If he doesn't play ball, get impatient and look at your watch. If all goes well you'll walk out with a good piece of equipment far cheaper than anywhere else in town.

To bargain successfully in the bazaar is cause for celebration. So, take time out for a leisurely lunch at one of the charming little restaurants along West 13th Street just off Sixth Avenue. There is La Tulipe, one of Manhattan's most praised (some say overpraised and overpriced) establishments, plus live entertainment at Zinno, huge budget lunches at Spain, a little Cockney class at Covent Garden, and excellent bistro fare across Sixth Avenue at La Gauloise. Or snack your way down 14th Street nibbling tamales, plantanos fritos, pasteles, papas rellenas, and empanadas at the tiny sidewalk counters, or really splurge at one of the establishments in the city's newest and most elegant restaurant enclave. Many of the big-name places are within a couple of minutes of Fifth Avenue and 14th Street: Johanna's (18 East 18th Street); America (9 East 18th Street); Café Seiyoken (18 West 18th Street); Gotham Bar and Grill (12 East 12th Street); Downtown (Fifth Avenue at West 17th Street); Fifth Avenue Grill (102 Fifth Avenue near 15th Street); Union Square Café (21 East 16th Street); and the Metropolis Café (16th Street and Union Square).

What used to be a rather sleepy corner of the Big Apple after 5 P.M. is now a romping nucleus of night life attracting every strata of society. Danceteria (30 West 21st Street), Palladium (126 East 14th Street at Irving Place), and the Underground (850 Broadway at Union Square) feature dancing until the early-morning hours. Live rock bands perform at The Ritz (119 East 11th Street), live country-and-western bands at the Lone Star (Fifth Avenue at 13th Street), live blues at Tramps (125 East 15th Street) and Dan Lynch (14th Street at Second Avenue), live comedy revues at Comedy U (70 University Place at 11th Street), live jazz at Bradley's (70 University Place at 10th Street) and Knickerbocker Saloon (33 Univer-

sity Place at 9th Street), and odd nighttime antics at the hip Bowling
Club (110 University Place at 12th Street). Not to forget the burgeoning NoHo bars down Broadway between 12th Street and Houston Street.

We have now reached Union Square itself, until recently a murky,
battered space with drug-pushers lurking in shadows and bag-ladies
sharing broken benches with hookers and winos, ceaselessly passing
on their brown-bagged bottles. Today, the square is an open, friendlier space, with new ornate subway entrances and news kiosks, a
hectic greenmarket featuring the finest produce, specialty food
items, and plants on Wednesdays, Fridays, and Saturdays, and a
sense of new possibilities in the form of top-flight bar-restaurants,
most notably Metropolis and the Union Square Café, and the ambitious redevelopment of S. Klein's department store site.

Union Square has always been an important hub of New York
life, whether high or low, and was once described as the "social
center of Knickerbocker society, first home of opera, theatrical
rialto, authentic Bohemia, platform of patriots, rostrum of liberals
and communists." Tammany Hall and the Academy of Music were
located where Con Edison's "Tower of Power" rises to a tall embellished point. Macy's once had a department store close to the square
that was famous for its revolving toy displays. Tiffany's also flourished nearby, and the famous "Ladies' Mile" continued down
Broadway as far as 8th Street, with John Wanamaker's department
store and James McCreery's Dry Goods Emporium at the corner
of 11th Street. Billy Watson and his Beef Trust (a famous chorus
line of two-hundred-pound damsels) appeared from time to time in
one of the burlesque theaters adjoining Tammany Hall, and close
to Third Avenue "Good Old Doctor Grey" (a VD quack) opened
his grizzly "Museum of Anatomy" to a curious public.

Union Square itself, once a private enclave for such residents as
the Roosevelts, Van Beurens, and Pennimans, found its true voca-
tion as a center for political rallies in the 1860s following the out-
break of the Civil War. In 1870 the iron railings were removed and
the square became truly public—a meeting place for such groups as
the Anarchists and the Wobblies. On the night of August 22, 1927,
a vast crowd gathered to express indignation at the execution of

Nicola Sacco and Bartolomeo Vanzetti. The police, fearful of riots, mounted machine guns on what was the roof of Klein's department store. Although the guns were not used, dispersal of the crowd was unusually rough and subsequent gatherings, supported by the Communist newspaper *The Daily Worker,* vigorously protested police brutality.

Following the crash of 1929, the square saw scores of unemployment rallies. A particularly large meeting of 35,000 people on March 6, 1930, was again broken up by police. More than a hundred people were seriously injured, but with the impending threat of total civil disruption the police repented and finally recognized the square as an official meeting place for dissident groups.

By this time, however, the area was declining. There was a brief flicker of bohemian life in the thirties followed by a long period of stagnation as the flourishing midtown area leeched businesses away to more prestigious locations and the street people made the square their home.

But nearby there's still much of historical and commercial interest. Past the superbly ornate Moorish structure at 33 Union Square West (it once boasted a minaret-type tower, but this was deemed unsafe a few years ago and dismantled) there's a budding nucleus of bookstores consisting of Barnes and Noble (on both sides of Fifth Avenue at 18th Street and possessing a sales annex guaranteed to keep you enthralled for at least half a day), a large center for French and Spanish books just north of Barnes and Noble, Revolution Books at 13 East 16th Street with one of the widest selections of counter-culture books in the city, and the delightful incense-perfumed East-West Books at Fifth Avenue near 13th Street, where you can browse for hours, exploring new options in religions and alternative life-styles.

Union Square has a long history of association with books and publishing. Brentano's first store was situated at the top end of the square, and many left-wing newspapers and magazines were produced in adjoining buildings. In fact, the *Daily World* still exists nearby on 19th Street. Farrar, Straus, & Giroux also has its offices at 19 Union Square, the Arco Publishing house is located across from the square on Park Avenue South, and Charles Scribner's Sons is located at 115 Fifth Avenue, close to its first headquarters on Fifth Avenue between East 21st and East 22nd streets.

Perhaps the area's most memorable feature was "Book Row" on Fourth Avenue, a string of dusty stores selling used books south of the square, where devotees could browse for hours among floor-to-ceiling shelves in search of some elusive first edition (something missed by the hectic store owner, something for the price of a cheap lunch). Although much of Book Row no longer exists, a true stalwart remains at 828 Broadway (at 12th Street) where the Strand's tiny frontage disguises ten thousand square feet of display space (bigger than the average suburban supermarket) and "eight miles of books"! What a treat awaits first-timers here. This is no marginal establishment with an indifferent owner and an even more indifferent collection of books. This is a venerable institution, a haunt of famous authors (one of the managers, Bert Britton, has produced a book of caricature self-portraits by the hundreds of celebrities who have browsed the stacks over the years), loved by students, and a source of nourishment for reviewers who regularly supplement their income by selling their review copies to the store. Come here with time to spare and, for the sake of your sanity, with some specific field of interest in mind (customers have been known to leave in a state of tearful confusion after hours have been lost through the constant distraction of tens of thousands of books). Across the road lies the Forbidden Planet (the windows tell it all), equally as confusing with its vast collections of horror and science fiction comics, games, and masks, and posted warnings that "shoplifters will be disintegrated!"

Even those allergic to bookstores (I have known individuals threatened and psychologically belittled by these impressive repositories of information and learning) should venture down Broadway and its side streets and explore the clusters of antique stores, mainly wholesale, that have become a distinct feature of the neighborhood. Watch out for public auction sales (usually advertised in Saturday's *New York Times*)—they can be great fun, as can a visit to Blatt Bowling and Billiards (809 Broadway between 11th and 12th streets, 674-8855), which claims to house the world's largest collection of antique and contemporary pool tables. You can see a few magnificent specimens at street level, and guided tours

Grace Church Rectory

around the upper floors are offered if sales staff are available.

Also don't miss the superb Gothic Revival grouping of Grace Church, Clergy House, and Memorial House at 800 Broadway and Fourth Avenue at 10th Street, designed by the engineer James Renwick, Jr. The spire is one of the most delicate in the city and the church actively encourages public access with its free Thursday organ recitals (12:30 P.M.) and Sunday guided tours (around mid-day, following the morning service).

Farther east along 14th Street we find the sad shell of Lüchow's (closed in 1982), that once-magnificent center of Germanic cuisine and beverages, a favorite with Lillian Russell and Diamond Jim Brady, and frequented by that master of pianos William Steinway, whose Steinway Hall was directly opposite the restaurant. Lüchow's was the only remaining link with an era when Union Square and vicinity was a nucleus of the German culture. Beer halls flourished everywhere; Tuesday's (Scheffel Hall) on Third Avenue and 17th Street, for example, used to be the famous Joe King's Rathskeller.

But if wursts, dumplings, and sauerkraut are too heavy for lunch, turn north up Irving Place, one of the most attractive streets in this part of town. Here you can sit in Pete's Tavern, an old speakeasy,

Pete's Tavern

opened in 1864 and loved by O. Henry, who wrote his "Gift of the Magi" in a booth by the door. Farther up the street on the left there's Sal Anthony's, an excellent Italian restaurant; nearby is Paul and Jimmy's Place, an intimate restaurant well-loved for its outstanding southern Italian cuisine (recently moved round the corner, next door to the rather elite 65 Irving Place Restaurant).

For those fascinated by New York's literary heritage, Irving Place and the Gramercy Park area offer a wealth of past associations with Washington Irving, Mark Twain, Theodore Dreiser, Horace Greeley, Herman Melville, and Henry James. Again, new life is enveloping this sedate cultural enclave where The Players and National Arts clubs keep watch over the carefully groomed gardens of the park itself. Access is limited to residents, each of whom carries a precious key, and in spite of all the new restaurants, bars, and gourmet food stores emerging in the neighborhood, the area has a twenties feel to it, particularly along East 19th Street between Third Avenue and Irving Place. This remodeled group of townhouses is a highlight of the Gramercy Park Historic District and one of my favorite nooks.

Another cherished spot very close by is Theodore Roosevelt's Birthplace (28 East 20th Street), which must be one of Manhattan's least-frequented landmarks. "Teddie's" memorabilia fills the hallway, and the five furnished rooms reflect a Victorian family's refined tastes (Roosevelt's two sisters and second wife aided in the restoration). On Saturdays at 2 P.M. from September–June, free concerts and recitals are offered to the public (call 260-1616 for details).

Back on 14th Street continue east to Third Avenue, the Times Square of that area. Lines of flashing lights and badly drawn silhouettes of naked ladies pinpoint porno stores and theaters showing various kinds of erotica. The Bijou, a couple of blocks south, is entirely gay, whereas Panascope 35 boasts the largest porno screen in the city. A couple of others are more traditional—cramped, sweaty pleasure-pits showing badly scratched editions of *Schoolgirl Capers* or *Swedish Swingers* with dubbed soundtracks, full of groans and sighs of simulated ecstasy. For the hard-core clientele anxious for live action there is usually an interesting selection of suitably dressed ladies of the street around Third Avenue. Occasionally a police shut-down sends the women scurrying up Lexington Avenue for a few days and brings a minor period of financial hardship to the seedy hotels down the side streets. But things return to normal fairly quickly.

Peering down on all the local antics is Henry Hardenbergh's Con Edison Tower at 14th Street and Irving Place, where a well laid-out Energy Museum offers an educational alternative to the rather raunchy street scene. A short distance to the north stands the Police Academy at 235 East 20th Street (at Second Avenue), which invites the public to call for tours of the large academy museum (477-9753).

Just down Third Avenue at 13th Street is the famous Kiehl Pharmacy, mecca for the health-food crowd and homeopathic enthusiasts since 1851, and still dispensing unique iron tonic remedies, authentic musk oils, herbal laxatives, and botanical cures. The live Yugoslavian leeches, alas, are no longer in stock. "No real demand nowadays," says Aaron Morse, the owner. But otherwise, nothing much has changed in the last hundred years or so.

A brief diversion on 15th Street east of Third Avenue leads to the recently renovated Stuyvesant Square—actually two squares on either side of Second Avenue, originally a gift to the city from Peter himself. At the western side, the Rutherford Place Friend's Meeting House and Seminary (1860) is a large, plain, red-brick structure with an elegant portico, which perfectly expresses the straightforward honest ethics of pure Quakerism. On the adjacent corner, however, the overbearing and confused jumble of styles and influences in J.P. Morgan's St. George's Episcopal Church and parish house leaves one wondering about the clarity of church doctrines!

At Second Avenue and 14th Street, a neighborhood feel begins to emerge again. Churches reappear, along with bakeries and small supermarkets. The Tifereth Israel Town and Village Synagogue, complete with Russian-style domes, offers the public a wide range of lectures and films on Jewish culture. Next door is the Emanu-El Midtown YM-YWHA where nonmembers are welcome to visit the photo exhibition gallery and attend theatrical productions, many of which are revivals from the old "Jewish Rialto" days (see chapter 3, "The East Village"). Nearby, the charming Roman Catholic Church of the Immaculate Conception provides a richly carved drinking fountain for "everyone that thirsteth!" Unfortunately, it never works. Inside is that smell of incense and the flickering half-light of a thousand prayer candles. A chapel, set to one side, has been Hollywooded into an artificial cave complete with life-size statues.

Across the road the brick bastions of Stuyvesant Town and Peter Cooper Village rise up behind a sickly, low line of maple trees. The street is ending, coming closer to the East River and the vast Con Edison plant. Behind the little stores is the last great ghetto in this part of Manhattan—a dense neighborhood of dark buildings, part of the old "Gashouse district," and ominous even on a sunny day. It's time to turn around and start back.

No one word can really describe 14th Street. It's a kaleidoscopic strip, full of contrasts, full of ironies. A few yards away from large, plush apartment complexes the street people drink their Ripple or bourbon from greasy bottles. It has more churches than almost any other street in the city, yet at the same time vice is flagrant and porno shops flourish. The great Centennial Memorial Temple of the Salvation Army, west of Sixth Avenue, has an entrance framed by the immortal words of General William Booth:

> *While women weep, as they do now*
> *I'll fight. . . .*

yet the temple is hemmed in by cheap appliance stores and discount cosmetic outlets, and bowed bag-ladies still trundle by with their overloaded shopping carts as they have done for decades.

But for all its brashness and contradictions, 14th Street possesses links with almost every facet of Manhattan's history. It's truly a "slice of New York" and the hub of a burgeoning revitalization.

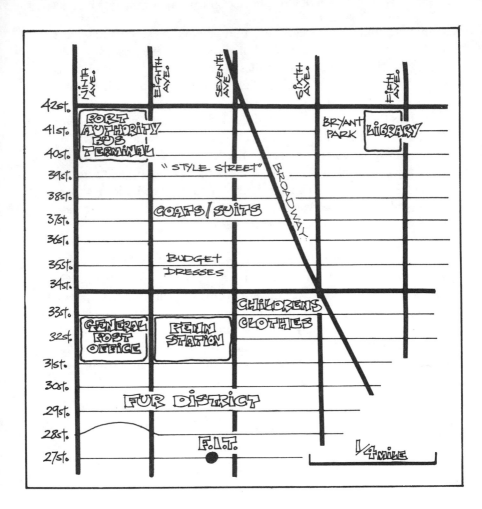

6 | The Garment and Fur Districts

"Imports are killing us!" So says Jasper Peyton of the International Ladies Garment Workers Uniion (ILGWU). This may be true—but the garment and fur districts still seem to be flourishing in their gloomy midtown canyons where every day is a "hot-number" day. So take a none-too-leisurely stroll here during your next Macy's outing.

"So where's your hat? You come to talk to me 'bout makin' hats an' you got no hat. Okay, okay, so sit down. Wad y'wanna know? C'mon, c'mon I ain't got all day—hey, Irv, you seen this guy, he ain't got no hat and he comes to talk to me 'bout hats. Thas'a trouble today—the goyim don't buy hats no more, so why do we bother? Oy, it could be worse. Maybe I could be dead—I should be so lucky. So wad y'wanna know, I'm sittin' here waitin' an' you ain't opened your mouth yet. Here, have a cigar. You don't want one—hey, Irv, this guy don't smoke cigars. You wanna talk to Irv? Hey, siddown, siddown—Irv's no use, he don't know nothin'. But least he wears a hat. Hey, Irv, show him your hat." Irv solemnly brings out a shiny Chassidic hat, broad-brimmed and very black. He doesn't smile. It's some kind of ritual. The large man with the cigar slaps the desk with

☞ DIRECTIONS

As no specific walk is planned, any subway or bus stop between an area bounded by 28th and 40th streets and Fifth and Eighth avenues will place you within the garment and fur districts

stubby fingers and bursts out laughing. "Now there's a hat for you." He gasps for breath between the chortles. Irv replaces his hat, still unsmiling.

I'm getting nowhere with the interview and loving every minute of it! At least it's a respite from the streets, although maybe *street* is the wrong word. They're really outdoor corridors, extensions of the cramped workshops that fill every corner and niche of floor space in the gray, grimy buildings of the garment and fur districts between 28th and 40th streets and Fifth and Eighth avenues. Certainly through traffic has no business here. Anybody trying to negotiate his way in a car across this area on a typical weekday should be quietly led away in a straitjacket. He probably would be anyway. People have been known to collapse, suffer nervous breakdowns, and burst blood vessels just trying to get between Seventh and Eighth avenues on 38th Street. Vans on both sides of the street are double-parked, sometimes triple-parked. Tiny pushcarts laden with bolts of cloth and large cardboard boxes or piles of garment pieces emerge without warning from between the double-parkers. The "pitchmen" (pushcart pushers) seem totally oblivious to the confusions of the street. They'll nip and twist between cars as nimbly as a squirrel climbing a thorn tree. Salesmen dressed with a touch of flash maneuver their wheeled suitcases between fenders. Sleek female models, aloof and seemingly lifeless, float along the sidewalks. A rack of half-finished dresses suddenly runs amok down a ramp out into the street, cartwheels, and spins a dozen flimsy satin things in all directions. The boy frantically scoops up the garments, picking one off a windshield, another off an old lady who doesn't quite understand what's going on, slams them all back on the rack, and scurries down the street. The drunk on the corner, who has perhaps wandered down from 42nd Street for a change of scene, bawls out, "Hey, take it eeeasy, man, jus' take it eeeasy!" slaps his thigh, and does a little dance. "Hey, was' all the rush, I say was'-is-all-the-rush, fellas? Wow! Jes' look at 'em go."

There is a decided craziness that pervades the area, but it's the craziness for which New York is so well known—and loved. It comes from a concentration, a distillation of energy, talent, money, and mutual interests. It comes from the need for contact and communication—direct and continuous—in every phase of the business. "You couldn't move the garment industry. It's far too complex," I was told by the owner of a small high-fashion house. "It took me twenty years to understand how really complex it is. I'm still learning. We all live out of each other's pockets. We curse about conditions, about labor rates, about the city, about the congestion—about everything. But not one of us would move. We need one another. We spy on each other, we play games, we bargain and barter, try to outguess one another, try to find out what's new before anyone else does—even try to drive each other out of business. But it couldn't work any other way. We're not like one of those conglomerates making long-range decisions in ivory towers. We're right in the middle of the marketplace—and it's a hell of a fickle market, let me tell you—and there's hundreds, thousands of tiny businesses all trying to get their piece of the action. Talk about competition being true capitalism—well, this is where it started!"

Garment manufacturing is still one of New York City's leading industries. Between Fifth and Ninth avenues and 34th and 40th streets is the heart of the "rag business." Fashion Avenue (Seventh Avenue) is the center of the most glamorous of all garment trades —women's clothing. Within or on the fringe of this area are the "kindred needle trades": the furriers, shoemakers, and glove manufacturers. The millinery industry can be found between 36th and 39th streets and Fifth and Sixth avenues—39th Street is known to many in the trade as "style street." Window-peering is interesting, although most stores serve the wholesale trade only, and it's usually impossible to get inside to see the manufacturing process. The furriers (between 27th and 30th streets) are especially nervous. At each shop and loft buzzers sound to admit every visitor and worker, and closed-circuit cameras are a familiar sight. Major crime has become a serious problem, and the area is gradually shrinking, due to early retirement, fear of robberies and break-ins, and a generally dwindling trade. Today there are about three thousand workers in the fur district; ten years ago there were eight thousand.

Down the dark side streets are grubby storefronts brimming with muskrat, raccoon, beaver, and mink pelts. The narrow workshops are dingy affairs. Paint flakes off the walls and the only light comes from a few random low-watt bulbs dangling on long wires from the ceiling. Old men and old-looking young men huddle in the shadows over sewing machines, rarely pausing. In the center of the floor is a coatrack on wheels, full of fur creations. Even in the most meager workshops along 28th and 29th streets around Eighth Avenue there's often more than $100,000 in furs lying about. Occasionally one of the workers will leave the shop carrying a magnificent $15,-000 creation to one of the Seventh Avenue showrooms. There's hardly a more disconcerting sight in Manhattan than little wizened men scurrying along the gloomy sidewalks of the fur district with minor fortunes in coats bundled under their arms.

While you're in the area you may find it fun (and educational) to visit FIT (Fashion Institute of Technology) at 227 West 27th Street at 7th Avenue (760-7760). Here at the Shirley Goodman Resource Center there are four galleries providing fashion-related exhibits for both students of the college and the general public. Pick up the *Revelations* paper from the information desk and see what's happening in the business. It's fascinating, as is the tour of FIT's amazing collection of over 1½ million dresses, hats, shoes, and handbags, many donated by celebrities, which trace the meanderings of fashion over the last century. A true hands-on history lesson (by appointment only).

Continue up Fashion (Seventh) Avenue past the children's-wear manufacturers on 34th Street (No. 112 houses scores of showrooms where buyers from all over the country come to check out the latest trends in children's fashions), up to 35th Street, where numerous loft showrooms and popular-priced dresswork shops fill the area between Seventh and Eighth avenues. Note the synagogue on the corner frequented by many of the garment workers. Services start at 7 A.M. and there are even lunchtime and going-home celebrations at noon and 4:30 P.M.

After passing 498 Seventh Avenue, one of the elite coat-and-suit manufacturers and showrooms, you may be ready for a snack at one of the many sidewalk delis where you can mingle with seamstresses, cutters, pressers, and clerks and listen to their lunchtime banter. You may get some useful tips on upcoming fashion trends or alternatively may discover whose daughter had a baby only last week or whose son has been accepted at which school.

One of the most popular hangouts, Dübrows, has gone the way of many New York landmarks. As Paul Tobin, grandson of the founder, explains, "They made me a nice offer I couldn't refuse"— so, farewell to one of the last old-time cafeterias, famous for its mushroom and barley soup, strudel, pirogi, kugels, and kasha dishes. As Eli Bernstein, a cutter, told me: "Thirty-two years and fifty million meals—that takes some beating!" If you choose to rub shoulders with the bosses, try Lou Siegel's at 209 West 38th Street where the well-bedecked dine on such traditional favorites as roast beef flanken, potted meatball and noodles, and stuffed derma, or join the younger whizz kids at the pink-and-gray Café St. Tropez (Seventh Avenue and 37th Street). If your craving is for kosher food take a walk over to Sixth Avenue and visit Jerusalem 2 (would you believe kosher pizza!) or Moshe Peking on West 37th Street between Fifth and Sixth avenues for kosher Chinese food and snacks. There's also a splurge restaurant in this area—Keen's English Chop House at 72 West 36th—where lamb chops are the specialty of the house and clay pipes signed by satisfied customers hang in jovial rows from the ceiling. Here you'll mingle with the famous, as the place tends to attract a gregarious crowd of columnists, fashion-world celebrities, and Broadway stars. It's unlikely you'll starve while touring the garment district.

Although it's usually difficult to bluff your way into the trade showrooms, there's plenty of movement and life in the surrounding area. Just walking the streets and bobbing into the occasional lobby, one can sense the excitement—and the uncertainty. Everyone seems to be wondering: "Is this the year to make that million, or is this the year we bust . . . !" Everybody watches the fashion barometer and hangs on their fingernails. Not too surprising that the rate of bankruptcy is high: twenty percent among the manufacturers and thirty-three percent among contractors (the people who make up the garments).

If you're interested in learning more about the fashion world, tuck *Women's Wear Daily* under your arm and head off to the International Ladies Garment Workers Union Education Department at 1710 Broadway (at 54th Street). Call a few days in advance (265-7000) and you can arrange to see a forty-five-minute film on the history of the development of the garment industry and the union, hear an interesting talk about how the area functions, and take a guided tour of the district with a representative from the union. You'll even visit one of the clothing factories, where, believe it or not, you'll finally see clothes under construction. While tours are mainly for fashion students, the public is welcome and enthusiasts leave clutching the union's kit of booklets tracing the Garment District's development from the earliest sweatshop days.

The sweatshop era stems from the mid-1800s when many German-Jewish refugees began arriving in America. For generations these people had dealt in new and secondhand clothes in their own country, and here they began as peddlers or fringe merchants, eventually finding their way into garment manufacturing. More and more refugees came—entire families from Poland, Italy, Czechoslovakia, and Russia. They settled in the Lower East Side, which inevitably became an enormous sprawling slum and the subject of published protests such as Jacob Riis's *How the Other Half Lives*. Women and children could be seen striding through the mud with bundles of "piece-work" on their heads, while men carried sewing machines on their backs to the dimly lit, disease-ridden sweatshops. Signs outside reminded the workers who was boss: "If you don't come in Sunday, don't come in Monday" (signed "Management"). Thousands had made their way via Ellis Island to work twelve hours a day, seven days a week, and take home a pittance.

Then came the strikes, particularly the general strikes of 1909 and 1910, which were both milestones of the American labor movement. There were vociferous demands for factory regulations, decent working conditions, hours, and wages. There was also a new sense of brotherhood among the immigrant workers, which ultimately led to the formation of the powerful ILGWU. As the union anthem explains:

> *We cut a dream within our head*
> *And then with needle and with thread*
> *We fashioned something great and good*
> *A union seamed with brotherhood.*

Gradually the industry moved to more spacious and conveniently located workshops. Searching for an area to establish a complete "garment center," the industry followed the theaters and newspaper offices uptown toward Herald Square, to an area known then as the Tenderloin District, full of dance halls, restaurants, bordellos, and bars that offered ribald frolicking fun—just what visiting salesmen and buyers needed. In 1904 the Pennsylvania Railroad began to thrust its way under the Hudson and in 1930 came the Lincoln Tunnel. Both helped to clear the slums that had characterized the Hell's Kitchen area to the west of the Tenderloin District. These transportation links also put the area on the map as an established stronghold for the garment workers—an ideal central position for commuter-labor and access to the newly developed department stores and hotels.

Today the garment industry is much less uniform than it was thirty years ago, although this tiny sector of Manhattan is still the hub of trade and activity. The lunchtime crush of workers in the street has in no way diminished, but the ethnic origins of the labor force have altered considerably since the early days when Eastern Europeans made up the bulk of the sweatshop population. There's also a larger proportion of designers and salesmen than before, and the actual assembly of garments is now often performed elsewhere —in small towns somewhere in Pennsylvania or South Carolina. But there is still a ghetto—three hundred hidden sweatshops in Chinatown where Chinese immigrants live and work in conditions little different from the pre-ILGWU days, before the industry left the Lower East Side.

Meanwhile each manufacturer prays that "this time" he'll have

a "hot number" or at least be able to produce some effective "variations" if his line doesn't sell. That's the spirit that holds this little
world-within-a-world together as the push boys crash their carts
along the sidewalks, workers gather by the thousands at the street
corners, models flit like fragile butterflies through the roaring confusion, and the drunk on the corner bawls out his words of reason:
"Hey, take it eeeasy, man, jus' take it eeeasy!"

7 | Manhattan Markets

Many long-established markets have vanished or been relocated, but a few of the hardy continue to thrive. Enjoy them while they're still around.

When the Washington Street Market was unceremoniously removed to make way for the World Trade Center, downtown's pristine twins, dour predictions were made about the fate of Manhattan's other markets. There were plans to bundle up the Fulton Street fish merchants and ship them off to Hunts Point in the Bronx along with all the other dislocated produce people. They say that as soon as 42nd Street is revamped and the new convention center gets established, Paddy's Market will bid a final farewell to Ninth Avenue. They say the secondhand book market on Broadway around 12th Street will soon be gone. They grumble about unsanitary and unsafe conditions at the Gansevoort Meat Market at the west end of 14th Street in the shadow of the West Side Highway and threaten yet one more transplant to Hunts Point. At one time or another they've had plans to get rid of every market in Manhattan or lock what little remains into sanitized brick boxes and gloat at the silence of the streets, the absence of odors, the smoother-flowing traffic, and the docility of once-tumultuous neighborhoods.

But "they"—the planners, highway engineers, federal specialists,

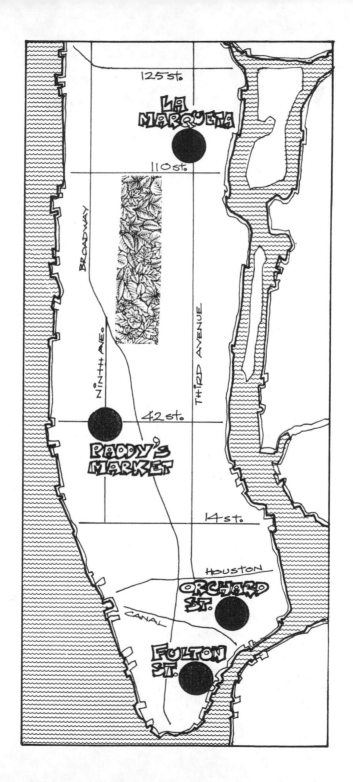

land peddlers, and great construction conglomerates—are finding the process of removal harder than they'd thought. Markets are not idle appendages stuck randomly on the body of the city. Each has a reason and a purpose and is linked to the city by vital arteries through which flows the very life blood of New York and its people. What would the Lower East Side be without Orchard Street? Where would the people of Clinton shop if Paddy's Market died? What about the Ukrainians around St. Marks Place and their tiny stores reflecting crucial aspects of an ancient culture? And how about the grubby, raucous, impromptu "thieves' market" at the east end of Canal Street, long considered an unnecessary annoyance by the "city-beautiful" people? Where would the Bowery boys and the street people go to exchange clothes, trinkets, and gossip if some enlightened idealist decided to remove "this unpleasant eyesore?"

The city is for people, not for planners. The city is the city—grandiose, brash, secluded, litter-laden, sweaty, tranquil, smelly, breeze filled, silent, and so damned loud it makes your head spin. Markets are concentrations of needed activities. If they weren't needed, they wouldn't be there. So the message is really very simple —let them be.

We're going to explore four of Manhattan's major markets—The Fulton Street Fish Market, Orchard Street, Paddy's Market, and La Marqueta—plus a few of the smaller affairs scattered throughout the city.

Fulton Street Fish Market

The market is located around the junction of Fulton and South streets.
Subway: BMT J, M to Fulton and Nassau streets; IND A, E to Broadway and Nassau Street; IRT 2, 3 to Fulton and William streets; IRT 3, 4 to Fulton Street and Broadway
Bus: M15 (South Ferry); Culture Bus II, stop 30

At dawn the masts and funnels of the old ships at the South Street Seaport Museum are silhouetted against the dim orange glow over Brooklyn. It's chilly. A breeze full of the Atlantic ruffles across the piers and down the dark streets. It's a time of day most New Yorkers never see—but it's the best time to visit Manhattan's Fulton Street Fish Market.

The deep chasms of downtown are silent. Only a few lights glimmer in the windows of the Southbridge Towers apartments. An old man wrapped in greasy blankets and newspapers is curled like a mouse in one of the dark doorways. His feet rest on a pile of empty liquor bottles.

The unmistakable odor of fish creeps up the narrow streets between the low brick buildings. The light from a single street lamp illuminates the rusted shutters and streaked windows of an old warehouse. Somewhere down by the river a truck trumpets its exhaust, and a group of men, huddled around the orange glow of a fire in an oil drum, turn briefly and then move in closer to the warming flames.

Suddenly, around the corner it's bright and bustling. Down one side a line of tiny stalls display their wares on tables and in tanks —shrimp, scallops, scungilli, clams, and mussels. Mounds of gray, green, and blue crabs thrash in buckets and boxes. Lobsters, their claws closed with wood wedges, churn in shallow sinks while buyers prod warily. The stall owners, fat and flushed, shout at customers as burly men in caps and rubber aprons trundle carts laden with boxes of pink fish with gaping mouths. Bright bulbs under the canvas canopies of the stalls reflect on the slippery sidewalks and cobblestones where buyers move in a continual throng—a hubbub of mumbles, barterings, and bawlings.

Across the street, under the elevated highway, is the big-time market where the *real* fish can be found—tuna, mackerel, dogfish, halibut, catfish, eel—you name it. A one-hundred-sixty-eight-pound jewfish, its scales as long as a man's thumb, lies by itself on a large wooden bench. A card tied through its dorsal fin reads: "From Florida, for Mr. Mariano."

"Charlie, get these fish outta here." A large man, presumably Charlie, ambles over with a steel hook, spears an enormous prong-tailed tuna just under the gills, and hoists it, dripping, on his back. He half drags, half carries the creature across the wet floor and with a deft flick of hook and shoulder sends it bouncing and slithering into the back of a refrigerated truck. Charlie returns several times to repeat the process with even larger fish, then, satisfied, he clips the hook over his shoulder and wanders outside into the street for a smoke.

"Charlie, where the hell are you going? Charlie . . ." The small man in rubber boots, almost lost behind mounds of mackerel, gesticulates violently and wipes his forehead with the stained sleeve of a once-white overall. He stuffs a grubby notebook into his pocket and sets off in pursuit of the elusive Charlie, almost tumbling over two large halibut embracing on the floor.

And then gradually the pace slows and the tumult eases. By late morning the market is closed and the South Street Seaport plays host to hundreds of tourists and three-piece-suited employees from the downtown towers who flock here for food, drink, and diversions in this imaginative redevelopment. All that remains are the little piles of fishbones in the gutter, pieces of shrimp, broken boxes, odd bits of heads and tails and scales—and a distinct aroma that wafts along the wharves and up the teeming streets, reminding us of the city's sea-related heritage.

Orchard Street and Essex Street

Subway: BMT J, M
Bus: M9, M14, M15, M21
(Avoid coming by automobile. The Bowery boys will hassle you at every step along "desolation row," parking is virtually impossible, and the local traffic police are the most alert in the city.)

If you prefer window-browsing and buying in relative calm (remember the word *relative*), come to Orchard Street during the week. There may even be a spare table at Katz's Deli at East Houston and Ludlow and only a short line of waiting customers at Guss Pickle Emporium. Alternatively, if you'd like to experience the real Orchard Street scene come on Sunday when the top end, from East Houston to Delancey, is closed to traffic, and people—thousands of them—take over for the day. If you can, find a place to pause briefly. It's a narrow street full of grim buildings, unwashed windows, and a filigree of fire escapes silhouetted against the sky. Bearded Chassidim scamper past the hundreds of tiny stores selling the widest, cheapest (and occasionally the best) variety of dresses, coats, shoes, handbags, shirts, jackets, blouses, and underwear in the city. Little square signs, all about the same size and all painted in the same reds, yellows, and blues, hang over every store. The better places (look for the credit-card signs) have neat window displays and electronically controlled doors to limit the number of customers inside at any one time. Lines of anxious customers wait outside. The other stores are less restrained. Their doors are flung wide open, clothes, bolts of cloth, and assorted boxes of socks and handkerchiefs tumbling across the sidewalk on a profusion of trestle tables. The owner's outside stalking buyers with the subtlety of a Central Park mugger —"Hey, you—you, yeah the one with the pimples, c'mon over here, let me show what I got here. Hey, you seen a blouse like this before? It's real silk. Touch it. Go on, jus' feel it . . ."

A bald man of gigantic proportions takes up most of the sidewalk, along with a large box full of packs of razor blades. "Three for a dollar, you can't beat it . . ." Lower down, an old, rather crumpled lady wrapped in a gray shawl sells handkerchiefs from a supermarket bag to sympathetic customers.

The Orchard Street area is the last real remnant of the Lower East Side and still possesses all the flavor of a Jacob Riis photograph. Nearby Grand Street was once the wealthiest shopping street in New York. Lord and Taylor had a large establishment at the corner of Chrystie Street, and Ridley's ran special coach services to bring customers from the Debrosses Street ferry on the Hudson side and the Grand Street ferry on the East River. At that time Hester Street and Orchard Street were a peddler's market. Hundreds of pushcarts lined the sidewalks. Their Jewish and Italian owners sold everything a local resident might need—wines, chicken, freshly made horseradish, fruits and vegetables, olive oil, cloth, eyeglasses (sold by the "glimmer men"), newspapers in every Eastern European language, suspenders, candles, candy, "broken chocolates," sweet potatoes, hot corn, nuts, halvah, umbrellas, pickles, bread, strange sweet drinks, and a wide array of hot snacks to be gulped down while peering and poking in the peddlers' carts. That was the era of penny knife grinders, "sniff cartes" (installment plans to buy steerage tickets for relatives back in the homeland), elaborate shoe-shine parlors, and bartering sessions unmatched outside the bazaars of the Middle East.

It all ended rather abruptly in 1938 when Mayor Fiorello La Guardia authorized the construction of the enclosed Essex Street market for the street traders and transformed peddlers into merchants overnight. The market remains, between Broome and Delancey streets. Inside the dull red-brick buildings (Open Monday–Saturday 7 A.M.–7 P.M., closed Sunday) the Spanish influence is pronounced, and many of the meat and vegetable stalls resemble those at La Marqueta up in El Barrio (110th–116th streets on Park Avenue). But somehow it seems a sad remnant of the old peddler-and-pushcart days and, like La Marqueta, badly in need of long-promised renovations.

Essex Street itself, though, still retains its distinct character. Guss Pickle Emporium ("Eat Guss's Pickles and Stay Young and Beautiful") just around the corner on Hester Street, next door to the H&M Skull Cap Manufacturing Co., seems to have provoked a flurry of competition. There's the Pickleman ("All our Pickles are Straight and not Crooked") with a mouth-watering display of pickled eggplants, olives, tomatoes, peppers, dills, cauliflower, and just about any other vegetable capable of being doused in vinegar. Then next to a kosher cheese shop is Hollander and Sons, a third pickle establishment that, for all the color of its display, lacks the solid authoritative appearance of Guss's, with its line of gray pickling vats and gallon jars of sour tomatoes.

Kossar's bakery, hidden away in a line of small stores on Grand Street just east of Essex, is famous for its bagels, onion breads, poppyseed and onion boards, and its delicious bialys. Of course, as might be expected in this touchstone of American Jewish culture, there is constant debate over the relative merits of the food in the area. Some claim that Ratner's at 138 Delancey Street is the only place for bagels, but there's general agreement that tiny Yonah Schimmel's at 137 is the best knish bakery in New York, that Russ and Daughters at 179 East Houston Street has the finest smoked fish and pickled herring, that Economy Candy Market at Essex and

Guss Pickle Emporium

Rivington has the best selection of confectionery around, and that Moishe's at 181 East Houston Street excels with its Russian bread. Finally, patrons insist that Bernstein's-on-Essex, with its kosher-Chinese cuisine, is not half as bad as it sounds. Their kreplach, potato pudding, kashavarnishkas, and goose dishes (during the November kosher goose festival) are particularly outstanding.

Which brings us back inevitably to noisy Katz's Deli (205 East Houston Street), decidedly nonkosher, but serving generous pastrami and corned beef sandwiches with plenty of chutzpah thrown in with the mustard and dills. There's a kosher place next door with a more restrained spirit, but most visitors seem to prefer the plastic tables, the yellow walls, the din and chatter, and the spirit of "eat, eat!" that is Katz's. After all, the place caters to those who enjoy the push and shove of Orchard Street, the waiting in line outside a store to buy a handbag, trying on clothes behind a blanket held to a length of string by clothespins, being shanghaied into stores and dragged out again by frustrated companions, and suffering the final indignity of being told "you're too fat, dearie." If you come to Orchard Street—come prepared for the fray.

And if the fray gets to be too much, take one of the Sunday tours at Shapiro's House of Kosher Wines (126 Rivington Street between Essex and Norfolk streets), complete with a full description of the Kosher wine-making process and free tastings. A perfect ending to the day.

Paddy's Market

Subway: IND A, E, AA or CC to 34th Street and Eighth Avenue (Penn Station) or 42nd Street and Eighth Avenue (Port Authority bus terminal)
Bus: M11

If you're hungry, start at Manganaro's (488 Ninth Avenue between 37th and 38th streets). It's a good idea for two reasons. First, you'll get one of the best hero sandwiches in town. Second, you'll buy less later if you're not hungry, and along this short section of Ninth Avenue, within the shadow of the Port Authority bus terminal at

40th Street, it's very hard not to go through a month's food budget in a couple of hours, mumbling clichés like, "Well, it'll keep and it's so cheap," "I've been meaning to have a party anyway," or the classic "Well, I'm down a few pounds, so . . ."

It's a pretty shabby area really—just as a good market should be. Fire escapes cast lengthy gray shadows on blocks of grubby buildings ranged along the avenue like the smashed teeth of an Irish bar-brawler. Traffic, avoiding the crush of Times Square or swirling around the ramps to the Lincoln Tunnel, surges by constantly. Packs of dogs chase one another across vacant building lots and buses roar overhead up the ramp to the terminal.

But along the sidewalks and in the crammed stores everyone is oblivious to the hurly-burly. This was once the market center of Hell's Kitchen (otherwise known as Clinton), and today there's still one prime focus of interest, one torchlike beam of enthusiasm and conversation—Food. At Manganaro's Grosseria Italiana the old wood floorboards creak as customers mingle, peer, and prod at the hams, sopresatta, and long, pear-shaped provolones dangling from the yellowed tin ceiling. On a table opposite the counter there's a display of cheeses all ready for cutting. High above, on bent shelves, are boxes of pastas—spaghettini, capellini, perciatelli, bucatini, mezza zita, cannaroni rigati, lumache medie, pennoni. It's not the kind of place to pick up a pound of any old macaroni. Perfectionists come here to buy their own ravioli makers. Gourmets come here to vie with one another. Gourmands come here to gush at the mounds of prosciutto, mortadella, pancetta, salamis (the finest Sicilian), pepperoni, and cotechini. Coffee lovers leave with espresso makers tucked under their arms and trundle up to the nearby Empire Coffee and Tea Company to select an Italian roast from a score of blends that include the real Jamaican Blue Mountain and green beans for do-it-yourself roasting enthusiasts.

What's the secret of Paddy's Market? Well, it's not a "fancy-foods at fancy prices" kind of area like some of the more elite streets on the East Side. It offers instead meat, seafood, Greek, Philippine, and Oriental foods, rare Italian delicacies, herbs and spices, cheeses, breads, and vegetables at some of the best prices in town. It does this without affectation, without snobbery, and with a respect for the knowledge and taste of the customer. There's the assumption that if you're not already a gourmet, you certainly will be soon and you'll obviously be coming back.

Of course, there may be many types of food not quite to your taste. Well-dressed West Siders frequent the little bakeries with windows full of golden fresh-baked loaves (my favorite is the Casa Italian bakery under the ramps), and hurriedly avoid the butcher shops displaying racks of smoked pigs' heads, goat meat, rabbits, brains, hoofs, trotters, tripe, and fresh "mountain oysters." But even for the squeamish or unadventurous it's hard to bypass Giovanni Esposito and Sons' pork shop on the corner of 38th Street, with its dry-cured Smithfield hams and its homemade sausages—parsley and cheese pork sausages, Italian links with fennel, and those pungent garlic sausages.

On both sides of the street there's Vinnie's, with its encyclopedic array of fruits and vegetables, and a little higher up on the west side of Ninth Avenue (between 39th and 40th streets), stores spill out onto the sidewalk with boxes and burlap sacks of paprika, crushed peppers, red lentils, dried fava beans, oregano, bay leaves, fresh tarragon, fennel seeds, and coriander. Slabs of salt cod, buckets of herring fillets, and bloaters mingle with baskets of garlic, nuts, dried fruit, and ginger roots.

Don't pass by the Philippine food stores if you like to experiment with your cooking. Many of the products are recognizably Chinese, but there are some unique specialities here, including a remarkable array of dried fish, sweets wrapped in banana fronds, fermented fish sauce, langkas (an odoriferous seasoning made from roots), and unusual fruit jams such as ube, mango, and jack fruit.

Alternatively, if these exotic goodies don't excite, visit the stalwart fish and meat stores on the west side of the street and enjoy the largest and freshest selections in the city. If you skipped Manganaro's at the outset there's a fish-fry store near Vinnie's that offers a tempting array of cooked whiting, porgie, mackerel, snapper, shrimp, scallops, and clams. Or, for splurgers, there's Giordano's Restaurant tucked down 39th Street around the corner from a fruit-and-vegetable store, and Jolsen's at Ninth Avenue and 42nd Street.

After 40th Street the market fragments but there are still places of interest to visit, most notably The Washington Beef Company (excellent prices here), Lois Lane's Natural Foods Restaurant, Mike and John Anagnostou's Poseidon Greek Bakery (wonderful phyllo nut cake, pistachio pastries, spinach and meat pies), the adjacent pork store famous for homemade pâtés and garlic sausage, and the Golden Sweet French Bakery.

For all the recent changes around the Port Authority Bus Terminal and along West 42nd Street, Paddy's Market continues to flourish and, every May, hosts the Ninth Avenue International Food Festival—one of Manhattan's most popular street fairs.

La Marqueta

The market is located on Park Avenue between 110th and 116th streets and is open Monday-Saturday 8 A.M.–6 P.M.
Subway: IRT 6 to 116th Street and Lexington Avenue
Bus: M1, M2, M3, M4, M101, M102

"Yessir, yessir—you wanna somma this, mister, *buenos días*—eh! Come 'ere I wanna to show this, *señor* . . . hey, mista, take a look at this tuna—yessir, you wanna pig—hey, how 'bout some chili peppers—hey . . ."

Frantic, loud, raucous, booming with Latin American music, smelling alternatively of abattoir, greenhouse, incense-filled churches, with overtones of the Fulton Fish Market—it was, until a recent decline, one of the noisiest places in town, deep in the heart of El Barrio, Spanish Harlem. Poor maintenance has led to poor business, and although the city is encouraging a major renovation project here, specific proposals have not yet been developed.

But there's still life in the old place yet. The main market is located in a series of block-long buildings directly under the tracks of the Penn Central railroad. Trains grate and squeal overhead, their commuter passengers oblivious to the tumult below. Everyone shouts. At the end of the day chaos reigns. The fruit and vegetable stands, so neatly arranged at eight in the morning, are a shambles. It's hard to separate the vast array of plantains, mangoes, coconuts,

La Marqueta

sweet potatoes, persimmons, chayotes, cassavas, papayas, sugar cane, and banana fronds (used for making pastelles, a kind of tamale). Higher up, in the meat sections, the butchers are gesticulating wildly, making last-minute reductions, trying to sell off whole pigs and every conceivable by-product—ears, tails, snouts, heads, feet, skin, chitterlings—even gallon bottles of blood for making blood sausage.

On Fridays the fish section way up at the top end near 116th Street is the busiest part of the market. The floor is a treacherous mass of ice, blood, and scales. A line of gaping tuna heads frames a pile of contorted black eels. There's red snapper, mackerel, salted codfish, gray gelatinous octopus, conch, lobsters, and huge gulf prawns. If you can put up with the stench, you'll get some of the best bargains in town.

Hidden among the bustling meat, fish, and vegetable stands are quieter stalls. One sells nothing but religious trinkets—statues, rosaries, brightly colored pictures of Christ on the crucifix (the eyes blink as you move by), candles, and all kinds of prayer cards embossed with saints smiling under their halos. Another specializes in grossly painted plaster products—purple owls, green dogs, madonnas of every hue, even a Christ figure in fluorescent pink!

Then there are the little hole-in-the-wall places offering strange concoctions of herbs and spices from old glass bottles, cheek by jowl with stands displaying six different types of rice and dried beans of every shape and color—"Hey, mister, I make my own chili sauce —real hot—the hottest." A little man with a greasy mane of curled black hair waves a container of murky gray-brown liquid in front of my face. I can see, dimly, the floating shapes of deadly jalapeño peppers. I smile and quickly pass into the street for some fresh air.

Outside is almost as chaotic as the enclosed market. Along both sides of Park Avenue and much of 116th Street there's a confusing array of coats, suits, shoes, dresses, and shawls, dangling from every doorway and awning or perched and piled on the sidewalks. Salsa music blares out from a score of perforated speakers. There is an amazing energy here—even dancing at the street corner. For an hour or so, lose yourself in the infectious spirit of the barrio. You might arrive home with a bag full of "chitlins" or even a pig's ear as a souvenir. You might blow your carefully structured diet in a lunch of fatty snacks—tamales, papas rellenas, legua, plantanos fritos, and empanadas, but so what? It's not every day you go to a carnival—and it's much cheaper than a trip to Puerto Rico.

Here's to a colorful and integral part of New York. Long may it prosper!

MINI-MARKETS

A few more delights for market-lovers:

The Flower Market

28th Street around Sixth Avenue
Subway: IND B, F to 23rd Street at Sixth Avenue
Bus: M5, M6, M7 (also M2, M3 on Fifth Avenue)

A delight for insomniacs or a splendid way to end a very-early-morning trip to the Fulton Street Fish Market. Most active times are between 5 and 8 A.M. The scurry and bustle is reminiscent of the opening scenes of *My Fair Lady.* One expects all the delivery boys, bawling warehousemen, demure female buyers, and bloated packers to suddenly burst into some rousing chorus. Even if you miss the wholesale antics, the street becomes a fascinating retail strip of palms, rubber plants, ferns, flowers, and dried fronds during the day. Intense and very New York.

During summer on Sunday mornings, when the neighborhood is a little less frantic, there's usually a flea market at 25th Street and Sixth Avenue, situated in a rather worn parking lot. For a small fee, enter and browse among the Art Nouveau lamps, wartime posters, battered cameras, old magazines, suitcases, records, perfume bottles, and all the paraphernalia normally found at a country rummage sale.

The Canal Street Bazaar

Between West Broadway and Lafayette Street
Subway: BMT N, QB, RR to Canal Street and Broadway
Bus: M1, M6, M10

110

Marvelous! Everyone knows about Canal Street and its hodgepodge of surplus stores and flea markets, but few have actually explored it. How many, for example, have visited the City Dump with its oscilloscopes, sweep generators, sound analyzers, and programmable regatrons, or the four plastic/plexiglass stores with their transparent skylights, plastic rods, tubes, and cubes of all sizes and colors, Styrofoam planks, and loads of free advice. Then there are the used office-equipment outlets, stores selling bits and pieces of transistor radios and tape recorders, the fabric and brass lofts (just up Greene Street), Abco's wonderful array of burglar alarms, Canal Rubber Supply's hoses, stripping, tubes, and three discount stationers. Best of all is the SoHo-Canal Street Flea Market at Canal and Greene streets with belt buckles, jewelry, prints, old clothes, records, books, hand-painted cards, teapots, lampshades, and glasses of cold lemonade.

Farther up, east of Lafayette, is a mini-diamond district—far less rich and raucous than 47th Street, but a diverting area nevertheless on the northern fringe of Chinatown.

STREET MARKETS

Often unreliable, fleeting affairs, especially if the local police are unfriendly, but a lot of fun, and even invaluable if you're looking for back issues of *National Geographic* or *Playboy,* secondhand leather jackets, instant self-portraits, simulated Gucci purses, or hand-tinted prints of the New York skyline.

The following might yield some surprises:

- Fifth Avenue in the mid-fifties
- Sixth Avenue around West 4th Street
- Avenue A at Tompkins Square Park (East 7th Street)
- Second Avenue around St. Marks Place
- Around Fourth Avenue and Astor Place

GREEN MARKETS

One of the best ideas for the city in the last decade! Thanks to the initiative of a group of private citizens, the Council on the Environment of New York City was established in 1976 to promote the concept of "greenmarkets" throughout the city, selling the best in produce from regional farms. Today there are eighteen such markets in Manhattan and Brooklyn (see list below), and more are planned in the near future.

MANHATTAN

Southbridge Towers *(Beekman & Pearl Sts.)*	Sat	June 1–Dec 21
City Hall *(Municipal Building South)*	Fri	June 28–Nov. 22
World Trade Center *(Church Street)*	Tues & Thurs	June 4–Dec. 24 June 6–Dec. 19
Independence Plaza *(Greenwich & Harrison)*	Wed & Sat	June 12–Dec. 18 June 8–Dec. 21
1st Avenue & 1st Street	Sun	June 16–Nov. 24
Tompkins Square *(9th Street & Avenue A)*	Sat	June 15–Nov. 23
St. Mark's Church *(10th St. & 2nd Avenue)*	Tues	June 4–Dec. 24
West Village *(Gansevoort & Hudson Sts.)*	Sat	June 15–Nov. 23
Union Square *(17th St. & Broadway)*	Wed Fri Sat	Year Round
East 67th Street *(bet. 1st & York Avenues)*	Sat	June 15–Dec. 21
West 77th Street *(Columbus Avenue)*	Sun	Year Round
East 87th Street *(bet. 1st & 2nd Avenues)*	Sat	June 1–Nov. 23

102nd Street *(Amsterdam Avenue)*	Fri	June 28–Dec. 20
137th Street *(Adam Clayton Powell Blvd.)*	Tues	June 4–Dec. 24
175th Street *(Broadway)*	Thurs	June 20–Dec. 19

BROOKLYN

Cadman Plaza West *(Montague Street)*	Tues & Sat	June 4–Dec. 24 June 1–Dec. 21
Columbus Plaza *(Jay Street near Myrtle)*	Tues & Fri	June 4–Dec. 24 June 7–Dec. 20
Flatbush Avenue *(Atlantic Avenue)*	Wed	June 26–Dec. 18

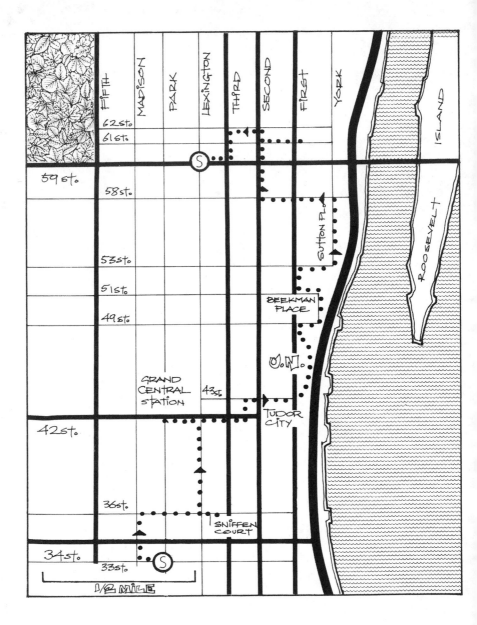

8 | The United Nations and Vicinity

At first glance the eastern midtown section of Manhattan may not seem to possess much to delight nook-and-cranny lovers. But more intimate exploration reveals a wealth of hidden surprises including a museum devoted entirely to dogs, a secluded court with all the dainty charm of a European mews, the last genuine automat in the city, tiny out-of-the-way parks and gardens, sedate enclaves of the rich and famous overlooking the East River, and an 18th century carriage house museum, prim and pretty, in the midst of burgeoning redevelopment.

Before we begin our tour, stop in at the Dog Museum in America (51 Madison Avenue between 26th and 27th streets, open Tuesday–Saturday 10 A.M.–5 P.M.; 696-8350. Donation). Here in the lobby of the New York Life Insurance Building you'll discover a delightful gallery of paintings and sculptures depicting the faithful creatures, which touch even the most indifferent of passersby!

On that note, we're now ready to start our walk in the furniture district, roughly defined by 29th to 34th streets between Third and Fifth avenues. It's more diffuse and less immediately spectacular than the Diamond District or the Flower District to the west. Many of the trade showrooms are hidden behind shuttered windows or located several stories up in ponderous buildings closed to the general public. Those places that are open to the casual passerby pre-

☞ **DIRECTIONS**
Subway: *Start:* IRT 6 to 33rd Street and Park Avenue *Return:* BMT RR or IRT 4, 5, 6 from 59th Street and Lexington Avenue
Bus: M1, M2, M3, M4, M101, M102

sent a tiny sampling of the district's wares and are often highly yet delightfully specialized. Deutsch, Inc., for example (196 Lexington Avenue at 33rd Street), is a bright, airy place filled with an extensive collection of wicker and bamboo furniture, and stores along 34th Street, between Madison and Park avenues, display endless variations on the convertible sofa theme. My favorite, and a favorite with anyone willing to invest a lifetime's savings in domestic comfort, is the Roche-Bobois showroom at 35th and Madison. One can quite easily spend several hours here, notepad in hand, brain swirling with design concepts for the ultimate bedroom or singles dwelling. There's even a bargain basement for limited-budget connoisseurs. I always leave refreshed knowing that there is indeed fine furniture available in Manhattan but with a vague sense of inadequacy at the thought of my own abode.

At the corner of Madison and 35th Street there's the Church of the Incarnation, a delightful place to pause and enjoy one of the frequent lunchtime concerts (preceded by a snack from the nearby delicatessen that looks as if it just arrived from the Lower East Side).

Nearby we come face to face with the presence of that great nineteenth-century individual, J. Pierpont Morgan in the form of his library at the corner of 36th Street and Madison, which became a public institution in 1924. The annex through which one enters the building (exhibition hours Tuesday-Saturday 10:30 A.M.–5 P.M., Sunday 1–5 P.M.; 685-0008. Contribution) is the site of Morgan's house. On the northern corner is his son's house, the J. P. Morgan, Jr., Mansion, now occupied by United Lutheran Church offices, and directly across 37th Street is the incredible DeLamar Mansion, now the Consulate General of the Polish People in New York. This miniature French chateau, complete with cherub-adorned entrances, was the work of architect C. P. H. Gilbert. If you peer in the windows, you'll notice that the interior detailing is even more extravagant than the façade.

In contrast, the Morgan Library, built in 1906, seems an austere creation, finely articulated in the Italian-Renaissance style by McKim, Mead and White, but lacking the exuberance once characteristic of the homes of the Four Hundred in this elite part of Murray Hill. Morgan had no interest in fleeting fashions. He wanted

Polish Consulate

a structure that was timeless in its design and reflected the finest craftsmanship. The great white marble blocks of the library itself were laid "dry" (without mortar), held together by weight and the absolute exactness of the fit. It's an admirable creation. The tiniest details on the iron railing in front of the library are exquisitely produced, and the two cheetahs, on either side of the main entrance, seem ready to spring at the slightest sign of inappropriate behavior from passersby.

I'm surprised how few residents of New York have visited this rich storehouse of literature and art. Admittedly, the library itself can be used only by accredited scholars, but the two public galleries and the exhibition areas contain what, at the time of Morgan's death in 1913, was considered to be the most splendid private collection in the country (in an era when collecting was a popular pastime of the super-rich, that was no mean achievement). There are illuminated manuscripts from the sixth to the sixteenth century, the Book of Hours of Catherine of Cleves, autographed manuscripts of Byron, Keats, and Milton, etchings by Rembrandt, and famous paintings by Tintoretto and Perugino. But those are only highlights. Stroll through the building and experience the solemnity of history, particularly in the east room, where enclosed shelves rise from floor to frescoed ceiling. There's a complete wall of Bibles and two blue leather boxes labeled modestly "Gutenberg Bible." The collection is priceless. One can only gaze in wonder at the knowledge and learning stored within those hundreds of worn leather bindings. In the west room, wonder turns to awe as one stands next to Morgan's carved desk in the tall red room he used as his study. His presence is almost tangible; the aura of unmitigated power fills the room. One of the guards told me how he loved being on duty in this room. "It always makes me feel bigger," he said.

In a haze of culture, continue east on 36th Street toward Third Avenue until you reach Sniffen Court, one of those unexpected surprises you'll find constantly throughout the walk. This delightful alley consisting of a mere handful of two-story homes was built in the mid-1800s by John Sniffen as a series of coach houses and stables for the gentry of the Hill. They were converted into dwellings in the 1920s; the building at the end was for many years the studio of sculptress Malvina Hoffman. There's also a small theater, an architect's office, and an abundance of decorative touches—lamps, flower boxes, odd chimneys, a lovely triangular bay window, brass bits and pieces, and lots of climbing plants. Unfortunately, an occasional car sits in the court and destroys the illusion of being in some Bayswater back garden or one of those quiet passageways that lace the French quarter of New Orleans.

A couple of blocks north on Lexington Avenue, at 152 East 38th Street, is another tiny remnant of nineteenth-century Murray Hill,

Sniffen Court

a delightful townhouse set back from the street behind a flourishing garden. In contrast, at Park Avenue and 35th Street is the J. Hamden Robb House, a solemn edifice of brick and terra-cotta in various shades of burnt sienna and umber. The house, once described by a celebrated architectural critic as "an ideal setting for a wealthy young bachelor," was for many years the home of the Advertising Club. Adjoining streets lined with well-maintained rows of townhouses give this section of town an air of dignity and grace—one can almost hear the clopping of hooves on the cobbles and carriages rumbling by, transporting their frilled and feathered occupants on ceaseless rounds of social engagements.

Stroll north along Lexington, past a series of attractive restaurants and pubs, to 42nd Street and into the hubbub around Grand Central Station. Here we can wander and explore the foyers, passageways, and great halls that seem to characterize the architecture of this bustling enclave. Guided tours are frequently available and details can be obtained at the information desk in the main concourse. Tens of thousands of scurrying commuters pour through every day, but one wonders how many pause to admire the great 140-foot-high ceiling painted with the constellations of the zodiac, where each star becomes a pinpoint of light after dusk? How many have enjoyed the magnificent New England clam chowder, a meal in itself, served in the refurbished Oyster Bar, or played "whispers" under the vaulted arches outside the restaurant entrance? How many realize that this is one of the few enclosed shopping malls of any significance in the city? And don't forget to take note of the adjacent Grand Hyatt Hotel. Once the dowdy Commodore, the hotel's recent transformation by Gruzen and Partners brings a bit of glassy sparkle and dazzle to this rather shadowy part of town. You can now sit in the greenhouse like Sun Garden lounge, cantilevered over the 42nd Street sidewalk, and watch the crowds below.

Across the street you may find respite from all the rush and din in the lobby of the Philip Morris Headquarters on the southwest corner of Park Avenue, where a branch exhibition space of the Whitney Museum of Modern Art houses a permanent sculpture display. An adjacent room often has shows of New York-inspired art, including works by individuals of the famous Ashcan School.

Across from Grand Central on the south side of 42nd Street is the Chanin building, an elaborate example of Art Deco creativity tinged with flourishes of Gothic, constructed in 1929. Note particularly the rich fourth-floor terra-cotta frieze of floral patterns, and the convector grilles, elevator doors, and floor motifs in the lobby. A profusion of polished Istrian marble, elaborate bronze moldings and even bas-relief mailboxes enthusiastically reinforce the primary theme of the Chanin—"New York, City of Opportunity." (Ironically, the building was completed in 1929, the year of the Great Crash.)

Then we come to my favorite building, the great Bowery Savings Bank at 110 East 42nd Street. Through the enormous arch one enters an elaborate Romanesque basilica with columns, each of different-colored marble, rising seventy feet to an ornate beam ceiling. You feel very tiny in such a space as this. Voices echo off the intricate marble walls and the equally extravagant floors. I happened to visit here one Christmas when a choir of sixty young girls presented a program of carols. Their voices rang pure throughout the hall, richly reverberating. People came in off the wet streets and stood listening. Everyone paused. The tellers looked out from behind their ornate cages. The customers relaxed a little. The spirit of the season filled the whole building. It was an experience I'll long remember.

Then on the east side of Lexington Avenue there's the famous 1929 Chrysler building, one of the finest examples of Style-Moderne in Manhattan. Everyone recognizes its tapering sunburst tower and its stainless-steel gargoyles, but few venture into its marble and steel lobby, bathed in surrealistic light, to admire the Trumbell paintings on the ceiling (now almost the same color as the marble) and the total unity of design, down to the smallest details—letterboxes, the guard's stainless-steel cubicle, and the elegant elevator doors. There are automotive themes galore, particularly on the façade of the building where setbacks are embellished with friezes of wheels and hubcaps, the spire is based on a radiator grille design, and the gargoyles themselves reflect the popular radiator cap created for the

1929 Chrysler. Another well-designed attraction here is the Con Edison Conservation Center, located at street level (Open Monday–Saturday 10 A.M.–5:30 P.M. Free).

Past a truly authentic Horn and Hardart cafeteria, at the corner of Third Avenue (slots, flap boxes, and fish-head coffee machines), the last one remaining in the city, we come to the self-contained *Daily News* building at 220 East 42nd Street. Unfortunately, the tours, particularly of the adjoining printing plant, have been discontinued, so you'll have to make do with a saunter around the great globe of the world in the lobby (there are occasional exhibitions) and brief reflections on our comparative insignificance, as pointed out by pungently worded plaques displayed around the slowly rotating sphere—for example:

> If the sun were the size of this globe (12 feet in diameter) then the great nebula in the constellation of Andromeda would be another globe 1½ billion miles in diameter and 10½ billion miles away.

Thoughts of this magnitude may require quiet digestion, so pause awhile at the Horn and Hardart or splurge at the nearby Helmsley Hotel, an elegant mirror-glass replacement of the Central Commercial High School. Alternatively, take a quiet stroll across the street to the twelve-story glass-enclosed garden of the Ford Foundation building. Again, public tours of the offices have been discontinued, but visitors are encouraged to lose themselves in the lush terraces, among full-grown trees, waterfalls, pools, and abundant shrubbery. This creation, one of the most sensitive and imaginative pieces of institutional design in Manhattan, was opened in 1967 and, as critics predicted, became instantly famous. *The New York Times* proclaimed it "one of the most romantic environments ever devised by corporate man." Kevin Roche, of the architectural firm Kevin Roche, John Dinkeloo and Associates, explains his concept as follows: "The conventional office building tends to isolate the individual and store him away in a cubicle with no means of communication other than electronics . . . and with no view other than that of the anonymous cubicles 100 feet away across the street." So Roche decided to design an environment that would allow employees to enjoy fresh and stimulating views and at the same time be aware of the presence of fellow employees—to create the sense of "a family of effort."

Roche's concern was also for the building's relationship to the external environment of the street. "It would have been easy for us to have designed another tower building, but we chose, rather, to keep the building as low as possible and to conscientiously observe the lines and planes created by other buildings that form the surrounding street." Result? The building is modest yet extremely powerful because of the integrity and clarity of the concept. How refreshing to see this kind of restrained statement in a city full of exclamation marks.

Then the mood changes. The encyclopedic array of Art Deco and Style-Moderne creations, along with some examples of twentieth-century glitz, abruptly gives way to the Elizabethan-styled fantasies of Tudor City, perched on a hilltop near First Avenue. Developed as a self-contained community in the 1920s, Tudor City expresses a vocabulary of architectural thought ranging from the sublime to the sublimely ridiculous—eleven multi-story apartment towers with such quaint names as "The Cloister" and "The Manor," topped with gables, turrets, and water towers disguised as miniature manors. There's also a Tudor-treated church, the Church of the Covenant, next to the 600-room Tudor Hotel. Fortunately, the complex also has its redeeming features. There are fine views between the towers of the United Nations and the East River, two intimate and shaded parks, pubs and stores, and La Bibliothèque, a small but popular dining establishment overlooking the river.

One could argue, I suppose, that Tudor City is at least an improvement on the Irish slums that blanketed the area in the late 1800s. In 1863, the infamous draft riots began near Tudor City and spread like windswept fire throughout the city. The wealthy, who had been permitted to buy draft exemption for three hundred dollars, scurried out of town while the mob rampaged the streets, burning and looting, lynching Negroes, and fighting with the police. More than twelve hundred people were killed in that four-day insurrection. Later, during the early 1900s the Tudor City area was home of Paddy Corcoran's "Rag Gang," while down in the flatlands by the river, where the real Turtle Bay had been (Poe once described a peaceful fishing expedition on its quiet shores), was the most noxious neighborhood in Manhattan, full of dank, smoke-filled streets, slaughterhouses, glue factories, breweries, rendering plants, and gas works. All this was cleared out for the construction of the United Nations complex in the 1950s, but was still very much in existence when Tudor City was built—hence the lack of windows on the east face of the towers.

Down the steps near La Bibliothèque, pause briefly in the tiny, tree-shaded Ralph J. Bunche Park, located directly across from the United Nations building. The park honors the memory of a prominent United States UN official who was awarded the Nobel Peace Prize in 1950 for his efforts to resolve problems in the Middle Eastern countries. A plaque on the park's curved Isaiah Wall is a permanent reminder to all the delegates, politicians, diplomats, and protest groups who pass through this park:

> *They Shall Beat Their Swords into*
> *Ploughshares, and Their Spears into*
> *Pruning Hooks . . .*

And there she is—the 544-foot-high Secretariat building, New York's first major glass "curtain-wall" structure. Conceived by a group of internationally renowned architects including Oscar Niemeyer (of Brazilia fame) and France's Le Corbusier and completed in 1950, she is still one of the city's most graceful contemporary creations. Rising cleanly from the long, low conference building and the curved bulk of the General Assembly Hall, the unadorned Secretariat seems to symbolize man's hope for a better future in an era of renewed cooperation and understanding.

It seems that regardless of how toothless, confused, and contradictory the United Nations may appear as an international organization, one cannot remain unmoved by the amazing profusion of art, sculpture, and gifts from all nations that adorn the interior spaces.

Well over one million visitors come every year to the United

Nations; described as "one of the world's most popular attractions" by the New York Convention and Visitors Bureau. Many join the hour-long tours, witness General Assembly sessions (free tickets in the lobby), attend the film showings on the work of the organization, and shop in the bookstore and gift shop—a true world bazaar of products from most member nations, including brass trays from India, Mexican jewelry, Venetian glass, Delft ceramic earrings, Scottish scarves, Indonesian shadow puppets, and gold filigree from Israel. Philatelists flock to the UN's own post office, which always offers new commemorative issues, and true enthusiasts request reservations in the Delegates Dining Room to sample its distinctly international (and inexpensive) cuisine. (Daily information—754-1234.)

But there are two little niches here that even frequent visitors tend to miss. The first is just inside the Assembly building, to the right of the U.S. Moon Rock exhibit. It is the Meditation Room, "a room devoted to peace and those who are giving their lives for peace. It is a room of quiet where only thoughts should speak." Come here and sit in the near-darkness in front of a smooth block of iron ore. A tiny needle of light shines on its upper surface. Behind is a simple mosaic representing the concepts of harmony, freedom, and ultimate balance. The significance of these three elements—the block, the light, the mural—depends on individual interpretation, but everyone seems to leave a little quieter in spirit.

Allow time to explore the United Nations gardens, one of the most refined and carefully conceived spaces in the city. Note how the curve of the riverside esplanade reflects the roofline of the General Assembly building and how, while the massing of the complex always changes as you move about the park, it is always in balance. In the park the knife-edged lines of shaped bushes contrast with the free grouping of trees at the northern end and provide a foil for the two heroic pieces of sculpture, gifts from the USSR and Yugoslavia to the UN.

Hidden in the trees at the far end of the park is a memorial to Eleanor Roosevelt. A semicircular stone seat faces a pink marble tablet on which is inscribed her famous epitaph:

She would rather light a candle than curse the darkness and her glow has warmed the world.

Look closely for this secluded niche. It's easy to miss.

Leave the park by the north entrance if the gate is open and continue up First Avenue to Mitchell Place in quest of a midafternoon rest or repast. Visit the lounge at the top of Beekman Towers and enjoy the splendid view over midtown, or take afternoon tea at the green glass-clad UN Plaza Hotel at First Avenue and 44th Street. Enjoy the grand piano recitals in the lobby, or try to find your way through the multi-mirrored corridors to the Ambassador Grill where everyone seems to dine lavishly on OPM (Other People's Money). If you prefer to keep the mood cultural, visit the African-American Institute at First Avenue and 47th Street (modest but exciting displays—call 949-5666 for details) or the Japan House Gallery nearby at 333 East 47th Street between First and Second avenues. Here is a little world apart, a tranquil oasis of Japanese art, sculpture, and photography, simply presented in the second-floor space (daily 11 A.M.–5 P.M.; 832-1155. Donation).

And—talking of oases—we now leave behind the tumult of First Avenue and wander slowly through one of New York's most refined residential enclaves, beginning at Beekman Place—one of those niches full of the aura of the old Four Hundred days. Although cramped by tall apartment buildings, this row of townhouses still possesses a distinctly aloof and refined character. As Oscar Wilde once remarked, "Breeding can never be disguised."

Many New York notables have lived here—the Rockefellers, Ethel Barrymore, Irving Berlin, Katharine Cornell, and other famous theatrical personalities. The area is named after William Beekman, a contemporary of Peter Stuyvesant. They sailed to America together and his son, James, built his Mount Pleasant Mansion here on the hill overlooking the East River and Turtle Bay. Some of the furnishings of the house are on display in the New-York Historical Society building at Central Park West and 77th Street. (The exhibitions here and at the Museum of the City of New York, Fifth Avenue between 103rd and 104th streets, are excellent and should be a regular part of any New York exploration itinerary.)

Beekman Place abounds with historical tales: General Howe established his headquarters on the Mount Pleasant Estate, Nathan Hale was captured and hanged nearby, and arrangements were made here by the British to accept the assistance of Benedict Arnold. Today it's all very quiet and restrained. Uniformed doormen officiously watch every stranger on the street. Limousines glide silently to chandelier-adorned foyers, and the only disturbance comes from the occasional overfed poodle, yapping at some other equally pampered specimen in the street.

At the end of 51st Street there's a footbridge over the tiny roadside park, across FDR Drive, to a riverside walk. Here residents occasionally gather to watch the East River scene (those residents, that is, without their own river view) or sunbathe while traffic roars by a few feet away.

Continue northward to Sutton Place South and Sutton Place, a unique corner of the city where short cul-de-sacs end in tiny parks and play areas. Select groups of townhouses on 57th and 58th streets nestle together, oblivious to the great blank blocks of apartments nearby and the continuous rumble from the Queensboro Bridge. It's a world apart. One of the rooms above the street on 58th has on display the heads of various types of deer and gazelle. Two Lamborghinis (his black, hers white) purr outside a gray Georgian-style house with canary-yellow shutters. Little gnomes hide in the shrubbery of enclosed gardens overlooking the river. The smell of pollen-laden flowers wafts over the walls. There's no sign of life in the houses and somehow that too is appropriate. People would seem far too intrusive in this setting. And yet the place is peppered with celebrities (present or recently past), including Marilyn Monroe, who married Arthur Miller at her No. 2 Sutton Place South apartment, Senator James Buckley, the Kissingers, Greta Garbo, the architect I.M. Pei, the UN Secretary General, and the President of the American Museum of Natural History.

My favorite niche here is Riverview Terrace, a tiny cul-de-sac tucked behind Sutton Place, formed by six small row houses, none more than sixteen feet wide. The best view is from the elegant Sutton Square with its Georgian houses and limousine-lined sidewalks. You can peer past the white gateposts, topped by two rather worn creatures (seemingly combinations of fish and goat), into a little unspoiled enclave of yesteryear.

Stroll westward to Second Avenue. Turn left to 56th Street and visit a fascinating antique complex in this neighborhood of antique stores—the Manhattan Arts and Antique Center (Open Monday–Saturday 10 A.M.–6:30 P.M.; Sunday noon–6 P.M.). Here are more than eighty-five unusual stores and galleries displaying all manner of silver objets d'art, Oriental artworks, icons, ceramics, jewelry, crystal, porcelains, Wedgwood, furniture, chandeliers, contemporary fine arts—even African sculptures and Tibetan temple ornaments. One can tell just by the Rolls-Royce and Ferrari showrooms nearby that this is a monied enclave. The two lower levels of the center contain some of the most magnificent displays of antiques and art treasures in the city. According to one of the eloquent store owners it's a "veritable vortex of vicarious experiences!"

If you find all this wealth beginning to pall, take a ride in the Roosevelt Island cable car from Second Avenue and 59th Street and regain your perspective on the city as the yellow wheels turn, sending the little box climbing high above the rooftops and the avenues. Down below, there's a virtual jungle on the top of a large warehouse nearby (Terrestris)—a hothouse filled with trees and shrubs surrounded by black roofs and odd groups of chimneys. Then comes the East River with its chubby tugboats, views of the Roosevelt Island residential complex, and the descent to the terminal. It's quite a change from subway travel. Everyone seems to know everyone else. The operator of the car is on a first-name basis with many of his passengers. For most of the journey he discusses the care of azaleas with a distinguished-looking gentleman in a vicuña coat.

If you'd like a sidetrip through the growing community of Roosevelt Island, take one of the jitney buses to Northtown and stroll along the curling main street between the high-rise blocks, past the preserved 1889 Chapel of the Good Shepherd and The Green Kitchen restaurant, then down to the East River steps where you can watch the flotsam float by while casually dressed islanders toss their frisbies between the baby strollers.

There's a feeling of country here—a sense of security, family, and quiet evenings, while Manhattan continues to bump and grind on into the night. The simple Blackwell Farmhouse, originally built around 1796 and restored in 1973, reflects, in architectural terms, all the basic qualities that must make life so peaceful for the island's 8,000 residents. By the time you arrive back at 59th Street you'll have a different view of the city. Maybe you'll want to go roaring off to the country to find places where trees don't grow in hothouses on rooftops.

Maybe instead you'll love the city a little more, in which case visit the Abigail Adams Smith Museum at 421 East 61st (at York Avenue, Monday–Friday 10 A.M.–4 P.M. Fee) for one of the prettiest surprises of the walk. Tucked between a parking garage and a new block of apartments is a 1799 stone carriage house built on the estate of Colonel William Stephens Smith, husband of John Adams's daughter Abigail and aide-de-camp to George Washington. Smith named his estate Mount Vernon in honor of his chief's favorite home, but after a reversal in his financial fortunes was obliged to sell all twenty acres. The coach house was subsequently used as an inn, a private home, and a Salvation Army soup kitchen until, in 1924, it was purchased by the Colonial Dames of America. Massive refurbishing was necessary, but today this remnant of Smith's folly, as the estate was once known, is a charming museum of early nineteenth-century life. It's usually quiet here, especially during the week, and guided tours are provided by a representative of the Dames. There are a few reminders of its original function, but the building has been successfully converted into tastefully decorated living space and is full of elegant furniture. In one of the upstairs rooms there are framed letters from George Washington and President John Adams who, in an awkwardly formal letter to his daughter, wrote:

> I have received your pretty letter and it has given me a great deal of pleasure, both as it is a token of your duty and affection to me and as it is proof of improvement in your handwriting and in the faculties of the mind.

Typical Adams sentiments!

This is a most refreshing place to spend an hour or so, and if you're a little foot-weary there's a small garden at the rear of the house where you can rest. But try to conserve enough energy for a final stroll up past the Rolls-Royces at Carriage House Motor Cars Ltd., and the infamous Chippendales (male dancers for female patrons), to the Treadwell Farm district, on 61st and 62nd streets between Second and Third avenues. Here are two of the most attractive streets in this part of town, so very close to, yet totally divorced from, the burgeoning 59th Street scene around Bloomingdale's. As one might expect, many of these elegant townhouses, built between

1868 and 1876 on land that was originally Adam Treadwell's farm, have been occupied by New York notables including Paul Gallico, Gertrude Lawrence, and Eleanor Roosevelt, and continue to retain their dignity and charm despite rampant redevelopment all around. It's a lovely place to end the walk.

NOTE: There were, at last count, ten institutions and societies in the east 60s that offer exhibitions and cultural activities to the public, and these are described fully in the Mini-Tours section at the back of the book (see Mini Tours, The Upper East Side Cultural Maze).

Abigail Adams Smith House

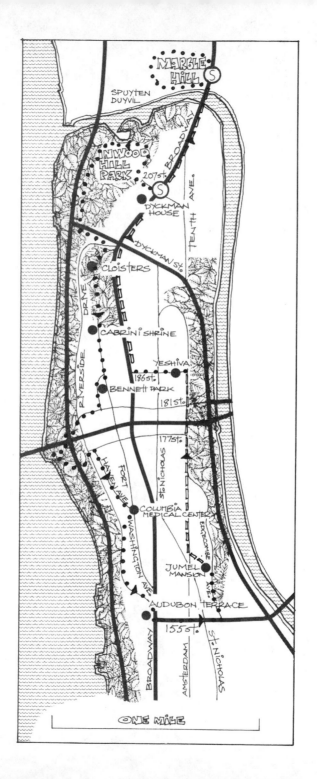

MARBLE HILL Ⓢ

SPUYTEN DUYVIL

IN WOOD HILL PARK

BROADWAY

207st.

Ⓢ

DYCKMAN HOUSE

DYCKMAN St.

TENTH AVE.

CLOISTERS

RIVERSIDE DRIVE

CABRINI SHRINE

YESHIVA

186st.

BENNETT PARK

181st.

177st.

St. NICHOLAS

FORT WASHINGTON AVE.

HAVEN AVE.

COLUMBIA MEDICAL CENTER

EDGECOMBE

JUMEL MANSION

AUDUBON TERRACE

155st.

BROADWAY

AMSTERDAM

St. NICHOLAS

ONE MILE

9 | Inwood- Washington Heights

Though not one of Manhattan's newly gentrified neighborhoods, Inwood–Washington Heights has its own very real and timeless appeal. There are museums galore, superb parks, a delightful enclave of Victoriana, fine churches, and one of the best nooks in New York around the old Morris-Jumel Mansion. So—let's go!

The balcony at the United Church, 175th and Broadway, shakes alarmingly as one thousand feet bounce to the beat of "Joy to the World." A large black woman in a gold-sequined hat three times bigger than her head grabs my hand and shouts into my face, "God specializes, God specializes." A man on my right is leaping two, maybe three, feet off the floor, tears streaming over his cheeks, mingling with sweat spinning off his nose and chin. A small girl turns cartwheels in the aisles. Both organs roar out the crashing chords. The drummer bobs and shakes with the rhythm. The choir, full of little bouncing boys, is a gyrating mass of blue and red gowns.

☞ **DIRECTIONS**
The walking tour starts at the Dyckman House, Broadway and 204th Street
Subway: *Start:* IND A to 207th Street and Broadway (Dyckman Street)
Return: IND AA, B at 163rd Street and Amsterdam Avenue
IRT 1 at 181st Street and St. Nicholas Avenue or
IRT 1 at 225th Street and Broadway in Marble Hill
Bus: *Start:* M100
Return: M2, M3, M4, M5, M100, M101

Above it all, on a dais, the Reverend Frederick Eikerenkoetter, better known as Reverend Ike, drinks from one of two sparkling silver goblets brought to him on a gleaming silver tray by an angelic assistant and watches the audience carefully. He raises a hand and the frenzy starts to slow. He raises both hands: "Lift up your hands as high as you can," he cries out to the audience. "Lift them up—up—and say after me: 'You cannot outgive God, you cannot outgive God.'" The response is full and unanimous. "God does not grow feeble with age and neither do I. C'mon," shouts the reverend, "Say it—say it loud, say it after me . . . 'God does not . . .'"

It's just another typical Sunday in the ornate temple, an old Loew's theater, in Washington Heights. Soon Reverend Ike—his curly black hair glistening with pomade, his voice as powerful as Little Richard's, his rings flashing in the spotlights—will begin his message of material wealth and well-being—the gospel of "green power." He'll read testimonials from followers who gave generously to his ministry and were blessed in return with Cadillacs, diamonds, mink coats—and good health. He'll tell them to "Think rich," he'll have them screaming out in unison: "You can't lose with the stuff I use." He'll have them loving him and coming back again week after week.

Not far away, on the line of benches below the old Dyckman Farmhouse, groups of elderly residents talk together quietly and enjoy the silence of Sunday streets. Over in Inwood Park, just past the Columbia Boathouse on Spuyten Duyvil Creek, a couple stroll arm in arm up the hill to the caves in the rock where Indians lived centuries before the first European settlers sailed up the Hudson.

At Audubon Terrace on 155th Street four young students are leaving the Hispanic Museum. "It's fantastic," says one of them. "I never knew this place was here."

In Morris Park visitors stand at the fence and look out over High Bridge Park, and across the river to Queens and Brooklyn. Behind them is the eighteenth-century Jumel Mansion—Washington's headquarters during September 1776—with its great white portico and delicate balcony. Over to the west, down under the towers of the George Washington Bridge, a child, hand in hand with his father, stands and smiles at the Little Red Lighthouse. Inside the

Mother Cabrini Shrine, near the entrance to the Fort Tryon Gardens, rosaries click and people pray, their eyes fixed on the remains of the saint in the glass coffin below the altar.

"You know, the crazy thing is, if you took this top part of Manhattan and put it down anywhere else, it would be one of the biggest tourist attractions in the country." I was chatting with Carol Silagyi, who with Heather Schweder, were founding members of Arts Interaction for this northern tip of the island. "There are more than one hundred sixty thousand people living up here, y'know. We're the same size as Syracuse. There are eight major museums, two world-famous universities, all kinds of historic buildings and landmarks, a dozen sites commemorating the Revolution, over six thousand acres of parks—and yet we're ignored. Many people who've lived in Manhattan for years have never been here—except maybe for that one visit to the Cloisters. Even local residents don't know the area."

The aim of Arts Interaction is simple—to put Washington Heights, Inwood, and Marble Hill on the map. Under the leadership of Joseph Hintersteiner, the group produces poster campaigns and directories, publicizes local events, operates an information hotline (927-5004), and runs a gallery offering free exhibitions, lectures, and readings (711 West 168th Street; Monday–Friday 10 A.M.–5 P.M.). "You could spend days exploring these neighborhoods—there's so much going on and so many places to see. Just give me a couple of hours," Carol told me, "and I'll show you what I mean." She did. I was taken on a fascinating journey and was introduced to one of the most interesting, and, in places, most beautiful parts of New York.

We begin at the Dyckman farmhouse (1783) perched on a rocky garden high above the sidewalk at Broadway and 204th Street (Open 9 A.M.–5 P.M.; closed Monday. Free). Many people tend to associate Inwood with somber blocks of gray apartments, the screeching of the el as it twists its way north to the Bronx, or grubby, overused parks devoid of grass. You might be surprised to learn that not very long ago this was verdant farmland surrounded by dense forests. You may also be surprised to learn that much of the natural landscape still remains. On a summer day the garden behind the old farmhouse is full of shade and the perfume of flowers. The traffic seems far away. Just down the street there's the great green bowl of Inwood Park with its hidden valley walks and views across to the rocky precipice of the Palisades.

Inside the farmhouse it's dark and cool. When the door is closed, you enter a little world of candlelight, of small, simple rooms furnished with eighteenth- and nineteenth-century pieces, many based on Chippendale designs. The ceilings are low, particularly in the basement, which contains the kitchen and a small display of artifacts from the revolutionary period. As you descend, head bowed

Dyckman House

to chest level, note the intrusion of Manhattan rock on which the farmhouse is built. Many of the objects, the clay pipes, old pieces of stained silverware, wine bottles, and even bone buttons from military uniforms, were found in the garden. It was used as a military encampment for much of the Revolutionary period, and a replica of one of the soldiers' log huts, complete with log roof, can be found down the path at the back of the house.

The old people of the neighborhood gather daily in ritual fashion at the benches below the farmhouse. They think it's one of the nicest places in the city and consider it their exclusive territory. While I was there a stranger strolled up, selected a bench at random, and sat down. One lady was most upset and murmured to her companions, "That's Mrs. Epstein's seat. He shouldn't sit there, you know." There was a brief flurry of discussion among the ladies. They decided that someone had to tell him that it was one of "their" benches. The ones at the top end, away from the corner, were for "outsiders." Fortunately, a bus came, the man left his seat, and the problem was resolved. Mrs. Epstein, who had gone around the corner to chat with a male friend, hurried back to reclaim her seat and the ritual continued.

Take one of the streets west from Broadway and stroll into Inwood Hill Park—one of the few unspoiled and undiscovered parks in Manhattan. Across the ball fields there's the Spuyten Duyvil Creek and the "new" stretch of the Harlem River. In 1895 a shortened link was made to improve navigation around the top part of the island. The old arc of river that ran around what is now known as Marble Hill was filled in. Marble Hill was abruptly cut off from the city and became a continuum of the Bronx. The residents, however, would have none of that and demanded to remain Manhattanites. We visit this strange little fifty-acre parcel later in the journey.

Down by the Duyvil Creek near Baker Field is the Columbia Boathouse, in demure contrast with the great apartment towers on the other bank. The rail line disappears behind a slice of hillside inscribed with a huge blue-and-white "C." Painting this creation, the largest piece of graffiti in the city, was a popular hazing escapade for Columbia freshmen and is now officially discouraged.

At the western edge of the park's grass fields, where the woods begin, there's a gray boulder set in the pathway. A plaque here marks the site of the largest Indian village on Manhattan, Shorakapkok, and claims this as the place where Peter Minuit reached agreement with the Indians for that famous twenty-four-dollar sale in 1626. There's much dispute about the authenticity of this site. Many historians believe the transaction took place at the southern tip of the island where the Dutch settled. But somehow this seems the more impressive location. One can visualize the Wiechquaeskeck Indian village here on the slope of the meadow, canoes lining the river-bank and smoke wafting through the maple and oak woods enclosing the natural amphitheater. Higher up there are caves in the hillside once occupied by the Indians.

Pick a path at random and stroll into the woods. Not many people come this way, particularly during the week, and you'll probably feel more secure with a friend along for company. There's a silence here you won't find anywhere else in Manhattan. As with many of New York's parks it needs some restoration, but the overgrown character of the place only serves to emphasize its sense of separateness from the city.

When I come here I normally head south through the woods, taking the western ridge with its occasional views across to the Palisades. After half a mile or so the land steeply slopes and the path leads out of the park, over a bridge alongside the Henry Hudson Parkway, around the curve of Riverside Drive, and into Fort Tryon Park. It's a nuisance that the parks are not contiguous, but the link is short and in no time you're walking up through the woods to the Cloisters (Open Tuesday–Saturday 10 A.M.–5 P.M.; Sunday 1–5 P.M. Contribution). I once made the mistake of taking the shorter route, up the steps. It was like the traditional mountain-climbing experience where the higher you ascend, the farther away the summit appears to be. Only choose this route if you're determined to make your life hard.

The Cloisters, of course, is a prime New York landmark, fully described in almost every available guidebook and pamphlet. Suffice it to say that it's also one of my favorite not-so-hidden places. I experience different sensations and discover new niches every time

I explore its cool rooms filled with medieval works of art—tapestries, altarpieces, icons, sculptures, chalices, statuettes, and, in the treasury, some of the most highly prized medieval religious works in the world. It's hard to imagine a more pleasant way to spend a hot afternoon than sitting in the St. Michael de Cuxa courtyard listening to the ageless Gregorian chants. Unfortunately, most New Yorkers visit Inwood just to see the Cloisters, Fort Tryon, and the gardens and then hurry back down to the 190th Street subway station. Those with a more adventurous bent should now join our walk southward into Washington Heights. Before leaving the park, however, pause on one of the terraces of the old fort and enjoy the fine views of northern New York, the Hudson River, and the Palisades.

Just outside the park on Fort Washington Avenue is the Mother Cabrini Chapel named in honor of America's first citizen to be canonized—Saint Francesca Saverio Cabrini, who attained beatification in November 1938 (Open Tuesday–Sunday 9 A.M.–4:30 P.M. Free). The wall around the altar is covered in mosaics depicting incidents in her life. She was a tiny person, full of unbounded energy, who founded orphanages, child-care centers, hospitals, and homes for the aged, and made twenty-five Atlantic crossings establishing similar centers outside the country. She died in 1917, and her remains are entombed in a glass coffin under the altar. The nuns who run the little relics-and-souvenir stand just down the corridor from the chapel speak of her as if she were still alive. It's a touching place.

Continue a short distance southward on Fort Washington Avenue to Bennett Park, site of the original Fort Washington. Built in 1776 by the patriots, it was soon captured by the British and remained in their hands until the end of the war. A wall inside the park is a partial reproduction of a segment of the original structure. The land was later owned by the Bennett family and was presented to the city in 1903 by James Gordon Bennett, Jr., errant son of the *New York Herald*'s stern owner. Known for his passionate indulgence in most of the conventional, and a few unconventional, sensual activities, James finally disgraced himself at a New Year's party given by the family of his bride-to-be. It was an occasion characterized by all the pomp and puffery of high wealth and the affair was a splendid success until Mr. Bennett, hailing the onset of 1877 through a brandy haze, decided to relieve himself in the main fireplace in front of the guests. Shortly thereafter he left New York for Paris, brideless, and returned to the city only when business required and/or to consult with the architect Stanford White about his proposed mausoleum—a 200-foot-high hollow statue of an owl where his body would be suspended in a casket hung from chains inside the owl's head. White was shot, however, before the project come to fruition and Bennett was buried in a far more modest manner at Passy, Paris. All we have left of him is his park, a delightfully urban enclave bounded on the west side by the medieval-style Hudson View gardens.

Although there's a "private" sign at the gate of the apartment complex, visitors often stroll along its quaint interior street lined with rockeries and rose bushes, and pause to admire the fine views across the river. Unfortunately, though, for many of the residents, the views are not what they once were. A new complex of tall red-brick towers known as Castle Village was built directly in front of the Hudson View gardens by a Dr. Paterno, on a terrace of land previously occupied by his private castle. According to a plaque on the wall near the office, the doctor was a most philanthropic developer:

> In apartments he built, he lightened burdens with labor-saving conveniences and lifted the spirit with the beauty of gardens.

Some say, however, that he built his village primarily for spite when a close friend was prevented from purchasing a property in the Hudson View complex. But whatever the story, there are certainly some lovely gardens and viewing platforms, although members of the public are not always encouraged to walk here.

Follow Pinehurst Avenue on the west side of Bennett Park south a short distance and then descend a palatial set of steps leading to 181st Street. Here, just briefly, walk up the hill to Fort Washington Avenue and note the building on the southeast corner. This is one of scores of buildings in this part of town richly adorned with sculpture. The larger-than-life figures here are splendid caricatures —but of whom? No one I talked to in the area seemed to know. Note the one on the corner, with glasses. Not far away at 165th Street and Broadway is the Audubon Ballroom, where Malcolm X was shot. That too possesses some magnificent ceramic details, including an almost life-size Viking ship above the main entrance. Many of the apartment buildings, somber and austere on the outside, contain hidden courtyards, fountains, lobbies rich in Italian marble, mahogany paneling, stained-glass windows, and in the case of the apartments on the corner of 159th Street and Edgecombe, a complete ceiling of stained glass thought to be of Tiffany origin. Gargoyle-gazing and lobby-loitering could become a popular local pastime.

But we digress. At the base of the steps on 181st Street, those with energy to spare should continue west to Riverside Drive, take the footbridge over the Henry Hudson Parkway, follow the path through the underpass to the base of the George Washington Bridge, and arrive finally at the famous Little Red Lighthouse sitting coyly in the shadow of the "Great Grey Bridge," just as described in the beloved children's story. "This is my fav'rite bridge," I was told by an Irish bridge painter, sitting in the sunshine drinking a lunchtime beer. "Why, I've worked on just about every one in the city, but this one, she's the best, 'specially when you get upstairs. That's a view worth braggin' about. 'Course it attracts the sad ones, y'know. Somethin' about this bridge that attracts the sad ones. A fella this mornin', 'bout seven it was, he jumped. Police came around. Couldn't find a thing. Hardly ever do. But it's still a lovely piece of work." He slapped the base of one of the great piers. "She's built to last, this one," he said.

Take time to explore the area around the bridge. On the north side there are creeks and shallows hidden from the path where you can spend a whole day undisturbed, oblivious to the city at your back. To the south there's a long riverside walk leading all the way to a footbridge at 155th Street that brings you up alongside Trinity Cemetery and Audubon Terrace. It's beautiful along the edge of the river, accompanied by ducks and sea gulls, but the bridge is not recommended. Instead take the alternative climb back up the

Heights, coming out at 177th Street and Haven Avenue. Of course, those who feel the detour to the lighthouse is a bit much just to dangle their feet in the Hudson will have slipped down Fort Washington Avenue from 181st Street. Either way, the route now leads southward past the new Long library building into the heart of the Columbia Medical Center.

At 163rd Street there's another choice to be made. Either follow Fort Washington Avenue south to Broadway and on to Audubon Terrace at 155th Street **or** turn right, walk to Riverside Drive, turn left and then follow the curve of the street past groups of ornate apartment buildings and smaller, but richly decorated, row houses. This is one of Manhattan's little baroque backwaters—too mixed architecturally to become a historic district but totally charming nonetheless. Closer to Broadway it becomes a little seedy, but that oasis of culture, Audubon Terrace, is looming up ahead, so scurry into the comforting confines of this refined neoclassic niche.

Like the Cloisters, Audubon Terrace is a well-loved, well-publicized attraction. For some reason, though, its diverse museums are often ignored and attendance during the last few years has been disappointing. The American Geographic Society gave up its premises here recently, and there's even been talk of relocating the most popular of the remaining museums, the Museum of the American Indian (Open Tuesday–Saturday 10 A.M.–5 P.M.; Sunday 1–5 P.M.; 283-2420. Fee), to a more nationally central site. Certainly it seems ridiculous that only a tiny proportion of its magnificent collection of more than four million artifacts can be shown here because of lack of space and limited museum funding. The largest part of the collection is now in a vast Bronx warehouse, closed to the public.

Next door the Hispanic Museum (Open Tuesday–Saturday 10 A.M.–4:30 P.M.; Sunday 1–4 P.M.; 926-2234. Free) boasts an extravagent collection of Spanish art, sculpture, and crafts from the Visigothic period to the contemporary era. Paintings by such masters as Velazquez, El Greco, and Goya (including a series of his bullfight etchings) highlight the collection, along with a magnificent series of huge vibrant murals depicting the varied regions of Spain by Joaquin Sorolla y Bastida, in the Sorolla Room. The library off the main court, richly decorated in terra-cotta, contains more than 100,000 volumes, including 12,000 published prior to 1700.

Behind the ornate bronze doors of the American Numismatic Society Museum, at the southern rear corner of the terrace (Open Tuesday–Saturday 9 A.M.–4:30 P.M.; Sunday 1–4 P.M.; 234-3130. Free) is one of the world's largest collections of coins, paper currency, medals, and medallions. Even those previously uninformed in the subtleties and complexities of currency will find the displays well-documented and fascinating. Visitors invariably emerge peering at their small change, looking for that rare Lincoln penny.

Finally there's the American Academy of Arts and Letters (Open Tuesday–Sunday 1–4 P.M.; 368-5900. Free) which, with its parent association, the National Institute of Arts and Letters (located directly opposite with an almost identical façade), recognizes and honors the American creative spirit. The National Institute has 250 writers, poets, architects, composers, and artists as members; the even more exclusive academy has 50 members, selected for their unique and enduring contributions to the arts. They include such celebrities as Pearl S. Buck, John Dos Passos, Aaron Copland, Carl Sandburg, John Steinbeck, Andrew Wyeth, and Norman Mailer. In addition to bestowing honors the academy presents regular exhibitions and, on special request, makes available to accredited scholars original manuscripts, first editions, and even the scratchpads, notebooks, and doodles of their famous creative members (call 368-5900 for details).

Ideally, a separate day should be given over to exploring the museums of Audubon Terrace. The displays and exhibitions are far too impressive and extensive to be enjoyed during a rigorous walking tour of the area.

Across from the terrace, at 155th Street, is Trinity Cemetery, resting place of many New York notables—Madame Jumel, John James Audubon (a tall cross next to a tiny bird box), Clement Moore (there's a candlelight procession here every Christmas Eve for the man who wrote " 'Twas the Night before Christmas"), and the unfortunate Alfred Tennyson Dickens, son of Charles Dickens, who died abruptly in 1912 of a heart attack at the Hotel Astor while making preparations for his father's centenary celebrations. The cemetery was part of the second-line-of-defense earthworks during the Revolution, hence its rather incongruous undulations. There's a plaque on the corner of the Parish House behind the neo-Gothic Church of the Intercession that illustrates the layout of the earthworks.

The church is an impressive piece of early-twentieth-century architecture complete with cloisters (the entrance to the cemetery is through here), parish building, a crypt, and even a secret "abbot's eye" window above the main altar. The remains of its architect, Bertram Grosvenor Goodhue, are contained in a wall vault adorned with a sculpture of the man reclining and bas-reliefs of his major architectural achievements—an immodest but impressive memorial. While much of the stained glass is disappointingly uninspired ("It was intended as temporary but was never changed," I was informed by an impromptu guide), the wood carvings, particularly around the chapel, are exquisite, and the roof, supported by massive wood beams, gives the nave an almost baronial banquet-hall flavor.

The Church of the Intercession is one of several religious centers in the immediate vicinity. In fact, Inwood and the Heights have a remarkable number and diversity of churches catering to a highly varied ethnic population—Chinese, Indian, Greek Orthodox, Armenian, Russian Orthodox, to name but a few. One of my favorite churches—the Church of Our Lady of Esperanza—is just across the road from Trinity Cemetery, along the north wall of Audubon Terrace. This has now become the cultural center for the area's burgeoning Puerto Rican population, and the tiny church, located up the stairs from the small entrance on 156th Street, is unusually restful and contains some lovely groupings of stained-glass windows.

Follow 155th Street eastward beyond St. Nicholas Avenue to a narrow footpath that turns north to join Edgecombe Avenue. Here begins what was once the island's most dramatic open space, the High Bridge Park. Regrettably, vandalism and the apparent lack of interest on the part of the Parks Department have resulted in neglect and abandonment. Few people walk through its wooded terraces. Junked cars litter the hillside and after-dark muggings are not uncommon. Yet there are still magnificent views across the East River, out toward Long Island Sound, from the park's rocky ledges. It is ludicrous that the city is allowing such a remarkable resource to deteriorate to the point where it will soon be inaccessible to the public.

Fortunately, there's still the Roger Morris Park and the Jumel Mansion at 160th Street and Edgecombe Avenue. This is one of Manhattan's most notable historic districts, offering a diversified range of late-nineteenth-century row houses, a narrow street of tiny clapboard homes known as Sylvan Terrace that ends in a set of stone steps leading to St. Nicholas Avenue, the Roger Morris Park, and the "Grand White Lady" herself, the 1765 Morris-Jumel Mansion (Open Tuesday–Sunday 10 A.M.–4 P.M. Fee).

The district is an important stopping point on city tours. While I was sketching the mansion some Newark residents were being shown the Jumel Terrace by an ardent black woman as part of the "Harlem As It Is" tour operated by the Penny Sightseeing Company. She proudly pointed out the house where Paul Robeson lived for many years and went on to describe in lurid detail past housing inequities in the area. The group listened silently and intently.

The mansion is a delight. Again, like the Dyckman House, it's one of those places where you can lose all sense of time and place. The large white door closes and you're transported into the eighteenth century, an era of decorous manners, exquisite craftsmanship and taste, a time of delicate sensibilities reflected in subtle hand-printed wallpapers, translucent eggshell china, and the restrained tick of perfectly crafted clocks. The mansion has been described appropriately as "a serene home." Washington found it "a most admirable place" and established his headquarters there for a brief month in September 1776. It subsequently became a summer camp for English and Hessian generals; then after the war, a tavern and a farmhouse. In 1810 Stephen Jumel and his wife Eliza purchased and refurbished the house, importing pieces of furniture said to belong to their friend Napoleon Bonaparte. After Mr. Jumel's death in 1832, Eliza briefly married Aaron Burr, but their union was a failure and the divorce decree was granted, ironically, on the day of Burr's death in 1836.

My favorite rooms here are the Blue bedroom bursting with

Napoleonic pomp, and the elegantly proportioned octagonal drawing room on the first floor, furnished in late-eighteenth-century style and possessing a remarkable spirit of dignity and calm combined with a sense of intimacy. Outside in the garden you can watch traffic churning along the expressways far below, planes roaring in and out

of La Guardia, subway trains clanking and screeching across the
East River bridges. Inside the mansion all remains quiet, and visitors leave looking a little less harried than when they arrived.

If you're now exhausted, there are regular buses on St. Nicholas
Avenue or subway trains from 163rd Street at Amsterdam Avenue.

Morris-Jumel Mansion

Alternatively, if you are still in the mood for exploring, take a bus up to Yeshiva University at 186th Street, where there's a small permanent museum and occasional exhibitions on aspects of Jewish culture (Open Tuesday–Thursday 10:30 A.M.–5 P.M.; Sunday noon–6 P.M. Fee). Take special note of the ten beautiful models of historic synagogues (not always displayed) and the year-long special exhibitions reflecting aspects of Jewish life and law.

Walk along the edge of High Bridge Park and visit the water tower off 173rd Street, adjoining the popular High Bridge pool and play center. This handsome campanile structure, recently restored, once supported a 47,000-gallon water tank and was part of the remarkable sequence of engineering accomplishments that brought water from the Croton River along forty miles of aqueducts, and an aqueduct-bridge spanning the Harlem River, to the distributing reservoir in Central Park. There has been talk recently of reopening the pedestrian walkway across the High Bridge aqueduct and improving the whole park environment around the water tower. We wait for action.

Here's one final pause for those enthusiastic souls who have enjoyed this rediscovery of a forgotten segment of Manhattan. Take a bus north on Broadway across the Spuyten Duyvil Creek into Marble Hill and ramble up the slope to the left, around the narrow curling streets. There are no major architectural landmarks here—just the spirit of a small town full of slightly worn Victorian villas and leaning verandas along Van Corlear Place, Adrian Avenue, and Fort Charles Place. The wood-shingled St. Stephen's Church overlooks the old course of the Harlem River, now filled in. Just across the street Johannes Verveelen operated his ferry over "the waterway of ebb and flow" from 1669 until the construction of the Kings Bridge in 1693.

This odd little community, cocooned in its past, is a fascinating reminder of how this area must have looked a hundred or so years ago. Across the river in Inwood it's possible to find an occasional old home with conical turret and high-pitched shingle roof, but most have been replaced by great gray apartment blocks. In contrast Marble Hill looks as if it might stay this way forever. "We're not really as old-fashioned as we look," a young resident told me. "We just like it this way—and d'you know, people have started to come and take pictures and write articles on these old homes now. They get all excited about them. Heck, who'd heard of Marble Hill a few years back? Now we're getting known and—you feel prouder, you spruce things up a bit more."

There are some marked signs of change and rejuvenation in the area. Down on West 225th Street and Terrace View, the Marble Hill Neighborhood Improvement Corporation is encouraging renovation of the dilapidated walk-up apartments overlooking the Harlem River, and the local community newsletter, *The Marble Hill Reader,* invites residents to "Be a Marble Hill-Nick." Great! It's good to see new life in this northern tip of Manhattan.

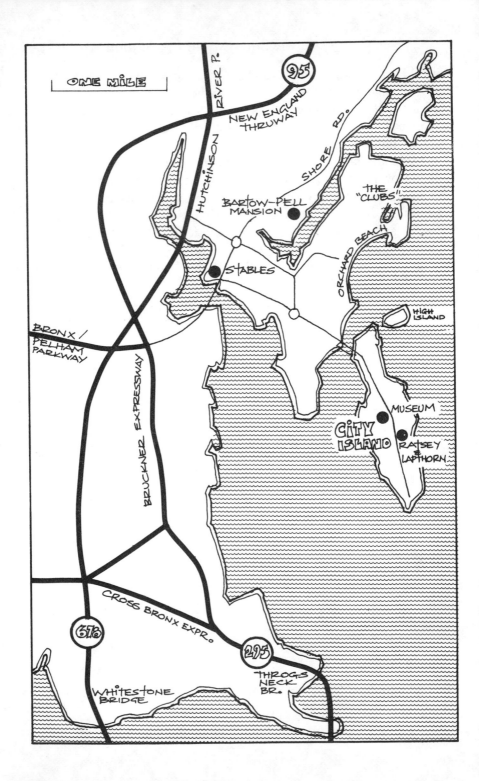

10 | City Island

There have been some changes here recently, including construction of The Boatyard condos and the opening of a couple of new restaurants, but City Island continues on as it always has —slightly sleepy and a most refreshing down-home interlude from hectic urban life.

To me City Island is always a surprise. I've been here in all seasons —at the first flicker of spring and when snowdrifts cover half of the Glover's Point Rock, just before the bridge. There's no buildup for what's to come. One minute you're traveling the highway, fendered in by traffic, tall apartment towers as far as you can see, jets screaming into La Guardia. Then there's the exit, a brief drive through the estatelike landscape of Hunters Island, and finally—the bridge, the bay, and the island. Church spires rise above the trees. A launch leaves one of the piers and ripples send a shower of gulls spiraling. Smoke curls from chimneys. Domes and mansard roofs rise above

☞ **DIRECTIONS**
Sailors can tell you exactly where it is—latitude 41° 51′ 0″N, longitude 73° 47′ 30″W. Many visitors do, in fact, arrive by boat—everything from dinghies to multistateroom launches. Landbound travelers use cars (City Island/Orchard Beach exit off the Bruckner Expressway or the Hutchinson River Parkway) or a combination of bus and subway (IND to Fordham Road/ transfer to Bx12, or IRT 6 to Pelham Bay Park/transfer to Bx12).
NOTE: If you come by public transport it may be best to limit your exploration to City Island itself

porticoed verandas, slightly bowed. There's the smell of seaweed, the smell of garlic from one of the seafood restaurants, the smell of resin from the boatyards. There are boats everywhere—lined up two, sometimes four deep along the wharves, peering between houses, over houses, out of garages, on front lawns. Red ones with white stripes, blue ones with black stripes, peeling ones, barnacled ones, upside-down ones, fat porky ones, thin sleek sloops, some with superstructures fifteen feet above the deck, white vinyl fishing chairs, and radar scanners. Richly detailed Victorian villas are surrounded by gaggles of diminutive clapboard cottages—a perfect "character-location" in the early days of filmmaking that attracted D. W. Griffith, the Keystone Kops, and Douglas Fairbanks, Sr. Later, one of the carpenter-Gothic mansions was the setting for the film of O'Neill's *A Long Day's Journey into Night,* starring Sir Ralph Richardson and Katharine Hepburn.

Delicate white paling fences and neatly trimmed hedges abound. A sturdy stone gatepost is embossed with a large *M* marking the driveway to the exclusive Morris Yacht Club, its manicured lawns sloping to the waters of the bay. The parking lot is full of boats, as is its once formal garden. Not far away are the other clubs—the City

Island Yacht Club, the Stuyvesant, the Olympia—all rigorously defended against the possible onslaught of outsiders. The same with the beaches. The short east-west streets all dead-end at the water, but the tiny beaches are for the sole use of residents. "It's the only bit of privacy we have," said an elderly lady at the end of Pilot Street, adjusting her beach chair, situated on her own patch of sand and pebbles. Visitors must join the crowds at nearby Orchard Beach.

Islanders stroll along City Island Avenue, chatting together ("clam-diggers," they call them, if they've lived on the island long enough). A fisherman, wrinkled as a walnut, peers into a sea-tackle store. Bob Borchers, owner of Thwaites Inn, is on the wharf gazing proudly at his new state-of-the-art marina while still insisting that the old island spirit is alive and well in spite of a recent influx of new and wealthier residents. And far away, out in the haze, you can see the towers of Manhattan between the forest of masts in the harbor. Many visitors liken the island to a New England village. Others sense a touch of Mexico in its *mañana* pace of life.

The great East Coast entrepreneurs chose City Island as a harbor to keep their magnificent boats and as a place to relax. Here one

City Island

could find Vincent Astor's *Nourmahal,* J. P. Morgan's *Corsair,* Jules Bache's *Colmena,* and Thomas Lipton's *Shamrock.* Many of the palatial yachts of the wealthy were built at the great yards that lined the shore—Nevin's, Minneford's, Kretzer's, and others.

There have been numerous visionary plans for this tiny 2½-by-½-mile island, known variously as Minniford, Minnewais, Mulberry, Great Island, and the Isle of Man. Before the Revolution there was speculation that it might well overtake Manhattan in importance. Then during the mid-1800s vast fortunes were made from the local oystering industry, followed a few years later by the emergence of the shipbuilding yards. August Belmont conceived a plan to convert the island into a huge race course, and there have been subsequent projects for casinos and Marina del Rey-type complexes along the waterfront, with apartment towers, multilevel malls, seafood markets, restaurants, and all the frolic and dazzle of a California oceanfront development.

The islanders and clam-diggers are consistent in their opposition to such glossy projects. They like the island the way it is. In fact, for many it's already too crowded, particularly on summer weekends. They blame nearby Orchard Beach, a Robert Moses creation, for the influx of day-trippers. They remember the days before the bridge. An elderly fisherman told me: "Now that was a time. My dad used to fish the oysterin' beds up the sound. Biggest and best oysters you'd ever seen. Why them Ches'peake Bay tooties got nothin' on these creatures. Fifty, sixty bushels a day. M'be more in a big season. Ev'body lived like kings in them days—some of 'em was richer'n film stars. Jes' from oysterin'!"

Another gentleman who'd lived on the island since he was a boy described the arduous process of reaching the island from Manhattan during the early 1900s: "Subway to 177th Street, trolley to Van Ness, railroad to Bartow, horsecar to t' City Island Bridge, stagecoach to t' police station. Then if you wanted to go onto Hart Island [farther out in the bay] you'd take a rig to t' pier and a launch to t' island. So's as you might expect, it was pretty quiet out here in them days!"

Today it's still quiet, especially if you come out during the week and avoid summer weekend crowds. Take time to stroll along City

Main Street—City Island

Island Avenue, peering into the stores selling ship supplies and nautical equipment—the Ship's Tender, the Square Rigger, and the Sailing Bag. Pause in one of the pubs and listen to the locals discussing island affairs. Invariably the conversation revolves around someone's idea for "makin' changes." Beer spills as glasses are thumped on the bar for emphasis. There was a controversy raging awhile back about whether the main street should be resurfaced. Islanders feared it would encourage more people to bring their cars onto the island. Last time I was there the conflict was still unresolved and the road was as rutted and scarred as ever.

Nestled among the pubs are antique stores, boutiques, a couple of photo galleries, and the Say Cheese, a delightful flower- and plant-filled wine-and-cheese restaurant featuring fondues, cheese desserts, and at least twenty different kinds of fresh-cut cheeses. Restaurants also abound along the avenue. No one will ever go hungry on City Island. For the limited-budget diner there are plenty of snack places and small cafés serving a representative selection of fresh seafood dishes, but if you're in the mood to splurge try Thwaites, Anna's Harbor, Sea Shore, or the Lobster Box. This Victorian-styled restaurant, (at the far end of the island, overlooking the sound), usually offers a small selection of budget dinners, but its reputation has been built on its lobster creations, twenty-five in all, with such appendages as à la Lemle, Luzianne, Fra Diavolo, and Salsa Verde, Texas-style, and Creole. There's also an authentic bouillabaisse that even residents of Marseilles would relish.

Many of the great boatyards are now gone, but occasionally employees at Minneford's or Consolidated will provide an impromptu tour of the wharves. Boatbuilding is a dying art here, and mostly servicing work is done today. Even the famous Ratsey and Lapthorn sailmaking establishment off East Schofield Street has recently closed. In England, where the company was founded well over two centuries ago, there were once hundreds of workers stitching, stretching, knotting, and testing the great sails that powered the tea clippers and the towering galleons of the British navy. This was the company that produced the sails for Lord Nelson's flagship *Victory,* and much more recently, for the Schaefer Brewing Company's re-creation of the famous sailing ship *America,* built locally at Minneford's yards.

If you enjoy museums, the islanders have recently opened the City Island Historical Nautical Museum in the old school house at 190 Fordham Street (Open Sunday 2–4 P.M. Weekdays by appointment; 885-1292. Free). It is like a mini-Smithsonian, a delightful repository of model ships, nautical flags, antique clothes, Indian artifacts, and a room full of paintings that depict City Island, created in the 1930s by Harold Vandervoort Walsh. It's all that a small-town museum should be and is staffed by a cadre of enthusiastic and knowledgeable volunteers. Here you could be a thousand miles from Manhattan.

A couple of miles to the west, along Shore Road (you'll need a car), there's the austere gray Bartow-Pell Mansion with its landmark interior and a fine formal garden, both open to the public (Tuesday, Friday, and Sunday 1–5 P.M.; 885-1461. Fee). The mansion was built between 1836 and 1842 by Robert Bartow on land acquired from the Indians in 1654 by his predecessor, Thomas Pell. The pamphlet about the mansion contains a copy of the original agreement with the local Indians complete with their "markes," and is full of rich Elizabethan language:

> [We] do sell & deliver to Tho. Pell his heyres & assignse to hould injoy improove plant as hee shall see Cause to his Best to be improoved ffor & to him & his heyres fforever wh out any molestation on our pt. This Wrightinge was signed & Wittnessed Beffore a great Multitude off Indvans & many English we who are under written do testify.

Times change, and in the early years of this century the house and garden were in appalling condition. Then, in 1914, the International Garden Club offered to restore the rooms and furnish them in nineteenth-century American and French Empire style, and to re-create the formal gardens, terraces, and fountain-pool, complete with dainty nymph. The result is an exquisite enclave of peace and history, little-known to New Yorkers—a perfect place to spend a warm afternoon strolling across the lawns and through the woods to the Hunters Island lagoon. There are no apartment towers to be seen, no bridges, no traffic noise to spoil the stillness of reed-edged water. It's a place for squirrels, mallard ducks, seagulls, and the quiet spirit.

For those who prefer more active pursuits there's horse riding at the Pelham Bit Stables on the north side of Eastchester Bay, golf on the Split Rock Golf Course opposite the Pell Mansion, miniature golf alongside the road to City Island, and, of course, the Orchard Beach complex itself—that great man-made arc of white sand complete with grandiose bathhouses and snack bars.

City Island is, as you might expect, a fisherman's paradise. The numerous wharves provide ideal places to settle for a few hours with a rod and line or, if you fancy something a little more adventurous, take a fishing cruise out into the sound after the big ones. Boats leave the docks from the west side of the island. One of my favorite sights off the southern tip is the Stepping Stone Lighthouse, said to be named after the small rocky islands that litter the bay like stepping-stones across a stream. The devil himself is said to have used these when fleeing from the ferocious Indians to safety on Long Island. Actually, the local Indians were a generally peaceable group. Their only major offense was the massacre of Anne Hutchinson, one of the first settlers to rebel against the strict Massachusetts colony and establish her own base here in 1642, near Split Rock. This courageous pioneer was killed accidentally during a reprisal raid by the Wiechquaeskeck Indians against Dutch settlers in the area.

Belden Point, at the southern tip of City Island, is home of the old pilot house, once headquarters for the Hell Gate pilots who used to navigate the ships through the treacherous whirlpools of the East River to the docks at South Street. Then a mile or so up the island on its eastern shore is the Pelham Cemetery, with some of the Pell family gravestones dating from the 1740s.

Not far away is the Hart Island ferry, a cheerfully painted craft fulfilling a cheerless mission. Hart Island, east of City Island, has been used since 1868 as New York's potter's field burial ground—home for deceased John Does, stillborn infants, and even amputated limbs. It's not open to the public. Hart Island prison is also located

here, a work camp for around thirty petty criminals serving short
sentence terms. Tom Madigan, one of the engineers, has been run-
ning various New York ferries for twenty-five years. Most of the
others have been abandoned—all that is left is this one and the
Staten Island run. He works his shift every day from a tiny office-
cum-kitchen-cum-lounge-cum-bedroom along with the ship's dog,
Brownie.

Although its aspect is peaceful when seen from across the choppy
channel, the island is, ironically, the most densely populated land
in New York. Over 700,000 bodies have been buried here on a
60-acre plot—more than 10,000 bodies per acre. And it's well util-
ized. After a twenty- to twenty-five-year burial period the land is
recycled for new burials and the new trenches are renumbered with
stone markers. Bits of bones and parts of skulls lie scattered like
seashells among the weeds. At the north end of the island, just
beyond the potter's field, is a large square monument with the word
PEACE inscribed on it. Nearby there's a granite cross that reads:
"He calleth his children by name." No irony was apparently intended in this final resting place for the nameless.

From the north end of Orchard Beach you can get a good view
of the island and the monument. You can also see the sound and
all its tiny islets, the Blauzes (after the Dutch *de Blauntjes*—"little
blue ones"). Over on Pea Island is an old radio station—currently
unused. The transmitting tower (NBC and CBS) is now located on
High Island, linked to City Island by a private bridge.

I like Orchard Beach best in the late fall. The crowds are gone;
the regulars take over. There are thirty of them at most, many of
them East Europeans who live in Brooklyn, the Bronx, even as far
out as Yonkers. They meet here most days to talk, play cards, and
read. When it's cold they huddle around picnic tables under the
great arches of the Orchard Beach Bath House, light fires, and chat
until dusk. If the sun is bright and the wind low, they sit out on
beach chairs in true Miami Beach style. "Oh yes," one of them told
me in a heavy accent, "we have been coming here for many times,
we are a group of friends. We sit together and talk and we're always
here. Even when it snows we come here. We don't like to be inside.
We like to be by the sea and we like to be together."

Stroll beyond the beach, northward across the beautifully colored rocks that roll like lava to the sea—pinks, pastel greens, and curling sinews of quartz—like thick cream swirled in soup. Follow the curve of the promontory until you come to a long set of stepping-stones leading across a patch of marshy ground to a small rocky island topped by twelve windswept trees. Here you enter another world—a little enclave unknown to visitors, unknown even to many residents of City Island.

I crossed the stepping-stones and met John Johnson. He was sitting in a little rock-built shelter protected from the chilly breeze. There was an old wooden bench, an oil drum with holes in it for use as a fire, a small pile of books and magazines covered by a tarpaulin to keep them dry, a worn pack of cards, and a battered coffee pot. He was waiting for his friends Big Jean and Henry to arrive. They were all in their seventies. They meet here, usually every day. It is their place, their own special "club": "Yeah, we built this ourselves. I've bin coming here since I was a school kid. We put up this wall 'bout ten years back and these trees—we planted these too, that's an apple tree there. Them two's cherry, at the side there. Usta have a roof too, and tin panels inside, real cozy like but they made us take it down. Said we couldn't have no roofs."

After showing me around the club, he led me up to the high point on the island and indicated the landmarks in the bay—the unused fort on Davids Island, the straggling white bulk of the New York Athletic Club across the lagoon, and the Execution Lighthouse out past Huguenot Island. It was on that island, so he told me, that British captives were tied to the rocks at low tide by their American captors during the Revolution and left to drown. Then he pointed across to the hill on Hunters Island and told me about the great Georgian mansion that once sat on the ridge overlooking the bay. John Hunter lived there in the early 1800s surrounded by his magnificent collection of Titians, Rembrandts, Raphaels, and Rubenses. Gradually the estate fell into disrepair, and the mansion was eventually razed in 1937. There are still a few remains up there—part of the huge gateposts and flat areas where the lawns used to be. "We get our water from up there, there's an old fountain. Best water anyplace."

John told me more about the Hunters Island and Twin Island clubs. "Used to be a lot more places like this 'round here—twelve, fifteen camps all along this side of the island. But they all died down; the old people, they died off and the young folks don't wanna bother coming out here on account of their cars—too much trouble for 'em. There's still a few left, though. They're not all gone." He pointed across the lagoon. "There's another gang on top of the hill. They play cards up there. Over on the point, that's the Russians, and there, where that smoke is, that's the Dutchmen's place, we call 'em the Führers—the Heinies. That's Henry over there now." He called out to a man on the far bank but he didn't respond. "We keeps to ourselves, y'know. We don't go in for socializin' much."

I crossed the lagoon by the old bridge to visit Henry (Wagner), one of the "Heinies." He was cleaning away the leaves on an old abandoned badminton court and told me how the club began. "Years ago, when we came to this country, all us Germans, y'know, no money, outta work sometimes, and this was the cheapest place. We like nature, y'understand. We used to come and play a Bavarian game—we called it 'plattel'—we used iron plates, we'd throw them, some were three or four pounds, we'd throw them fifty feet or more. Was healthy. Made you sweat." Henry showed me around his club —a bit more refined than John's place. He'd built most of it himself and was very proud of his workmanship: "Well, it's my bungalow," he said. Farther down near the rusted steel barge, beached in the reeds, the "Russians" were leaving their island for home, crossing the marshes on low bridges made from thick timber beams. I waved. They smiled and waved back.

What a strange little corner this is, unchanged for a generation. The same men have been coming here since they were school kids. Their numbers are dwindling slowly, though. More and more of the benches are empty on those bright afternoons. Soon only a few old residents of City Island will remember them.

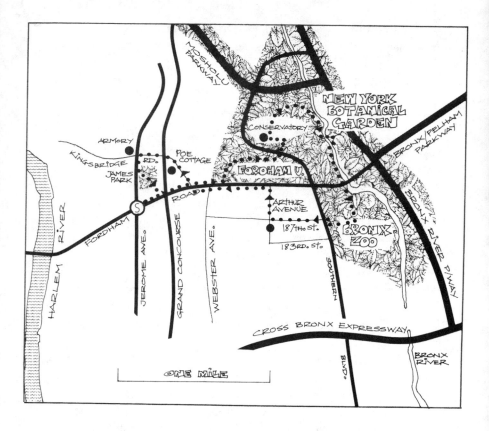

11 | Fordham

An experience not to be missed! There's a bit of everything for everyone here, from bargain fashion stores, a botanical garden, an old snuff mill, and a secluded gorge, to an English-flavored university campus, a slice of Little Italy, a zoo, and Edgar Allan Poe's tiny clapboard cottage. Come and explore.

To some Fordham Road is "Boogie Alley," a brassy strip moving to the beat of one hundred hand-held radios. To others it contains some of the best bargain stores in the five boroughs, a place to barter for fashionable clothes, boots, furs, kids' toys, and up-to-date clothing for the larger woman. There are always crowds here. Most of the stores stay open late, and the throng jostles along from Loehmann's on Jerome Avenue at Fordham Road (an incredible price-slashing garment store open since 1921) to Alexander's, Sears, Modell's, Gussini's Shoes, Crazy Eddie, VIP, and Children's World. It's 14th Street ten times over. The salesmen are out on the sidewalk "bringin' 'em in." The Palace Deli, with its genuine noodle pudding and hot knishes, bulges with pastrami-gorging customers and bawling kids, and crowds meander downhill to the sparkling new Fordham Plaza complex, which has put this part of the Bronx back on the map.

☞ **DIRECTIONS**
Subway: IRT 4 to Fordham Road/Jerome Avenue
Bus: Bx1, Bx2, Bx15, Bx17, Bx20, Bx25 to Jerome Avenue

163

Remnants of less hectic days remain. The great glazed edifice, Loew's Paradise, stands like a baroque palace on the Grand Concourse. Once, when the clock worked, the green copper horses in the tower above the main entrance pranced around to the ringing of bells. Today they're mute and motionless. Only the architecture itself is noisy. Back near Fordham Road there are elegant expressions of Classical Revival architecture, exemplified by the RKO Fordham Theater, but most shoppers never notice them. Some saunter by, swaggering to a disco beat; others, hunched and heads down, scurry from shoe outlet to snack bar to clothes shop in an endless search for the ultimate bargain.

It's busy, brash, and bustling. But the break is sudden. The strip ends at Webster Avenue, across from the Fordham University campus. Strolling through the gate just past Fordham Station, we enter a quiet world of green lawns, elm-shaded walks, and Oxbridge-style quadrangles. (Visitors are allowed in to see the administration building or attend activities at the campus center.) Students lie spread-eagled in the sun. Baseballs snap off bats near Collins Hall, but no one runs very fast. Three sophomores huddle over textbooks and notes and smile in unison at a stubby-bearded tutor strolling purposefully toward the administration building, originally an 1836 Greek Revival mansion known as Rose Hill (the 1950's white extensions on either side detract from its original grace and character).

There's a sense of longevity and tradition to the place, one of the largest Catholic institutions in the country, with an enrollment of 7,500 students. It was founded as St. John's College in 1841 by the Right Reverend John Hughes, who was later appointed New York's first Catholic archbishop. Later it came under the control of the Jesuits and was renamed a university. At that time the Bronx consisted of a straggle of tiny towns along the Boston Post Road—Mott Haven, Morrisania, West Farms, Eastchester, and Pelham. Significant development came later in the 1840s after the opening of the New York and New Haven rail service, although most of the area maintained its bucolic quality well into the latter years of the century. Even today, long after the hill-leveling, the highways, and the interminable tracts of tenement development in the southern portion of the borough, the Bronx possesses the finest system of parks in the metropolitan region. Not surprisingly, it was Frederick Law Olmsted, New York's master park planner, who conceived and helped implement this remarkable network of great open spaces tied together by tree-lined parkways. Henry Hope Reed called his work "one of the rare visions in New York's city planning." The Fordham campus abuts the Botanical Garden and forms an integral part of his concept.

We continue to stroll eastward past the 1845 St. John's Church (University Chapel). Note the elaborate copper tower over the nave and the elegant stained-glass windows bequeathed by Louis Philippe, King of France. Nearby is the somber bust of Orestes A. Brownson, a close friend of Emerson and Thoreau. The memorial is a classic summation of societal ethics in the late 1800s—"He loved God, Country, and Truth."

Passing the contemporary-style campus center (it's worth making a detour here to check on public events at the university), we emerge on the green swathe of Edwards Parade dominated at the far end by the tower-topped Keating Hall. Built in 1936 as the graduate school, it's a splendid hybrid in the "Collegiate Gothic" style. Students bask in the sun beneath the turrets and crenelations, and frisbees glide gracefully over the velvet lawns.

Leaving the campus by the parking-lot exit to the north of Keating Hall we cross Southern Boulevard and enter the New York Botanical Garden (daily 8 A.M. to sunset. Museum and conservatories close at 4:00 P.M. Admission charge. Free on Wednesdays). Here you're on your own. Pick up a map at the gate and select whichever features appeal most. Incorporated in 1891, the design was patterned after Kew Gardens in England and contains a glorious array of specialized gardens, a forty-acre hemlock forest, the Bronx River in a craggy gorge, an 1840 snuff mill once used by the Lorillard family, a museum, and, of course, the popular conservatory, which was recently completely refurbished and has become one of the main attractions in the Bronx. "Where else," effuses the brochure, "can you walk through two deserts and cross over a bubbling waterfall when it's cold outside? Or feel cool palms and

Bronx River Gorge

ferns on your face in the middle of summer? Take a trip to paradise," it urges. "Escape. Get away from it all to an oasis of jungles
and forests and gardens of dreams."

And it works. The city is forgotten as you saunter through the
eleven glass pavilions, each with its own distinct environment—The
Palm Court, The Fern Forest with its skywalk, The Tropical Pavilions, and The Orangery, plus herb gardens, an outdoor rock garden,
Northeastern native plant garden, and The Pinetum with adjoining
picnic area. Ironically, although the garden is a favorite haunt of
local residents, it's unexplored territory for many inhabitants of the
other four boroughs. "I never knew it'd be like this," gasped John
Travis, a Manhattanite who rarely leaves his cozy niche on the
Upper West Side. "She made me come," he told me, pointing to his
grinning girl friend. "She read something about the greenhouses
being open again with the palm trees an' all, so she said we had to
come." I asked if he was enjoying himself. "It's really fantastic.
Over there"—he pointed to the verdant hemlock forest in the northern portion of the park—"you can get lost it's so quiet. We walked
down by the river, by the waterfall, and it was just like being in the
country. Could have been a hundred miles away. Vermont or some
place like that."

I agree. I've had some of my best New York park walks here,
especially in the early spring and late fall when there are few people
in the more remote parts. If you don't mind sharing the attractions
with other avid admirers, though, be sure to visit Lord and Burn-
ham's conservatory building with its ninety-foot-high double-glass
dome supported on slender cast-iron columns, and the elegantly
columned Watson building, which houses the museum and botanical library. (Pick up a copy of the seasonal educational program
listing scores of courses and lectures in botany, gardening, landscape design, crafts, even winemaking and local history. It's an
incredibly active place.)

If it's quiet you're after, follow the paths through the forest and
the river gorge and across the delicately arched footbridge to the
unpretentious snuff mill near the rose gardens. Built around 1840
to replace an older mill, it was operated by Pierre Lorillard's sons
Peter and George who, according to a personal epitaph in ex-mayor

Philip Hone's diary, "led people by the nose for the best part of a century and made an enormous fortune by giving them to chew that which they could not swallow." For the weary there's a snack bar with a riverside terrace at the lower level of the mill, but don't eat anything here unless you really have to, as we'll soon be visiting one of the prime, though little-known, gastronomic centers of the Bronx.

Follow signs for the Bronx Zoo (Open daily 10–5 P.M.; 933-1759. Fee except on free days—Tuesdays, Wednesdays, and Thursdays) and cross the hectic Bronx and Pelham Parkway, heading for the towering Rainey Memorial Gates. This exotic fantasy of bears, deer, and lions was the work of architect Charles Platt and sculptor Paul Manship. "Some call it the Commodore Perry Gate," an elderly gentleman informed me as I stood admiring its exuberance. "He brought his animals through this way into the zoo. He traveled all over the world finding them." The man explained that he was a lover of Bronx history and went on to regale me with tales of Bronxdale, a little village that used to exist alongside the river not far from the gate. He also told me stories of the Indian moccasin paths that followed the valley northward to Connecticut and, pointing to the parkway bridge over the river, explained that it was named after Carl Linnaeus, the eighteenth-century Swedish botanist responsible for developing a system of botanical terminology in Latin. Our conversation touched on almost every aspect of Bronx history—dates, events, and personalities far too numerous to recount here. Then suddenly he burst into song. I remember one line: "I will look upon thy face again, my own romantic Bronx . . ." He explained, after what can only be described as a heartily confident rendition, that he'd taken Joseph Rodman Drake's famous poem and set it to music. "It came to me one night, all of a sudden. Sometimes I can't always remember the tune so I make it up a bit." Reluctantly I left the kind man, so in love with his native Bronx. Look out for him. He usually takes a stroll most afternoons around the lower end of the Botanical Garden. Be prepared for a lengthy and enjoyable diversion.

Admittedly, the zoo is no nook or cranny, but for most it's just too tempting a place to miss. (If the zoo doesn't inspire you today, however, follow the parkway west to Southern Boulevard and walk south to 187th Street. We'll meet you there.). Beyond the Rainey gates we're greeted by a frolicking group of mermaids and cupidlike children riding seahorses in the sprays of the Rockefeller Fountain. William Rockefeller was the donor. In 1902 he had this boisterous creation shipped piece by piece from Como, Italy, and in 1910 it was placed in its present location. In conjunction with the gates, it forms a most imposing entrance to this 252-acre woodland sanctuary.

The zoo is home to more than 3,000 animals, including such rare species as Siberian tigers, Mongolian wild horses, European bisons, snow leopards, and Pere David deer. Many exhibits are open-air re-creations of natural habitats—the African plains, South American pampas, the North American buffalo plains, elk forest, and wolf wood—others are splendidly imaginative indoor exhibits replicating The World of Birds environments, The World of Darkness, and the habitats of reptiles, crocodiles, and monkeys. It's a wonderland of experiences, particularly for children. There's a special touch-and-pet zoo for youngsters, the Wild Asia monorail ride on the Bengali Express over the Bronx River, the magnificent Jungle World complete with rain forest mists, and a cable-car skyfare crossing the central portion of the zoo, from the Southern Boulevard entrance to the African Plains exhibit in the southeastern corner. And more attractions are coming. At the time of my last visit the Baboon Highlands, Gorilla Forest, Wildfowl Pond, and Rhino Forest were all nearing completion, and the director, William G. Conway, claims to have a few more exotic surprises ready when funds are made available. Pick up a guide map at the entrance and select your choice of exhibits. Then after you've had your fill, leave by the Southern Boulevard exit at 185th Street (past the Buffet Terrace).

At 187th Street we enter another special little world, unknown to most non-Bronx residents. Walk slowly westward. Prepare your palate for a gastronomic romp and your pocketbook for merciless forays. Smell the air. The aroma of fresh-baked bread hangs thick above the street and wafts between the lines of wash dangling out of tiny windows. A fishmonger's display spills out on crates and tables—huge cream slabs of baccala (dried salted codfish), boxes of turquoise-blue soft-shell crabs, scungilli, oysters, clams, sea urchins, mussels, squid, butterfish, and evil-looking black eels. Porgies lie glistening and plump, salted whitefish fill a yellow plastic bucket, and hundreds of tiny whitebait, slivers of silver, are piled in moist mounds. After the silence of the Botanical Garden the racket here seems overwhelming. Everybody shouts at everybody. Greetings fly across the street like bullets. Motorbikes and mopeds crackle. Romantic love songs blare from tinny radios in the social clubs and kids tear down the sidewalks on skateboards shouting eloquent epithets at one another. It's Italy! It can't be anywhere else. It's the back streets of Naples, the eastern neighborhoods of Rome, the tenements behind Milan Cathedral.

Actually, it's the Arthur Avenue district of Belmont, New York's most authentic Italian neighborhood and one of the most colorful places I've found for Saturday shopping. If you've never been here before, spend a while just getting to know the place. Continue the stroll west along 187th Street to Arthur Avenue, then turn south as far as Crescent Avenue before reversing direction and returning along the opposite side of the avenue to 187th Street. Complete the reconnaissance with a brief detour to the left on 187th Street and then back again to the Arthur Avenue junction. By this time you'll have a reasonably clear idea of neighborhood structure, so repeat the process more slowly, pausing to sip, nibble, and sample whatever and whenever the urge takes you. Indulge a little.

Buy a fresh warm loaf of lard bread packed with bits of prosciutto, a few ounces of thin sliced Calabrian sopresatta salami, a bag full of green and black olives fresh from the barrel, a slab of Fontina cheese, and a straw-covered flask of chianti (a Ruffino or Frescobaldi). Adjourn to the little park at Arthur and Crescent avenues and *mange, mange, mange!* Alternatively, if you'd prefer to do your eating indoors, select one of the neighborhood Italian restaurants and enjoy a plateful of pasta with a choice of a dozen or more sauces —pesto, oil and garlic, sausage, calamari, anchovy, mushroom, marinara, lobster, à la Caruso, à la Mario, etc. Some of the restaurants, such as Mario's or Ann and Tony's, are obviously designed to appeal more to the visitor with paintings of Venetian canals and the sounds of soft guitar music. Dominick's, however, a tiny sweaty bar and eating room in the middle of Arthur Avenue, across from

Mario's, has no frills, and doesn't pander to elite tastes. What it does have are some of the best and most authentic dishes in the district, and a devoted clientele who attack the vast platters of pasta and sauces and meats and more sauces with endless elbow-to-elbow gusto.

Of course, if you weakened and ate during your exploration of the gardens or the zoo, you'll perhaps be more interested in browsing through the bakeries, the salumerias, and the noodle factories. So —browse. Peep in at the sacks of dried fagioli beans at Le Tre Corosse Importing Company, the bunches of army-green oregano, the clusters of chili peppers, and the carefully constructed pyramids of half-gallon olive-oil cans. Stroll through the poultry market, a richly redolent environment filled with guinea hens, rabbits, turkeys, ducks, and huge white cockerels. Admire the windows of pork stores filled with bright pepperonis, mold-flecked salamis, and fennel sausages. Best of all, spend time in the noisy retail market with its wonderful mounds of fresh vegetables, more sacks of beans than you've ever seen in your life, barrels of olives—all sizes and colors —and in the delicatessen-style outlets engulfed by wizened sausages and whole prosciutto hams. Mike Greco calls over from behind his pepperonis and provolones—"Hey, you wanna try some of this salami?" Alfio Gentile rattles off the names of all his dried beans, discusses the individual merits of his twenty-five different kinds of imported Italian pasta, and gives me an excellent recipe for preparing fava beans. Another man at a vegetable stall offers me an apple —"Try it. They just came in." I leave, weighed down with shopping bags.

Look out for the pasta stores, especially Mario Borgatti's, where it's almost impossible not to buy a box of his plump cheese, meat, or spinach ravioli, or his richly golden fettucini noodles. Then there are the pastry shops. Unless you have a will of iron, pass them by; once inside, it's too late. The aroma of crisp brown cream-filled cannoli, Italian cheese cakes, puff-pastry sfogliatelle, sweet panetone breads, and babas au rhum has sealed the doom of many a diet-bound customer.

The walk north on Arthur Avenue to Fordham Road enables first-timers to regain their equilibrium and seal their depleted pock-

Poe Cottage

etbooks. If you ate at Dominick's, maybe a brief jog would help restore the circulation and alleviate the guilt.

Passing the entrance to Fordham University again we proceed back up the hill and veer off Fordham Road to the right, at Kingsbridge Road. Poe Park is in front of us, a delightfully shaded summer oasis complete with bandstand and, unexpectedly, a diminutive clapboard cottage where Edgar Allan Poe lived from 1846 to 1849 (Open Wednesday–Friday 1–5 P.M.; Saturday 10 A.M.–4 P.M.; Sunday 1–5 P.M.; 881-8900. Fee).

The park is invariably full of noise, full of life, but inside the simply furnished house the mood is very different. Poe's beloved

wife, Virginia, died here in 1847 from tuberculosis. Poe could do little to save her. Ironically, the success of such major works as "The Raven" and "The Murders in the Rue Morgue" had in no way alleviated the poverty in which he and his wife had lived for years. His mother-in-law, Mrs. Maria Clemm, tried desperately to help by peddling some of Poe's more obscure manuscripts and even scavenging vegetables and herbs to feed the destitute family. But nothing could save Virginia, and she shivered to death under Poe's West Point coat, the only substantial blanket they owned. Afterward he began frequenting the boisterous taverns on Fordham Road until rescued from alcoholic oblivion by a friend, a Jesuit priest, who took him into St. John's College and spent long hours trying to help Poe reconcile himself to his loss.

But Poe could not accept solace. He almost seemed to welcome grief and sorrow as a birthright and entered his final period of decline, dying a "stranger" in a Baltimore hospital two years later. Somehow during this time he managed to produce one of his finest poems, "Annabel Lee," a memorial to his beloved wife:

> *For the moon never beams, without bringing me dreams*
> *Of the beautiful Annabel Lee;*
> *And the stars never rise, but I feel the bright eyes*
> *Of the beautiful Annabel Lee;—*
> *And so, all the night-tide, I lie down by the side*
> *Of my darling—my darling—my life and my bride,*
> *In her sepulchre there by the sea—*
> *In her tomb by the sounding sea.*

This tiny cottage reflects the spirit of this sad, brilliant man.

We're off again, west along Kingsbridge Road, past a series of Hebrew-lettered signs for kosher butchers, delicatessens, and cut-price lawyers ("Divorce $150; Bankruptcy $200; Name-change $50"), to visit the monolithic 258th Field Artillery Armory designed by Pilcher and Tachall in 1917. Originally home of the Washington Grays, formed as a guard of honor at President Washington's first inauguration, this towered and turreted structure occupies an entire block and is said to be one of the largest armories in the country. It is 106 feet high at its tallest point and boasts a drill floor measuring 300 by 600 feet. Unfortunately, visitors are not allowed inside.

We end our walk by wandering through the pleasantly shaded, if somewhat noisy, St. James Park, back to Fordham Road. The rush and tumble of the street continues and the crowds churn along the sidewalk while we remember the silence of the Hemlock Forest and the slow-moving Bronx River, chittering over the shallows beyond the gorge.

12 | The Brooklyn Waterfront

Change is coming about swiftly in Brooklyn, particularly along the East River shoreline, but you can still find a small-town ambience here, and some of the most delightful architectural idiosyncrasies in the five boroughs.

Forget the subway. Why not come the hard way and the best way —across the Brooklyn Bridge? (BMT N or RR to City Hall/Broadway; follow signs for Brooklyn Promenade.) There are few walking experiences in New York to match an early-morning stroll between the silver cables, between the great gray piers, above the traffic, looking out across the East River, the harbor, and Governor's Island. If you start early enough, you'll feel the city coming to life, the stirrings of Colossus (if you start too late you may find the noise and fumes on the bridge a bit overbearing). In all fairness though, I should warn participants in this walk that we cover quite a distance and you might prefer to save the stroll across the bridge for the end of the journey.

As you approach the Brooklyn side, down a long descent, the mini-city of the Jehovah's Witnesses Watchtower Society dominates

☞ **DIRECTIONS**
Subway: IND A or F to High Street/Brooklyn Bridge
Bus: B15 from Canal Street, Manhattan; B25, B41

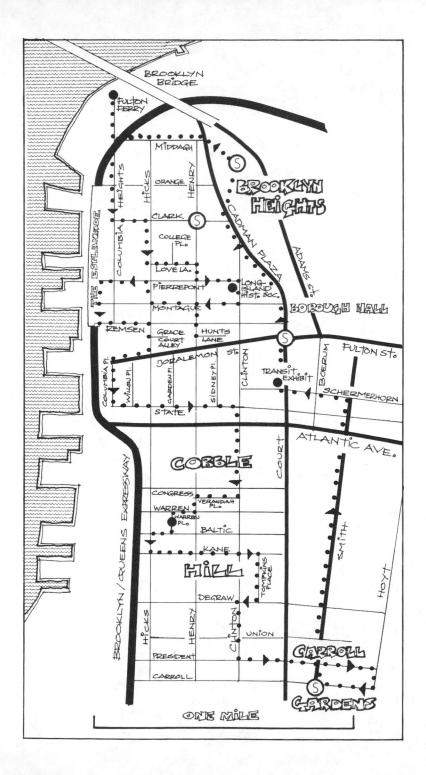

the waterfront. Farther along there's the Brooklyn Heights esplanade cantilevered over two levels of centipedelike traffic. In the foreground are the docks and the masts of sea-battered ships just in from Russia, New Zealand, and Latin America. Finally there are steps, an underpass, and you're out in the sunshine of Cadman Plaza, Brooklyn.

Cross over to Middagh Street. The formal sweep of lawns, statues, and the great white façades of the Civic Center gives way to a narrow thoroughfare lined with nineteenth-century homes, a few clapboard cottages, and refreshing shade from garden trees. There has been considerable restoration of the block, not all of it successful, but at the top of the street, at Columbia Heights, is the gray and prune-colored Eugene Boisselet House, "The Queen of Brooklyn Heights," built around 1824, complete with rear stables and carriage house. The whole structure is a little worn and slightly lopsided, with the main entrance's tiny windows and miniature columns tilting to the right, yet somehow this only serves to emphasize the dignity of a lovely place.

At Columbia Heights there's an interesting detour down the hill, between the Watchtower buildings (once the Squibb Pharmaceutical Factory), and into the Fulton Ferry Historic district. As early as 1659 there was a ferry across to Manhattan in the form of a rowboat. Demand was intermittent and the boatman, Cornelius Dircksen, spent most of his time farming nearby. A customer would signal a need for his services by blowing on an old coach horn that dangled from a tree on the riverbank. Later the operation was taken over by Robert Fulton, who provided a steamboat link in 1814. From that time on, the Heights developed rapidly as a fashionable residential area.

Today, the Ferry Plaza is a delightful corner of Brooklyn. The charming yellow fireboat house on the waterfront was, until recently, a ferry museum of the National Maritime Historical Society, and the huge Eagle Warehouse, with its sturdy brick arches, has been transformed into a residential complex. So far, not much else in the way of restoration has been undertaken, but the potential is obvious to anyone with a bit of imagination. Looking northward on Furman Street toward the old fireboat house, you sense the striking

Old Fireboat House

character of this historic district. Equally impressive is the Fulton Landing riverfront immediately north of the Brooklyn Bridge, which developer David Walentas recently purchased and considers one of the city's prime redevelopment areas. At the moment it's a mess of old industrial buildings and stumpy remnants of old piers, but his dreams of a riverside restaurant row, marina, stores, offices, and esplanade could soon transform the neighborhood.

Restaurants and pubs are often the major catalysts for change, and if the River Café and Harbor View are any indicators, this corner of Brooklyn has a bounteous future ahead. The former is sheer magic and romance, with spectacular skyline views of Manhattan seen through the windows of the docked dining room, and limousines lined up Water Street awaiting their wealthy patrons. Nearby a group of young musicians rehearse a particularly intricate piano trio by Shostakovich in the floating Bargemusic Center, which offers Thursday and Sunday concerts to a devoted clientele (call 718-624-4061 for details).

There are, of course, flurries of protest against all signs of change in the neighborhood. I recently saw a sign glued on the side of the fireboat house pleading for restraint—"No Pier Development. Leave the Heights alone!"—a reference to the city's interest in developing ninety acres of Port Authority land along the waterfront south of Brooklyn Bridge. At the moment there are six underused piers and several old warehouses, and Theodore Kleiner, the Port Authority's architect, claims this could be "one of the most exciting future projects in the five boroughs." Residents of the Heights and the thousands who enjoy the views from the esplanade over the Brooklyn-Queens Expressway are far more skeptical, fearing a wall of high-rise towers along the river. Norman Mailer, a long-time resident, is preparing for action: "Real estate developers will do anything to raise the height restrictions, but if they try to do anything against the interest of our neighborhood, the opposition here will make the fight over Westway look like All Souls Night!"

Similar rumblings have been heard about the Watchtower Society's plans for expanding their headquarters up on Columbia Heights, although recent additions are some of the most successful examples of infill architecture on the Brooklyn waterfront. The society is sensitive to public opinion and always anxious to promote their day-long tours starting at 8 A.M. from 124 Columbia Heights (call 718-625-3600 for details). Their enthusiasm, however, is not always shared by others.

I remember one day I happened to be passing the Watchtower residence just after midday when, without warning, and from every direction, scores of eager-faced young men appeared, heading for the main entrance. They apparently were the factory workers, all Jehovah's Witnesses, on their way to lunch. However, hardly had the front end of this stream of bodies reached the residence when a little man, obviously irate, came up Pineapple Street waving a handful of printed sheets. He stood immediately outside the door and began a long fire-and-brimstone diatribe urging the young men, whose minds were obviously focused on lunch, to mend their ways and join some other religious organization. He was greeted with tolerant smiles until the last worker had disappeared into the building. Briefly he spoke to the door and then, tying his pamphlets up with string, he marched back down Pineapple Street, still looking irate. "He's here most days," one of the young men told me. "He's really quite a nice guy, but I don't think he likes us very much."

As Brooklyn Heights is the most popular and best known of all New York neighborhoods outside Manhattan, we'll avoid some of its more famous landmarks and explore instead its nooks and crannies unknown to most outsiders—even to many of its residents. Of course, you may prefer just to stroll along the esplanade starting at Orange Street and rejoin the walk on Atlantic Avenue, in which case—enjoy yourself. Together with the Brooklyn Bridge, it's one of the finest walks in the city.

What I find most fascinating in the Heights are those hidden cul-de-sacs where old carriage houses and stables have been converted into charming cottages. Walking south down Hicks Street from Clark Street turn left into Love Lane and look out for the secluded College Place, a narrow alley of cottages marred somewhat by the parking garage at the bottom end. More attractive examples can be found a little farther to the south at Grace Court Alley and Hunts Lane, both of which we visit later in the walk.

At Pierrepont Street we enter the heart of the elite neighborhood.

Occasionally, some highly adorned mansion will appear in the middle of a sedate line of townhouses, like a bejeweled dowager duchess among her servants. The Herman Behr house, at Henry and Pierrepont, is a red sandstone creation full of massive arches, bays, odd chimneys, ornate steps, and a profusion of carved dragons, showing their fangs to the street.

Farther to the east, the imposing structure at Pierrepont and Clinton streets is the Long Island Historical Society building. The façade is decorated with terra-cotta busts of important historical figures, including token representations of a Viking and an American Indian over the door. A magnificent collection of material on Long Island, New York City, and New York State is available to nonmembers for a small fee, and there are exhibitions open to the public (Tuesday-Saturday 9 A.M.–5 P.M. Free). A visit here is highly recommended.

Everyone who knows the Heights knows Montague Street, the hub, the nexus. The spirit is effervescent and gay (in both senses of the word). It's less somber than some Greenwich Village streets, although the same kinds of shops are found here—some in basements, some up flights of steps overlooking the street. Restaurants and sidewalk cafés abound. There's music. Groups gather at corners or on the stoops. There are bulletin boards everywhere filled with wanted, for sale, for rent, lost kitten, and cheap-typing notices, all handwritten on grubby index cards. There's a sense of community. One feels that the people who live here really care for and love their neighborhood.

A short detour south along Henry Street leads us to Hunts Lane, another of Brooklyn Heights's hidden mews. I chatted with one of the residents, an elderly lady, who had spent much of her life in London. "I lived just off Kensington High Street and d'you know, I could still be there, this place is so much like my old home. I was in a mews, just like this, and all the stables were converted into flats with pretty flower boxes on the window ledges. There's something very comfortable about living in a little hidden street like this. We all know one another. It's like sharing a secret with friends."

If you have left a visit to the esplanade until now, then stroll west along Pierrepont Street past what many consider to be the most

Hunts Lane

refined structures in the Heights: numbers 2 and 3 Pierrepont Place.
There's some disagreement as to whether the architect was Frederick Peterson or Richard Upjohn, who was responsible for a number
of churches in the area and who lived nearby in Cobble Hill. However, there's no disagreement that the view westward past the mansions, out over the East River, is one of the finest in New York.
There's a remarkable sense of "hereness" and "thereness." In the
foreground are delicate iron railings, an ornate gas lamp, the shade
of small garden trees, a bench or two. Then beyond the esplanade
is the panorama of the Manhattan towers, the East River bridges,
Governors Island, Staten Island, and way in the distance, past the
Statue of Liberty, the rolling landscape of New Jersey. Whatever the
time of day, whatever season, whatever kind of weather, this view
cannot fail to touch the observer. Even if you've been here a dozen
times before, come again and enjoy the sudden contrast with the
intimate, human-scaled streets of the Heights.

Leave at the Remsen Street end and notice, to your left, the lovely
Montague Terrace possessing all the grace and relaxed dignity of a
Kensington street. Thomas Wolfe lived here while writing *Of Time
and the River,* as did Jules Feiffer and W. H. Auden. In fact, this
was just one of Wolfe's many apartments in the Heights during the
1930s. At one point he lived at 101 Columbia Heights and, in a
letter, remarked that he had a "nice view of New York harbor and
of the skyscrapers"—an unusual piece of understatement. Impressive premiums are paid for such views today.

The Heights, of course, has long enjoyed a literary reputation,
and the list of its writer-residents reads like a Who's Who of twentieth-century American literature: Truman Capote, Hart Crane,
John Dos Passos, Norman Mailer, Arthur Miller, and Henry
Miller, to name but a few.

Strolling south down Hicks Street, pause at Grace Court Alley,
a third secluded mews, before moving on to explore the tranquil
"places" south of Joralemon Street. Each is a mere one block in
length and terminates at both ends in cross streets, Joralemon to the
north and State to the south. There's virtually no through traffic,
and large London plane trees provide an almost continuous canopy
of shade. Most of the townhouses were built in the mid-1800s and

reflect the fashionable revivals of that era. Although Sidney and Garden places are the more refined, Willow Place boasts a most unusual terrace of simple row houses, whose modest appearance has been transformed by the addition of a long, columned portico. The whole odd affair has been painted white and looks like some hybrid from the Deep South. Ironically, though, the naïveté of the concept creates a charm that the more self-conscious designs on adjoining streets could never possess.

Columbia Place has an even odder collection of clapboard cottages with fragile porches, left over from a longer row built in the mid-1800s. On the opposite side are the Riverside Houses, one of Alfred Tredway White's projects in this area and partially emasculated by subsequent construction of the Brooklyn-Queens Expressway. White was impressed by attempts in London to provide inexpensive yet sanitary and pleasant apartments for low-income families. He saw no reason why the idea could not be adapted to meet New York needs and yet still provide reasonable profit to the developer. So, with his motto, "Philanthropy plus 5 percent," he financed the construction of a number of these projects (we'll explore two more in Cobble Hill) and not only provided a much-needed housing resource but also never failed to make his profit.

The charm of this southern corner of Brooklyn Heights has been noticed even by the power companies. Near the corner of Joralemon and Hicks there's a small electrical station disguised as a house, and along Willow Place a larger structure blends in well with the street. Brooklyn's fire companies went one better. Way over on Jay Street near the Civic Center is the Old Brooklyn Fire Department Headquarters, one of Frank Freeman's creations, which, both in scale and style, reflects the stately character of adjoining governmental buildings (visit this at the end of the walk). In contrast, the delicate firehouse of Engine Company No. 224 on Hicks Street, between State and Joralemon, is sensitive to the overall character of the street, although the architects (Adams and Warren) overindulged in their use of ornate trimmings. But, as we've seen, that kind of extravagance was hardly unique in the kind of neighborhood that can produce streets as handsome as Garden Place and as charmingly eclectic as Sidney Place.

Jay Street Fire Headquarters

Immediately to the south of State Street, the Heights ends abruptly in a gush of galleries, health food shops, Syrian bakeries, and Middle Eastern restaurants. Atlantic Avenue, though, has none of the warm intimacy of Montague Street. Architecturally, it's a messy street without spatial character, unity, or style. Yet it has its devotees, Heights residents who think it's the best street around, less self-conscious than Montague, less brash than Fulton. The restaurants—the Adnan, Atlantic House, Tripoli and others—are all reasonably priced and serve authentic Middle Eastern cuisine, but it's the honeyed confectionery, the homemade ice cream (try the pistachio), and the fresh-baked breads that are most tempting. The windows of the import-export stores brim with water pipes, caftans, trays, samovars, Turkish coffee contraptions in gleaming copper— even ornate camel saddles. Then there are the olives in vats, dried beans, sacks of almonds, grains, cooked figs, couscous, and bottles of thick flavored syrups. And finally the phyllo creations and minced lamb pasties at the Damascus Bakery and Pastry Shop—an enticing diversion.

Go south from Atlantic Avenue, down Clinton, into the second historic district along this walk, Cobble Hill. Actually, the name is a bit misleading. The British are said to have lopped off a good portion of the hill after Washington used it as a vantage point during the Battle of Long Island. Nonetheless, it's a most attractive area of brownstone terraces with Romanesque-Revival and Queen Anne detailing. It lacks the sparkle and the visual surprises of the Heights, but has a far more harmonious appearance—a sedate spirit made additionally attractive by fine rows of shade trees.

Don't mind the first couple of blocks south of Atlantic Avenue on Clinton. The neighborhood improves rapidly as you stroll down toward the tiny Cobble Hill Park, at Congress Street. Here's a delightful place to pause awhile if you resisted the restaurants along Montague Street and Atlantic Avenue. On the north side is an imposing terrace, spoiled somewhat by insensitive modifications. On the south side there's a line of smaller row houses, obviously not designed to face directly onto the park. They were once part of a mews when the park was occupied by more elegant townhouses. Yet, like those tiny carriage cottages in the Heights, they possess, through their very simplicity, an integrity unmatched by the ornate "Revival-style" terraces.

The same might be said of Alfred Tredway White's Warren Place Workingmen's Cottages, which can be reached by a short detour west along Verandah Place to Henry Street and a right turn on Warren Street. Here, facing each other across a narrow garden full of rhododendron bushes and replanted Christmas trees, are two rows of cottages reminiscent of some of the homes built by industrialist-philanthropist Sir Titus Salt in his famous model factory town at Saltaire, Yorkshire, England. It's a charming concept and a fashionable place to live. A little farther up the street are the Tower Buildings, the third of White's developments along the Brooklyn waterfront. They are similar to the Riverside Houses on Columbia

Warren Place Cottages

Place in the Heights except that in this case the central recreational courtyards are still in existence and apparently much used. A block farther south, between Baltic and Kane streets, there's a final complex, the Home Buildings.

Back on Clinton Street take a look at the Christ Episcopal Church on the corner of Kane Street. This was one of Richard Upjohn's works prior to Trinity Church in Manhattan, and it contains furnishings designed by Louis Comfort Tiffany, son of the famous glass craftsman. Note in particular the beautiful pulpit and lectern. Continue south on Clinton to Degraw Street, then stand and look back. This is one of the best sections of streetscape in Cobble Hill, with the finely detailed Upjohn tower rising above the tree-shaded street and the refined row houses. Also take a look at Tompkins Place, one block east of Clinton, between Kane and Degraw streets. It would have taken very little to spoil the harmony of this scene—a poor piece of modernization, a break or two in the terrace, the intrusion of a gas station. Note some of the other streets in this area and you'll recognize how very delicate this kind of environment is and how it needs to be protected. The creation of a historic district is obviously a partial answer, but even more important is the care and concern of the area's residents. Where this involvement is lacking, no amount of publicity and moaning from outsiders will make any difference. The spirit must come from within.

Three blocks south of Degraw Street, take President Street eastward (turn left) and follow it past Carroll Park to the Carroll Gardens historic district. In what is obviously a marginal neighborhood, President Street and Carroll Street east of the park have maintained their totally unique charm, and in recent years have been enthusiastically refurbished by young new residents. Although built at different periods by different developers during the mid- and late-1800s, both streets possess a remarkable unity of revival design. Carroll Street is the more dignified space, characterized by the even height of the terraces, the deep front gardens, the regularity of the front garden walls, the lines of street trees, and the rhythm of steps and stoops. President Street is less even in character and has a more informal feel. The view north is particularly appealing as the street frontage continues along the north side of the park and up to the austere United Church of Christ at Court Street. Alas, this historical district needs to be expanded and nearby streets require extensive renovation. To the north, Union, Sackett, and Degraw streets all retain their essential character, particularly east of Smith Street, but their distinctive quality will fade unless new funds are invested in the area.

How are the feet? If you've had enough walking, there's a subway at Carroll and Smith streets to whisk you home. If, however, you feel like trundling on, you could go north on Smith Street through a rather poor but colorful Spanish neighborhood full of Puerto Rican bakeries, noisy record stores, fish markets, Chinese restaurants with a Latin overtone, social clubs, butchers' shops with rows of smiling pigs' heads in the window, and the many trinket stores selling garish plaster madonnas, lions, parrots, and buddhas. To the right, down Union Street, are the remnants of the Gowanus Canal, once described by the journalist McCandlish Phillips as "a richly aromatic avenue of steadily declining commerce." (And he wasn't referring to the aroma of spices!) There's not much to see except a stretch of murky water and a lock gate but, when this whole section of Brooklyn was a flourishing port, the canal was one of the busiest stretches of water in the harbor, and teams of bargemen supplied the factories and warehouses along its length.

An alternative, and more attractive, route north to the Brooklyn Civic Center takes us along Court Street, past the Italian stores advertising "Latticcini Freschi" and "Jersey Pork Sausages Made Daily," and up to the crossroad with Atlantic Avenue where you'll find a remarkable grouping of restaurants—Mexican, Moroccan, Indian, French, American, and Middle Eastern.

Past the ominous House of Detention, pause awhile at the New York Transit Exhibition (Open daily 9 A.M.–4 P.M.; 718-330-3060. Fee), which offers a splendid panorama of transportation history in the five boroughs. Down on the lower level, the platforms are lined with old and new subway cars—the BMT Triplex 1927 through to the BMT-IND R 46 1976 cars, capable of 80 mph. Upstairs there's a slide show (it ends with a convincing plea for subsidized transport), bus engines, models of trams and trolley cars, early subway maps, fly-blown architects' renderings of subway-station designs à la 1930s, and a particularly archaic restroom which, it turns out, is not part of the exhibition but intended for current use! The whole presentation is excellent even if you're not a subway buff.

On the return leg of the journey stroll up past Borough Hall, past the Federal Building and Court House and the splendidly ornate General Post Office, back into Cadman Plaza. Note the statue of Henry Ward Beecher, considered by many to be the finest work of John Quincy Adams Ward, and one of the most impressive civic sculptures in New York. A short distance to the west, down Orange Street, is the delightfully New England-styled Plymouth Church of the Pilgrims, where Beecher delivered his dramatic sermons for many years during the mid-1800s. He, along with his sister Harriet Beecher Stowe, author of *Uncle Tom's Cabin,* were ardent abolitionists, and this modest church became a mecca for the noted liberals of his day. Appropriately, there's also a bust of Robert Kennedy in the plaza, a modern-day "abolitionist" of those injustices that still plague minorities today. Maybe this is a good place to end the walk (unless of course you skipped the Brooklyn Bridge section, in which case, enjoy the rest of your stroll). Relax at Cadman Plaza, or even better—take your shoes off and massage your feet.

13 | Park Slope and Prospect Park

The flurry of architectural renovations and modernizations continues apace, but this distinguished neighborhood has been able to maintain its character, dignity, and charm. A very rewarding place to explore.

In 1891 the first president of Brooklyn's newly opened Montauk Club declared: "A club should be an integral part of daily life. A man has his own church, and he should have his own club. It fills a need that cannot be met in any other way." At that time the great mansion and apartment residences around Grand Army Plaza and also Prospect Park West overlooking the park itself were collectively known as the "Gold Coast." Wealthy lawyers, merchants, and men of professional distinction lived in the elegant rows of townhouses that sloped downhill from the park.

Most of the dwellings were built after the 1883 opening of the Brooklyn Bridge and reflected the varied architectural influences in those affluent days—Italianate, French Second Empire, Victorian Gothic, Queen Anne, Romanesque Revival, and a frivolity of "neo" styles. "Wealth," said one millionaire physician of the times,

☞ **DIRECTIONS**
Subway: IRT 2, 3 to Grand Army Plaza
Bus: B41, B69, B71 to Grand Army Plaza

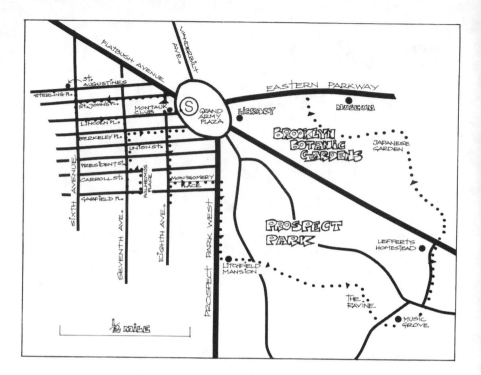

"should be apparent but not obvious. One's city house should be possessed of dignity and refinement. In one's country house, idiosyncrasies may be allowed to show. It is expected in fact." So, appropriately, Park Slope was developed with dignity and taste. Lower down the hill, however, toward the Gowanus Canal, far less care was taken and fragmented rows of brownstones mingled with noxious industrial plants and warehouses. Below Sixth Avenue was considered "blue nose" territory, named after a colony of Newfoundland fishermen who lived here and fished from Sheepshead Bay to the south. A local lady diarist wrote in 1903: "We do not journey below 7th [Avenue] and we instruct the servants to go about their shopping in other places. Here on the hilltop the breezes are fresh. We look over the farms and orchards and take our walks in the park. On Sundays a group of us visit the [Brooklyn] museum and rest by the fountain in the plaza. There can surely be no finer place of residence in the whole city."

In this last respect at least, Park Slope has changed little since those idyllic days. Contemporary residents are as proud of their property as were their counterparts almost a century ago. "For Sale" signs in the windows of local real estate agents emphasize not so much the space and internal characteristics of available townhouses as the quality of external detailing, the name of the original architect, and any little titbits of history that give the place distinction. For example—"Superb four story neo-Grec 1907 townhouse with four-columned doorway, Corinthian capitals, and copperfinished mansard extension. Work of a Stanford White student. Hart Crane lived here and it was originally home of the founder of the Gage and Tollner restaurant [a famous Brooklyn landmark]." Obviously, such details as the number of bedrooms and condition of fixtures are regarded by purchasers as mundane and seemingly irrelevant.

In the last ten years Park Slope has bounded back from the doldrums that afflicted it after the Depression. The "Buy a Brooklyn Brownstone" slogan worked its magic on the imaginations of scores of Manhattan residents, and the renaissance began bringing the new people up Flatbush Avenue to begin a fresh life on these airy slopes. "We still got problems, though," one elderly resident told me.

"Some streets below Seventh Avenue and down round Ninth Street are real bad—junkies, muggings, the lot. I'd never go down there, even in daylight. But the new people are helping. We get lots of those block-party things in the summer. That's real nice, 'specially for us that have been here a long time. Reminds me of how things were when I was a kid. There was the rich folks right on top of the hill. They kept to themselves mostly but the others lower down were really nice. It was like a village then. You knew everybody in your street. It's getting to be like that again."

Writers, architects, artists, musicians, and editors at Manhattan's prestigious publishing houses live happily alongside large Italian and Irish families, the neighborhood's more traditional residents. Places like Ryan's Bar at Garfield and Seventh Avenue are the stout and whiskey headquarters for the older Irishmen; not far away The Santa Fe Grill, The Coach Inn, P.J. McFeely's, Snooky's, and Minsky's attract the newer residents. The Hopper-like Purity Café and the Economy Restaurant appeal to a cross-section of patrons, with conversation stretching the gamut from dogs (the racing kind) to Degas. Garden shrines of pastel madonnas contrast with diminutive art galleries, grand pianos in parlor windows, and carriage lamps on the stoops. But the most important ingredient—harmony—is here. You can feel it in the spirit of the clean streets, the polished door-knockers, the proud new owners of old brownstones carefully patching heavily detailed cornices, and in the hearty bonvivant atmosphere of the Seventh Avenue strip.

Let's begin our walk at the Montauk Club (Lincoln Place and Eighth Avenue), focal point of the old and new in Park Slope. The architect, Francis H. Kimball, based his design on a Venetian palazzo with motifs strongly reminiscent of the Doge's Palace on St. Marks Square in Venice. The ornate and imposing structure contains a wonderful array of terra-cotta bas-reliefs on three of its four façades. Note the frieze depicting the history of the Montauk Indians, after whom the club was named. Various other panels contain carved Indian heads, a picture of the club's founders laying the cornerstone, and, on the Lincoln Place façade, elaborate gargoyles supporting the balcony. Inside it's all a club should be—finely paneled walls, creaking floors, hazy light filtering through subdued stained-glass windows, framed and aging ocean navigation charts, etchings of Park Slope in the 1890s, and an almost tangible sense of decorum and propriety. Although the club has had to liberalize its membership policy, welcoming women and children, the flavor remains masculine and "leathery."

Down St. Johns Place toward Seventh Avenue we experience the architectural unity of these sloping streets, the evenness of the stoops, the regularity of the roofline interrupted by occasional eccentric extensions that add a unique touch. The flavor is slightly formal, yet lively music drifts from open doors, a girl sits half out of a window combing her hair, and, farther down, kids chase one another with frantic determination, bawling and bellowing. The street, like most in Park Slope, is an essay in subtle browns, beiges, and other earth tones.

Around the junction of St. Johns Place and Seventh Avenue we find a cluster of churches. Park Slope has long been noted for its crenelated skyline of church towers and spires. On the northeast corner is the Grace United Methodist Church, a chunky red stone creation built in 1882. Note the stubby flying buttresses and the thick tower, which once supported an elegant spire. Occasional theatrical productions are offered here and most Saturdays there's a flea market (11 A.M.–4 P.M.) in the adjoining building. Across the road, its stone steeple still intact, is the Memorial Presbyterian Church built in 1882, with an adjoining chapel added in 1888. Its most notable features are the Tiffany stained-glass windows and the delightful sculpture of an angel and three young children, softening influences on an otherwise stern structure.

A little farther west on St. Johns Place is the English country-style St. John's Protestant Episcopal Church. Set back behind a small lawn, its flavor is delightfully rural in this intensely urban setting. "I got married in there." A broad middle-aged lady in a wide-brimmed hat stopped to watch me sketching the two magnificent 1888 townhouses opposite the church. "I was only twenty-three then." She sighed. "He was thirty-one—or -two—I forget which. But it was a lovely wedding. Lost him last year. Heart attack. Very sudden. He was such a lovely man too." We both paused. I

St. Johns Place

don't know what it is about a person sketching that attracts people, but I invariably find myself a captive audience listening to anecdotes, long life stories, or opinions on every imaginable subject. The tales only make my sketching more enjoyable.

The most elegant church in Park Slope and, from my experience, one of the finest in the five boroughs, is St. Augustine's Roman Catholic Church at Sterling Place and Sixth Avenue. This 1892 essay in Victorian Gothic extravagance was the work of the Parfitt Brothers, prodigious designers of churches in the area. Rarely has such harmony of design been achieved with such a wealth of materials and detailings—brownstone, brick, copper, marble, turrets, towers, gargoyles, statues, full columns, semicolumns, and windows of all shapes and sizes. Inside, the flavor is equally exuberant. The richly carved white stone altar wall stands at the end of a cathedral-like nave. The colored rays of light streaming through the elaborate stained-glass windows bounce off the delicate supporting columns and reflect on the ornate hand-painted ceilings and walls. A mosaic of a pelican feeding the young from her own blood dominates the open floor area in front of the altar, and finely detailed angels, madonnas, and prophets provide an almost baroque setting for Sunday observances. Unfortunately, the church is closed during the week except for masses at 9 A.M. and 4 P.M., but if you're really anxious to look inside, someone at the adjoining rectory will normally try to oblige.

Walking back up the slope along Lincoln Place, we arrive at Seventh Avenue, hub of the district. The elegant sounds of pianos, violins, and voices waft from the windows of the famous and well-loved Brooklyn Conservatory of Music, a rather aloof brick building on the northwest corner. Stroll down the avenue and enjoy its flavor. There's a neighborhood feel here, a sense of camaraderie among the shoppers and the browsers. The art galleries, the One Smart Cookie store, the Leaf and Bean (a wonderful array of teas and coffees and all the paraphernalia for making the brews), Big Cheese, beloved Bellamellio's, and a scattering of other shops reflect the tastes of the "new people," and rest comfortably alongside the more traditional grocery stores, older restaurants, and the staunchly Irish taverns. Streetcar tracks are still visible in certain places. A large Italian lady surrounded by a bunch of tugging kids waddles along the sidewalk carrying two enormous bags of groceries with loaves of crisp bread sticking out of the top. A young professional couple make their way to Ann and Richard Hayton's popular Village Green plant store (Union Street and Seventh Avenue). On walls and windows are the posters and flyers that tell the nook-and-cranny explorer so much about a community—a craft fair, flea markets, meditation sessions, weekend encounter groups, pedigree dogs for sale, folk music in one of the nearby taverns, an experimental theater group beginning its first season, a new health-food restaurant opening soon. Other signs for bingo evenings at a nearby Catholic church and a Guinness stout flyer on a store window reflect the interests of the more indigenous residents.

Seventh Avenue lacks the architectural unity and the decorous flavor that characterize many of Park Slope's east-west streets. A brief loop up Garfield Place and along Polhemus Place is a reminder of the utter tranquillity of the side streets. Note the interesting groups of townhouses designed to appear as large individual mansions. But the life and the vibrancy of the avenue is more than adequate compensation for its physical deficiencies. Spend time here browsing before returning to Eighth Avenue via Berkeley Place.

Stroll up toward Grand Army Plaza and look out for the elaborate mansion (274–76) dwarfed by the thirteen-story block of apartments facing the park. Architects are often entranced by its unusual combination of Romanesque Revival and neoclassic influences—an "inspired idiosyncrasy." Others find the bold detailing combined with its ponderous granite bulk of huge rough-cut blocks the perfect reflection of many early "Gold Coast" residents—strong-willed businessmen and merchants who had wrenched their way to the top of the money pile and didn't mind displaying the fruits of their labor. The more sedate residents, those blessed with inherited wealth, normally chose less demonstrative expressions of their status, but not George P. Tangeman, owner of the Royal and Cleveland Baking Powder Companies. He had the firm of Lamb and Rich design a house befitting his concept of himself, and 274–76 was the result.

He was not alone. Note the splendor of the mansions along Eighth Avenue as we head south toward Montgomery Place. Each is a totally individual expression of architectural style, yet there is harmony here. Magnificent detailing characterizes each one, even down to the intricate door-knockers and elaborate terra-cotta ornamentation. The array of capitals, crenelations, stained glass, towers, bays, wrought iron, fanlights, unusual brick-laying techniques, and stonework is virtually encyclopedic. Note the massive bulk of the pentagonal Temple Beth Elohim, whose character is also in keeping with the architectural flavor of the Street. Just down Union Street, though, the houses at 905–13 almost carry their joyous Queen Anne and Romanesque-Revival frivolities to an extreme. As an architect friend of mine remarked, "One more bull's-eye window and you'd have a fairground."

Residents in this part of the Slope have included such notables as Thomas Adams, Jr., owner of one of the largest chewing-gum factories in the country, Charles L. Feltman, who supposedly introduced the hot dog to America, and members of the F. W. Woolworth family. The term "Gold Coast" was certainly appropriate to this particular part of the neighborhood.

Montgomery Place has a totally different character and is the result of an interesting experiment in townhouse design. Known as the "block beautiful," it was developed in the late 1880s by Harvey Murdoch and reflects his attempt to introduce a wide variety of styles to alleviate the repetitive nature of typical Park Slope streets. Unlike adjoining Carroll Street, where a similar effort undertaken by at least ten of New York's leading architects resulted in a somewhat disjointed whole, Montgomery Place relied heavily upon C. P. H. Gilbert's unifying influence. He designed almost half of the individual structures with his typical flair for large unadorned areas contrasted with exquisitely rich detailing. The other designs were also doubtless supervised by him, as there's hardly a discordant element in the whole creation. More recent development, however, in the form of apartment structures facing Prospect Park West, has destroyed some of the street's spatial charm. The houses at the top end appear a little dumpy against the towering brick walls of the high rises. The view west, looking downhill, is far more satisfying.

On Prospect Park West we find another splendid selection of individually designed mansions. At the corner of Montgomery Place is an elegant residence of exquisitely laid Indiana limestone. In comparison to other houses in the vicinity, the structure is rather small, but what it lacks in bulk it makes up for in the richness of its decorative trimmings. Note the copper-topped tower above the dormer window—just the right touch of refinement.

A little farther south is the Henry Carlton Hulbert Mansion, built in 1892 and again reflecting the power and wealth of many of the "Gold Coast's" residents. The Ethical Culture Society purchased the property in 1928 along with the adjoining, and equally interesting, William H. Childs Mansion, and uses the buildings as its school and meetinghouse for members. The City Landmarks Commission waxed eloquent over both structures in its descriptive reports, so before we finally leave the historic district, spend time examining these turn-of-the-century creations. The Childs Mansion particularly contains an unusual range of gargoyles, Flemish-bond brickwork, a distinguished finial, bay windows, and two prominent chimneys. Guarding the door are twin lions, an idea repeated on the other side of the road at the entrance to Prospect Park, except that these are panthers proudly standing on vast granite pedestals. At least some people think they're panthers. The artist, Alexander Phimister Proctor, always referred to them as pumas, and Stanford White, who designed the pedestals, called them "those magnificent cats." Whatever they are, they rank alongside Edward Clark Potter's twin lions at the New York Public Library for sheer force of personality.

The Litchfield Mansion sits in Tuscan splendor on a knoll just inside the park. It was completed in 1857 from designs by Alexander J. Davis, one of the leading American architects of his time, and was the first mansion to be erected in the Park Slope area. The railroad entrepreneur Edwin C. Litchfield lived here until 1882, although for many years he rented the property from the City of Brooklyn, which had purchased it for eventual use as headquarters for the Brooklyn Parks Commission. Regrettably, the use of the mansion as an office building over the years has diminished its internal fascination, although one can still sense the grandeur of the place in the entrance rotunda and main staircase. Visitors are also bemused by the ornate cornstalk capitals on the columns at the side of the mansion.

If you intend to take the rest of the walk across Prospect Park and up through the Brooklyn Botanic Garden, pick up the free map here, which lists the prime points of interest. There's also usually a photographic display of the park's delights in the foyer.

Olmsted and Vaux's Prospect Park is undoubtedly one of the most beautifully landscaped creations in the five boroughs, with a wonderful array of meadows, streams, lagoons, pools, and playgrounds. The architects McKim, Mead and White and Frank J. Helmle are well represented here, and the park contains a wealth of revival-style creations—the Grecian Shelter, the Boathouse, the Tennis House, the Picnic House, and the Shelter Pavilion, all finely articulated structures in complete harmony with the rolling estate-like setting. The problem here is finding a relatively quiet walk through the park that avoids the more populated sections. On summer weekends, of course, it's almost impossible. Even the most inaccessible recesses contain their share of snuggling, romping, ball-playing park-dwellers. However, during the week or out of season, I find that a stroll directly through the heart of the park from the Litchfield Mansion to the Willink entrance on Flatbush Avenue, by way of the Picnic House, ravine, Music Grove (site of the free summer Goldman Band concerts) and the Palladian-style Boathouse, is a delightfully tranquil experience. The ravine, with its tumbling stream and waterfalls, is a lovely place to find a wooded spot off the path and rest awhile.

The Lefferts Homestead (Open daily 1–5 P.M. Free), near the delightfully intimate zoo at the eastern entrance, is a re-creation of a late-eighteenth-century Dutch-style farmhouse, with the exception of the huge Federal doorway that obviously has little relationship to the rest of the diminutive structure. Its charm is also best appreciated during a quieter hour. Like the Dyckman House in upper Manhattan, it possesses a steeply pitched roof supported by six delicate columns. Inside are typical room settings of the seven-

Ravine—Prospect Park

teenth and eighteenth centuries, featuring a Gilbert Stuart portrait of George Washington, a Hepplewhite sofa, a Chippendale highboy, and several ancient Dutch Bibles.

Across the road is the Brooklyn Botanic Garden (Open Tuesday– Friday 8 A.M.–6 P.M.; Saturday and Sunday 10 A.M.–6 P.M. After September the garden closes at 4:30 P.M. 718-622-4433. Free). This is one of my favorite niches in the borough and a delightful way to complete our loop back to Grand Army Plaza. The lower gardens and the conservatory tend to attract the majority of visitors, which leaves the Japanese Garden and the various tree-lined walks in the upper section relatively quiet. Pick up a pamphlet at the entrance and select your own route. Your pace tends to slow immediately after passing through the gates and reading the sign in the Children's Garden:

> *He is happiest who hath power*
> *To gather wisdom from a flower.*

In addition to beds of carefully nurtured plants and flowers there are the quiet corners like the Herb Garden, the far side of the lake in the Japanese Garden, The Cranford Rose Garden (with almost 1,000 different varieties), the Shakespeare Garden, and the beautiful Fragrance Garden especially designed for sensory exploration. "Rub, touch and smell" urges the sign. Braille notations throughout the gardens make this a particularly rewarding experience for visually impaired people.

A short distance from the man-made rain forest in McKim, Mead and White's conservatory is the remarkable Ryoanji Temple Stone Garden, a replica of a 500-year-old garden in Kyoto, Japan. Referred to as the "meditation garden," this skillful blending of raked sand and large rocks standing independently in an enclosed courtyard has a quality of total peace and harmony. As the leaflet explains, harmony is the prime expression—"that Harmony which underlies the universe, the world, and man; the Harmony of force, of nature and of spirit; the Harmony that makes man to know himself a brother of the rocks and the wind and the sun." Rarely in this sprawling bustle of a city does one discover a place like this, a place where people sit quietly without talking, without the restless shuffle that characterizes so much of life in New York. They sit, sometimes for an hour or more, absorbing the "knowingness" of this utterly peaceful place. As a prominent American architect said: "It is deceptively simple in design, but this is what gives it power." And there is power here—an almost tangible sensation of silent, infinite energy.

Just outside the courtyard is the Roji Garden, based on a traditional network of Japanese teahouse paths. The subtle interplay of textures underfoot, ferns and shrubs, water, and lanterns conveys a sense of variety integrated by a broader mood of harmony and completeness.

Here in the garden people tend to walk slowly, enjoying the surprises that await even the regular visitor. An elderly lady beckoned me over as I ambled toward the crabapple arbors. "Look, do you see him?" She pointed excitedly to a beautiful red-feathered bird singing deep in the bushes. "It's a red cardinal!" she gushed. "It's the first time I've seen one here—ever. I've been coming every week for fifteen years and I've never seen one here before. Isn't he absolutely wonderful!" The cardinal must have known he was being admired and sang even louder. The lady and I smiled at each other and at the bird. I realized that if I had smiled at her in the street she probably would have ignored me completely, suspecting some motive of a most ulterior nature. But here in the garden, it's neutral ground. People can feel safe to smile, to talk to strangers, to sit quietly looking at rocks and sand, to watch streams cascade in tiny waterfalls. Try to end your walk here, in the shadow of the Brooklyn Museum. The garden is just one more reminder that the city is still a lovely place in which to live.

14 | Flushing

There's new life in this once sleepy corner of Queens. Recent arrivals of Korean and Taiwanese families are changing the neighborhood and creating a new gastronomic center for adventurous diners.

After emerging from the subway at Roosevelt Avenue and Main Street, I usually have my shoes shined. It's a ritual. It gets the day, and the walk, off to a good start, especially when my shoes are shined by none other than Tony Avena himself. His stand is located under the Long Island Railroad bridge, just up Main Street from the subway. Small, wiry, and always sparkling, Tony can instantly detect the mood of his customers and carefully molds the conversation to the moment. Grumpy individuals full of the woes of the world leave with polished shoes and shining spirits. "Where else can a fellow have such a good time meeting interesting people," Tony told me. "I can listen all day to stories about other people's lives. Everyone's different, everyone's got something to say." Tony's enthusiasm is shared by his brothers, Charlie and Jimmy, who work in the

☞ **DIRECTIONS**
Subway: *Start:* IRT 7 to Main Street, Flushing
Return: IRT 7 at Shea Stadium
Bus: Q13, Q14, Q15, Q16, Q28, Q44

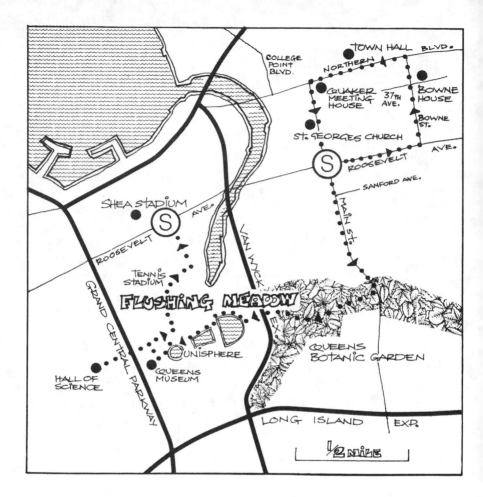

stand with him. Between the three of them, they offer a remarkable range of services, including the sale of flower arrangements, key duplicating, hat blocking and cleaning (note the custom blocks on the shelves to the right of the shoeshine "thrones"), and an inexhaustible supply of information on local history, neighborhood characters, and the changing features of "lovely Flushin'."

Tony and his brothers were all brought up in the Hell's Kitchen district of Manhattan, learning street wisdom at an early age. Their father was also a notable "bootblacker." ("Forget 'shoe-shiner',," Tony told me, "that's not the right word.") By the time his father died in 1937, Tony had become a master of the art. He moved out to Flushing originally at the time of the 1935 World's Fair in Flushing Meadow and stayed on. "It was a lot different then," he told me. "There were all apple orchards and farmlands round here. Not much housing and stuff in those days 'cept for fancy mansions with captains' walks and suchlike. Nowadays"—he gestured with his arm—"well, just look at it. Busy as hell. Gets busier all the time, too." I asked if he planned to retire. "Retire! I'll retire when they carry me out. What should I do, stay home and vegetate? I couldn't do without people."

Jimmy Avena smiles at his brother from behind vases of chrysanthemums and daisies. "Things are changin' fast; new faces all the time now. Last five years 'particular—you wouldn't believe the changes!" He points out the new Oriental signs and shop fronts on Main Street. "Take a walk on Roosevelt and Union. Whole new neighborhood—Koreans and Taiwanese love this place. Good people, too, pay top dollar for property and work like crazy—everybody in the family gets involved. There's been a few problems but mostly it's quiet nowadays. Everyone's got used to the changes— and Tony keeps 'em all smilin'!"

It's an exciting place—a dozen new Oriental groceries and butchers, Korean newspaper offices, and sushi restaurants, plus the unusual Stonywok on Northern Boulevard, with its Mongolian hotpot banquets featuring poach-it-yourself selections of more than forty different items including venison slices, fish head chunks, quail eggs, sliced jellyfish, and ox stomach. And don't forget King's Wok on Main Street, offering a tantalizing array of lobster dishes, plus such delicacies as sea cucumber in brown sauce, boiled eels with red pepper sauce, and sautéed conch and seaweed in garlic sauce. Then there are the new gastronomic possibilities, particularly at Foliage (136–11 38th Avenue, just off Main Street. Open until 2 A.M.), which claims to be "the first authentic Taiwanese restaurant in New York City." The palate pops with fresh flavors: eel casserole with garlic and sesame in a wine sauce; clams with golden mushroom soup; five-flavor octopus; pan-fried tape fish; sautéed silver fish with peanuts and chili; chicken with lily flower "firepot," and the popular midnight appetizer of preserved duck egg and pork. A taste treat.

But in spite of all the changes, old Flushing is still intact and as charming as ever. Tree-shaded Bowne Street is a three-minute stroll east from Main Street, a place of tranquil spirit and a perfect setting for the diminutive Bowne House at the corner of 37th Avenue (Open Tuesday, Saturday, Sunday 2:30–4:30 P.M. Free). Inside you begin to appreciate the long and fascinating history of Flushing and its once-staunch Quaker community. The town was actually named after Vlissingen in Holland. Many of England's persecuted Quakers had found refuge there before sailing to the New World in the 1640s and 1650s. But even in America they discovered religious freedom to be somewhat harder to achieve than they had expected. Peter Stuyvesant regarded the Quakers as "an abominable sect" and in his edict of 1657 declared that the only permitted religion in the New Netherlands was the Dutch Reformed Church. He forbade the assembly of other groups and threatened imprisonment of anyone found entertaining a Quaker or holding a Quaker meeting. But the people of Flushing objected strongly. Selected lines from their famous "Remonstrance" to the Governor on December 27, 1657, possess the same firmness of tone and intent as the Declaration of Independence itself:

You have been pleased to send up unto us a certain prohibition or command that we should not receive any of those people called Quakers because they are supposed to be by some, seducers of the people. For our part we cannot condemn them in this case, neither can we stretch out our hands against them, to punish, banish or persecute them . . .

Therefore if any of these said persons come in love unto us, we cannot in conscience lay violent hands upon them, but give them free egresse and regresse unto our Town, and houses, as God shall persuade our consciences. And in this we are true subjects both of Church and State, for we are bounde by the law of God and man to doe good unto all men and evil to noe man.

(The complete text of the Remonstrance can be found in the "Freedom Mile" brochure available at the Bowne House, and also on a plaque in the garden.)

John Bowne arrived here in 1651 and later, after joining the Society of Friends, he openly invited Quakers to meet in the kitchen of his pleasant English-style country cottage. As a result, he was subsequently deported to Holland in December 1662. Stuyvesant thought he had rid himself of "a troublesome menace," but he had failed to recognize Bowne's resilience and sense of outrage. Within a short time he was back, having argued his case before the Dutch West India Company, who sent a disciplinary note to Stuyvesant instructing him to insure that "the people's conscience should not be forced by anyone, but remain free in itself." From then on the Quakers, and many other budding religious sects, experienced increased freedom of worship. The founder of the Quaker faith, George Fox, preached under the shade of two oak trees outside the Bowne house in June 1672, and praised the residents of Flushing for their faith and fortitude. A large gray rock marks the site today.

Spend time inside the Bowne House. The simplicity of its structure and its fittings reflects the austere life of many early Quaker families, although the kitchen suggests that, while unimpressed by material abundance, they were well aware of the importance of ample sustenance. The fireplace is large enough to roast an ox (and obviously was used regularly for this purpose, hence the unusual width of the kitchen door), and the oven with its domed rear section could bake as many as forty pies or loaves simultaneously. My charming guide explained, almost defensively, "They had to work ever so hard in those days, so I suppose they needed a lot of food." She then went on to point out the hidden entrance to a tunnel that linked the Bowne house to the Aspinwall House (originally located on Northern Boulevard near the present YMCA). This was part of the underground railroad system in the years preceding the Civil War that provided runaway slaves with a safe, if occasionally circuitous, route from the South to New England and Canada. "The Quakers were very active in that movement," she explained. "That's why they call this part of Flushing the 'Freedom Mile.' So many things happened here that helped establish our basic freedoms— freedom of worship, freedom of slaves, freedom of education (the nearby Flushing High School is the oldest free public high school in Greater New York), and freedom of public assembly. It's quite amazing, really. People don't normally think of Flushing as being a hotbed of freedom movements!"

Farther east on 37th Avenue is the colonial-style Kingsland House (Open Tuesday, Saturday, Sunday 2:30–4:30 P.M. Free), originally built in 1774 as a farmhouse almost two miles east of its present location. The name *Kingsland* was derived from Captain Joseph King, an English sea captain who inherited the house in the early 1800s. His daughter subsequently married Lindley Murray, after whose family Murray Hill was named. Various generations of the Murrays lived in this sturdy structure. Most of the permanent collection of furnishings and paintings is maintained upstairs in the Victorian Room; the other rooms are used for regularly changing exhibitions and as the headquarters and library of the always-active Queens Historical Society.

Outside in the garden behind the house we find the magnificent Weeping Beech Tree, a rare mutation brought as a cutting from Belgium in 1847 by the farmer-horticulturist Samuel Parsons. Today, with a circumference of fourteen feet, a spread of almost ninety feet, and a height of more than sixty feet, this unique creature is now an official landmark designated by the New York City Landmarks Preservation Commission. In summer when the leaves are full, it becomes a gentle cascade of greens, moving in the breezes blowing off Flushing Bay—without doubt one of the most beautiful trees in the city.

In the adjoining park there's another tree worthy of note, a splendid cedar of Lebanon. Once again we are indebted to Samuel Parsons, after whom nearby Parsons Boulevard is named. He and an equally renowned horticulturist, William Prince, both selected these fertile hills above the bay as suitable locations for their famous nurseries. George Washington recorded a visit in 1789 to "Mr. Prince's fruit gardens and shrubberies" and was entertained royally by the citizens of Flushing on that occasion except for a slight mishap with a cannon, which blasted off harmlessly while Washington was delivering his address—sending the father of our country scurrying for cover. The official title of the nursery was the Linnaean Botanic Garden, and following its inauguration in 1737 Prince developed one of the largest arrays of tree specimens in the country. A century later, in 1838, Samuel Parsons's nursery began to flourish on the site of the present playground adjoining the Kingsland house. Like Prince, Parsons specialized in unusual species of trees, and the results of his labor can still be enjoyed throughout the town.

Passing the Collegiate-Gothic crenelations of Flushing High School, we stroll west on Northern Boulevard to the odd cluster of historic buildings around the Civil War monument. Most notable is the cream-and-chocolate-brown Town Hall, officially a Romanesque-Revival creation, but with all the idiosyncrasies of late Victoriana. Its history is equally eccentric. Built originally in 1862 as the Flushing Town Hall, the building has functioned as a municipal courthouse, theater, bank, ballroom, Supreme Court chamber, and headquarters of a local artillery company. Guests within its halls have included Tom Thumb, Jenny Lind, Samuel Clemens (Mark Twain), President Ulysses S. Grant, Theodore Roosevelt, P.T. Barnum the impresario and circus king, and scores of other prominent persons in politics, the theater, and the arts.

After long years of nonoccupancy, Steve Phillips and a number of other dedicated citizens assured its preservation by opening it as a nineteenth-century-flavored restaurant and theater in 1975. "God, we thought we'd never get the place going," Steve once told me as we strolled through the Town Hall's paneled corridors. "Eighteen months of paperwork—eighteen months! And that was just to get it to public auction. We could have lost it even then if someone had bid higher. As it was, we were the only nuts who wanted it." It took a lot more work before the place could be opened. "You should've seen the pigeons, hundreds of them, great mounds of droppings

Flushing Town Hall

. . . the place was a real mess. But then, that first night when we turned the lights on the stage and the audience watched our first play, hell, I could have wept. Just to hear laughter in the building after so many years . . . it was beautiful. It made everything worthwhile."

However, the last time I passed by, the place looked ominously shabby and there were no new production posters; Steve Phillip's creation had died due to lack of local interest. "Right now its future is a little difficult to predict," Elliot Semel of the Flushing Council told me, "but we'd love to have another theater or a restaurant there —anything but offices!"

Past the Masonic Temple and the "fairy-castle" brick armory on the other side of the road (now a women's shelter) is an austere, gray-shingle structure rich with the patina of age. This Friends Meeting House, built in 1694, with subsequent additions in 1717, is one of the oldest houses of worship in the nation. Except for a period between 1776 and 1783 when it was used by the British as a prison and a hospital, it has been an active meetinghouse and is open to the public Tuesdays, Saturdays, and Sundays (2:30–4 P.M.). The

Friends Meeting House

restful serenity of the cemetery, shaded by the elm tree planted to commemorate Washington's visit to Flushing in 1789, and the utter simplicity of its interior provide a sense of peace rarely found in the more ornate churches. The doors from the front porch are moved by weighted ropes and pulleys and open directly into the main room. Open-back wooden benches face the center of the room. The second floor is supported by forty-foot oak beams, hand-hewn from individual trees. Ships "knees" taken from an early sailing ship secure them to the wall timbers. The typical Quaker meeting is characterized by silence and absolute integrity, and these qualities above all predominate in this memorable place.

Nearby, various statues and memorials commemorate the Spanish-American War, the Civil War, and World War I. The landscaped oasis in the center of Northern Boulevard is named in honor of another notable Flushing resident, Daniel Beard, naturalist and illustrator and one of the founders of the Boy Scouts of America. The ponderous bulk of RKO Keith's theater, once a famous home of vaudeville and a showcase for rising stars of the time, looms ahead.

We turn abruptly south back onto Main Street, which, as we climb slowly uphill, seems to possess some of the flavor of typical small-town main streets all over the country. Flickers of Art Deco mingle with ceramic-tiled single-story businesses, clapboard façades, and pudgy, pompous banks. There's an elegant street clock, fifteen feet of baroque cast iron, occupying part of the sidewalk. Nearby is the prominent spire of St. George's Episcopal Church. This is the third church on the same site, the first having received a charter from King George III in 1761. Francis Lewis, one of the signers of the Declaration of Independence, was vestryman here from 1765 to 1790.

Those already feeling weary from our walk around the "Freedom Mile" might wish to return to the city. We shall continue, however, on the second leg south on Main Street, past Tony Avena's shoeshine stand and another tempting array of Oriental restaurants, toward the Queens Botanical Garden (Open daily 10 A.M.–5 P.M.; 718-886-3800. Free). Note the groups of civic-style buildings at Sanford Avenue—the proud-columned post office, the colonial mansion now used as a private high school, and the magnificent domed synagogue built in 1926.

Although this particular botanical garden is the most recently developed in New York City, it offers a wide variety of exhibits, lectures, demonstrations, and workshop courses in home gardening, tree care, flower arrangement, and even how to attract different species of birds into your own garden. At regular intervals throughout the year there are shows and festivals—the Tulip Show in April, the Spring Plant Sale, the Rose Festival in early June, and the chrysanthemum and yuletide plant sales in fall and winter, respectively. If you're interested in small-scale gardens, pick up the descriptive pamphlet at the entrance. This provides details on the more than twenty individual exhibits in the garden, including the fifty thousand roses in the Jackson and Perkins memorial garden; the subtle fragrances of the Herb Garden and the more exotic species in the Exhibition Greenhouse; the displays in the new orientation center; the Wedding Garden complete with murmuring stream, lily pond, white bridge, and dainty little gazebo; the Bee Garden, and the popular Arboretum loved for its spring extravaganza of crabapples and cherry trees.

The bee-buzzing little gardens gradually give way to open parkland, and the path continues under the Van Wyck Expressway into the vast panoramas of Flushing Meadow. Remnants of the 1964–65 World's Fair, impressive but underused, rise up above poorly maintained gardens. Except for hot summer weekends, it's usually pleasantly quiet here. The highway traffic provides only a distant background hum. Breezes ripple the broad ponds, and dogs romp across the lawns. The Versailles-style tree-lined boulevards and great spaces were, of course, designed for tens of thousands of visitors and were originally home to exotic architectural displays from more than fifty nations.

Watch for the notable pieces of sculpture scattered throughout the meadow, including Donald De Lue's *Rocket Thrower,* the vast *Unisphere* (a hollow steel globe built and donated by the United States Steel Corporation), and Paul Manship's elegant fountain sculpture depicting the zodiac signs, hidden in a little wooden dell in front of the New York Pavilion. My favorite, José de Rivera's

Free Form, is a thin, curved construction in polished metal which seems about to float off its marble plinth. Not far away and in complete contrast is the single unpolished "Column of Jerash" from the "Whispering Columns" of the Jerash Temple, built by the Romans in Jordan in A.D. 120. It was given as a gift to the fair by Jordan's King Hussein.

Today, all that remains open to the public is the Queens Museum in the Skating Rink (worth a visit just for the city panorama model), the diminutive Queens Zoo and Children's Farm, the Hall of Science, and the Queens Theatre. (Events and times keep changing, so call 718-291-1100 for the latest information on all of these attractions.)

When you're ready to leave the park, head north toward Shea Stadium and the adjoining subway station (IRT 7 train), following the footpath past the Singer Bowl (now the U.S. Tennis Association Courts—home of the annual U.S. Open Tennis Championship held all during August through the Labor Day weekend). Look back at the towering rockets of the Hall of Science exhibit. If you stand in the right place you'll see the outline of the Empire State building immediately between them. Close your eyes halfway and it's difficult to distinguish the skyscraper from the rockets—an appropriate reflection on twentieth-century life.

15 | Jamaica Bay and the Rockaways

The Rockaways have their bleak sections, particularly to the east around Far Rockaway, but Jamaica Bay and the western beaches offer undeniably simple pleasures and refreshing diversions for the city-weary. And when they finally decide to put some real *investment into the Gateway National Recreational Area, what a wonder-place this will be!*

In the middle of Jamaica Bay the subway train stops. It's strangely quiet and the handful of passengers look a little disconcerted. They're accustomed to the clanking, rumbling, screeching of the train as it lumbers under the East River and across Brooklyn, and this sudden silence is unexpected. One little man with a green felt hat pulled down over his ears looks around, sniggers briefly, and studies the wrinkles on his fingers with intense concentration.

You can hear the gulls. That's something—sitting in a subway train with all the windows closed and you can still hear the gulls. Across the bay the planes at JFK are huddled like somnolent swans

☞ **DIRECTIONS**
Subway: IND A or E to Broad Channel and Rockaway Park (double fare)
Bus: Q21 to Broad Channel and Rockaway Park
Q22 (east/west) to Jacob Riis Park/Playground and Far Rockaway
Auto: Cross the North Channel Bridge via the Jamaica Bay Wildlife Refuge to Rockaway Park and return via the Marine Parkway Bridge and Sheepshead Bay

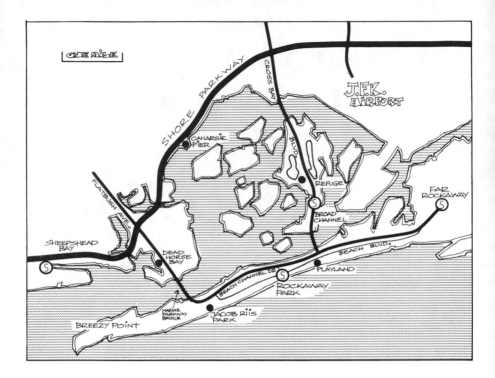

and the wavy haze makes their bright white fuselages ruffle like feathers.

It's all too brief. A moment of stillness. The train jerks and slowly rolls on across the bay. The passengers look up and the little man in the hat stops peering at his fingers and stares officiously at a guard walking through the car.

I leave the train at Broad Channel and walk into what looks like a Maine fishing village. Lines of tiny shacks are perched on shaky wooden piers. A few are lopsided. Small boats bob in the waves rolling under the piers. Nets and floats lie discarded in piles and the smell of seaweed wafts down the narrow streets of this unusual little community. To the west and rising in shimmering silhouette behind the ticky-tacky shacks and the bobbing boats and the piles of shells and strands of seaweed are the towers of the World Trade Center.

There are some citizens who find the anomaly intolerable. They would like to see Broad Channel eradicated forever and replaced by some more regionally oriented facility, reflecting the future scale of Jamaica Bay's proposed Gateway National Recreation Area. The inhabitants of Broad Channel, a determined bunch of Irish Catholics, react to such proposals with deep-felt derision. One elderly lady, her weathered face wrapped in a black shawl, said heatedly: "The city'll never get us out of here. We call this place our 'island kingdom' and we'll fight with everything we've got to keep it."

A store owner explained the problem to me: "Y'see, the city owns all this land, has done so since 1915, and we lease it from them. So I suppose they could close us all down in a flash if they wanted. They keep talking about it. They say it's too expensive to bring us up to standard. Who needs it? Things are okay just as they are. This is one of the safest places in the city. Why the hell won't they just sell us the land and have done with it?"

The residents live under constant threat of eviction. Many are reluctant to carry out needed improvements to their homes because next year—well, they may not have a home. Improvement loans are unavailable because of the lease situation, so everyone helps everyone else keep the place livable. Inevitably, the place has a rather worn, patched look, but there's a charm that's unique in the metropolitan area. The twelve hundred families who live here more or less permanently are a breed apart, a tiny tribe of Jamaica Bay natives with their own customs and social norms and a very direct view of the world: "As I see it," one elderly resident told me, "this is America, an' the reason I'm here is because I can do my own thing in peace as long as I don't disturb no one else and well, I ain't disturbin' nobody—so let me get on and do what I'm doin'. Heck, all I want is my house and the sea and some quiet—an' I got all that right here."

Take a stroll around Broad Channel, along narrow paths with names like Fifth Avenue, the Bowery, and Broadway. Dogs run loose among the marsh grasses and chase minnows in the shallows. An old gentleman with white whiskers sits in a creaking rocking chair overlooking a neat garden with a statue of the virgin Mary in the middle surrounded by thick bushes of red roses. Three fishing sloops sit on wood blocks above a barnacle-encrusted wharf. Piles of lumber are stacked everywhere.

The natives' real fear is the ambitiousness of the federal government, with its grandious plans for the Gateway Recreation Area. "Hell they've told us they want our village for a bird sanctuary," remarked an old man who'd lived in Broad Channel since it was a quiet fishing island prior to World War I. Plans are indeed ambitious. Voluminous tomes, filled with colorful architectural renderings, propose massive new beach and picnic areas on the Rockaway peninsula, along the northern marshy fringe of the bay, and down the eastern coast of Staten Island. "Gateway Villages" are envisaged, providing year-round educational, recreational, and cultural programs at Fort Hancock on Sandy Hook, Fort Wadsworth on Staten Island, and Floyd Bennett Field just across the Marine Parkway Bridge in Brooklyn. Expanded and improved wildlife reserves in the central portion of the bay are planned. Other projects include hostels and camping facilities, as well as new marinas, fishing piers, wetland areas, and even the provision of extensive water-transport facilities linking all parts of the recreation area. No wonder the residents of Broad Channel are worried: "Lord knows what it'll do to the traffic through here. They've widened the road once and split our community right down the middle. They may try and do it again, and that could just about kill us off!"

Broad Channel

Just a mile or so up the road from the village is the entrance to the Jamaica Bay Wildlife Refuge located on the famed Atlantic flyway. Here is a different world, a place of silence and beauty where one can sit by marsh paths and enjoy the slow curve of a flight of geese over the feather-topped reeds, the rustlings and scurryings in the undergrowth, blue herons lifting themselves languidly from still pools, the wild cry of sea gulls cavorting in a stiff breeze, the calls and chirrups of scores of different birds, some of them rare species on the American continent. It's almost a two-mile walk around the main lagoon (pick up the map given out by the refuge guides that pinpoints places of interest). Many disinterested visitors have returned from the walk as budding ornithologists. There are also the confirmed devotees such as Cheyenne Bode, an Indian painter of birds and one of the most familiar figures in the refuge. Like other regulars he uses the dial-a-bird service (212-832-6523) to check on the latest arrivals at the refuge.

Enthusiasts scamper over Cross Bay Boulevard and visit the fresh-water pond on the other side of the island. Here the trails are less developed and one can easily find a niche in the reeds to watch life on the lake, undisturbed except for the occasional passing subway train at the far edge of the marsh.

It's hard to see why Broad Channel residents are so upset about

Gateway proposals in this particular area. To date most of the park staff has been involved in developing programs and courses for schoolchildren and residents of the five boroughs. Even longer-range plans for a major expansion of public beach on the Rockaway peninsula, linking Jacob Riis Park with the tip of Breezy Point, should not directly affect the small community. Yet the lingering fear of ultimate doom persists. "They'll get us somehow," said an old fisherman living in one of the shacks at the end of a shaky pier.

I catch the subway again and take it to Rockaway Park, the final destination on the western leg of the peninsula. Just before we reach Beach Channel Drive I quickly sketch another strange little community of shacks stuck out in the water near Barbadoes Basin—remnants of the old summer cottages once so popular on the peninsula. At Rockaway Park it's warm outside and a breeze filled with the freshness of the sea wafts across the platform. Although still

Barbadoes Basin Cottages

early in the day, the sign for Gallagher's Seafood and Steak Restaurant, half stripped of its neon trimmings, flickers on and off erratically, and fat sparrows guzzle the garbage outside the kitchen.

The beach is empty. Just me and the clams. Thousands of them: half clam shells, broken clam shells, crabs, starfish, and seasnails. I love strolling on deserted beaches. This one's pretty clean, too. Better than Coney Island. I take my sandals off and walk in the oozy part where my feet sink into the wet sand and it squelches and gurgles between my toes. I stop and sit on one of the breakwaters and feel the waves. The wood is worn and the grain reads like contour lines. It's very deep brown with rusty bolts sticking out like old worn limpets. A dog lolls up, sniffs the wood, and lolls off lazily to the next breakwater. I keep looking at the waves.

The other way is the boardwalk and a score of those dull brick apartment buildings, all about the same height, all looking exactly alike. Farther down it gets better. Some of the old pre-World War II summer cottages have been converted into year-round houses. Anywhere else they'd look like slums, but here they're respectable, especially the ones that seem to be slowly rolling into the sand. An elderly couple sitting on the porch smile and wave. I smile back and remember, I've hardly seen anyone younger than sixty since I got off the train. No wonder I've got all this beach—and all these clams —to myself. The Rockaways are full of old people. Someone once told me, "It's like Coney Island—except here the dogs have got crutches."

It was a wild place back in the 1880s when the Irish made this their own weekend resort. Extravagant hotels, with names like "The Tack-a-Pou-Sha," and dripping with gingerbread trimmings, rose up behind the elaborate bathing pavilions that graced the beaches. The resort was popular with politicians of all guises. President Taylor and his daughters spent a summer at the magnificent Marine Pavilion, described by one enthusiast as "a large and splendid edifice in a style not excelled by any hotel in the Union." Longfellow and Washington Irving were also devotees of the place until it burned down in the hot summer of 1864. But it was the Tammany politicians who gave the Rockaways real flavor and a reputation for indulgence in the grandest of manners. Lillian Russell, long accustomed to extravagant living as companion to Diamond Jim Brady, loved the place and often arrived there on the Long Island Railroad, which crawled to the beach at a mule's pace, whistle screaming, the engineer bawling at the bemused spectators, "She's here—she's back!"

Hotels were built, burned, and built again—larger and more grand, with such fashionable English names as the Bayswater and the Windsor. In 1881 a group of wealthy investors, using more than one million dollars of Tammany funds, erected a vast self-contained "hotel-city," five blocks long from First to Fifth avenues in Rockaway Park. This enormous structure boasted numerous ballrooms, restaurants, arcades, enclosed gardens, vast suites, a rooftop observatory, and even its own private gas and water plants.

Just off the Far Rockaway coast, linked by five-cent ferries, was Hog Island, otherwise known as "The Irish Saratoga." This narrow sandbar only a few feet above sea level was the favorite haunt of the Tammany boys. They covered every buildable inch of the islet with bathing pavilions, bathhouses, bars, and restaurants. Thousands flocked there to lie on its white beaches or to concoct avaricious schemes for city-swindling in the cool confines of Patrick Craig's Dining Emporium. Then suddenly, as if by direct command from on high, the island became a latter-day Sodom-and-Gomorrah, in a tumultuous storm on September 10, 1896. Residents on the mainland couldn't believe their eyes. The *Brooklyn Daily Eagle* reported: "What was formerly the islet is now one mass of floating debris, composed of bath houses, chairs, tables and other fixings and furniture of the pavilions and restaurants on the outer beach!" But not only were all the buildings gone—the island itself had totally disappeared. The current was so strong that the sandbar had been washed away—nothing was left.

It was a blow, but the Rockaways recovered and expanded. Piers were built, hundreds of summer bungalows were constructed, the six-mile boardwalk was erected in 1924 (at that time it was the largest in the country), and in 1937 the huge Jacob Riis Park was opened, named after the famed Danish photographer and author of *How the Other Half Lives.*

But gradually fashions changed. Other resorts on Long Island

and to the north along the Connecticut coast began to attract the crowds. The Rockaways became slightly old-fashioned, a little seedy. The flimsy summer cottages started to be used as year-round homes, the boardwalk began to deteriorate, the beach was not cleaned as regularly as before.

Today, Jacob Riis Park (Q22 westbound) still attracts the summer crowds. Bathing here is strangely but voluntarily segregated. Each breakwater section is occupied by a distinct group. Go take a look on a hot summer afternoon—it contradicts the old melting-pot myth. The boardwalk is still usable, if a bit shaky in places, and the beach is usually quieter than Coney Island or Jones Beach, except when the summer craft shows line the mall here, or Joseph Papp brings one of his free Shakespeare productions to the park.

Nearby, Fort Tilden is being spruced up as part of the Gateway project and offers a wide variety of nature and history walks. If you feel like a long, lonely stroll, sample the empty dunes of Breezy Point, where you can lose yourself for a day in the infinities of sun, sand, and sea (call 718-474-4600 for information on organized walks, etc.).

Back in Rockaway Park, the Irish are still in force. Liz Mahoney's Pub, Hickey's Blarney Stone, and the Leprechaun Bar still maintain their draft Guinness signs and occasional smatterings of the old brogue. Plaster madonnas, painted in heavenly pastel shades, adorn front yards around Rockaway Park. And a local newspaper carries an invitation for "The Shannonaires, sponsored by St. Brendan's Gaelic Society of Rockaway Park at St. Francis de Sales Auditorium," while another reads, "St. Patrick's dance and bon-voyage party by the American Irish Society at the clubhouse, 1 Shamrock Lane." . . . Begorra! And the Guinness is good.

I catch a bus (Q22 eastbound). A sign reads "Come to Playland," so I get off and wander into this little bubble of fun. It's lively, but too small. Surrounded on three sides by oppressive streets lined with flaky shacks, it's not the kind of place I'd come to regularly for a wild weekend. The walls are high, though, and you can't see too much on the outside, and the music pounds from a hundred squeaky speakers. Have a hot dog, take a ride, lose a buck, win a prize, sing a song, smile a smile, drink a beer, and then go and stretch out on the beach again before the sun goes down.

If you've come by subway or bus, Rockaway is a good place to end the journey and return home. If you're traveling by car or bicycle, however, there are a few other places around the bay well worth visiting. Just over the Marine Parkway Bridge, for example, opposite the Floyd Bennett Field, is Dead Horse Bay, a wild area of dunes and sea unknown to most visitors. If you can find a place to leave the car (possibly near the marina), stroll westward over the sand hills crusted with brittle marram grass and wander around the bay. It's one of those places ideal for an afternoon's quiet contemplation. Manhattan Beach and Coney Island are to the west, but farther to the south, beyond the sandy tip of Breezy Point, is the great gray-blue Atlantic, stretching over a thousand horizons to Europe and Africa. It's one of my favorite places.

If you fancy a spot of fishing, continue north along Flatbush Avenue and take the Shore Parkway as far as Rockaway Parkway and the Canarsie Pier. Here's a small parking lot and a regular

Sheepshead Bay

contingent of fishermen religiously casting into the murky waters below the pier rail, with the familiar furtive exchange of informative tidbits, the boasting and braggadocio, the sense of kinship and the studied calm on the face of a man who knows he's got a big one at the end of his line. Fish are more plentiful in the bay and pollution levels are slowly being reduced. Fluke, "schoolie" bass, whiting, bluefish, sand porgies, hackleheads, and cod are common. There are even reports of American lobsters as large as three pounds in the shallows, although I've yet to see one. If fishing isn't your pastime of choice, the popular free weekend concerts and entertainments here during the summer usually offer something for everyone (except the fishermen, of course, who grumble that all the hullaballoo scares off the fish).

Those unfamiliar with this part of New York should follow the Shore Parkway to the Sheepshead Bay waterfront. If you can, come very early, around 6 A.M., and watch the fishing boats leave their wharves along Neptune Avenue. Better still, take an ocean-fishing trip. It's a competitive business. There are signs galore all along the

sidewalk: "Whiting Tonight," "Whiting and Cod—Guaranteed," "Short and Long Cruises," "Captain Jones—leaves 5:30 A.M.—the Earliest," "Captain Simpson Departs 6:30 A.M.," "The Longest Cruise—Leaves 7 A.M."

If that sounds a dauntingly early time to be up and about, visit Sheepshead Bay in the evening and dine at one of the waterfront restaurants. The famous Lundy's once served excellent shore dinners in dining rooms as big as Munich beer halls, but it is now a sad shell, so the lively trade has been taken over by Randazzo's, Joe's Clam Bar, Captain Walker's, The Houseboat, and several others.

To the east, at the far end of Emmons Avenue, is an entrance to Plum Beach, another one of the lesser-known beaches in the area. Before or after a stroll on the sand, pop into Shatzkin's and try one of the knishes—there's usually a choice of at least ten unusual varieties, including boodumm (potato knish with salami slices), beef frankfurter knish, pizza knish, chow-mein knish, kasha knish, fish knish, and cheese knish. Or take some of their frozen delicacies, such as potato blintzes, blueberry blintzes, potato pirogen, and mini-knishes, home for dinner—a splendid way to round off an exploration of Jamaica Bay.

16 | Staten Island

Staten Island must have once had the power to inspire great men. Poets and writers collected here, the Vanderbilt empire began here—even sailors ensconced at Snug Harbor became young salts again, full of tales of prowess and daring on the high seas. The island still has much of that invigorating quality left, so come and soak up its history, its open spaces, and the feeling that Manhattan must be at least a hundred miles away.

"It's that damned bridge. That's been the trouble." I was on a steep rise at the far end of the old Moravian cemetery in Dongan Hills, Staten Island, chatting with one of the groundskeepers. "Why, I remember less 'n ten years back when all this was jus' fields 'n' woods—all the way down to the beach there. Look at it now. It's rubbish, all rubbish. Wouldn't give you a dollar for those frilly things they call houses. There's not a bit of green left."

It's alarming to study maps of the island and see how fast the land has been used up. At the turn of the century there was almost

☞ **DIRECTIONS**
Ferry: From Staten Island Ferry Terminal on Manhattan to St. George (25¢ return/$1.50 auto)
Bus: From St. George Ferry Terminal buses leave for all parts of the island. Trains also stop at most communities along the eastern side of the island as far as Tottenville
Auto: Brooklyn-Queens Expressway to Verrazano Bridge
NOTE: This tour is best undertaken by car. If that's not possible, I suggest you select those places that appeal most and work out a public transport itinerary at the St. George bus-terminal information office

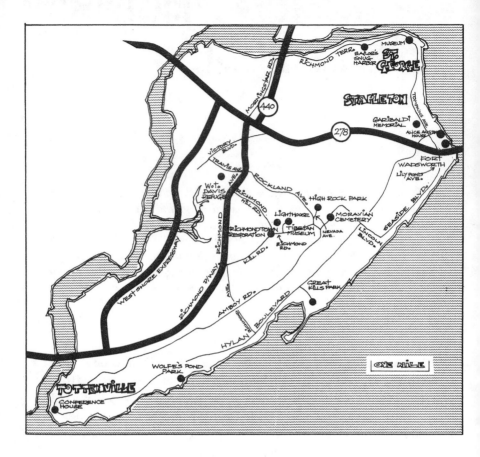

nothing here—just a few farming communities nestled in the folds of a rolling landscape. The only real town of any size was New Brighton, to the west of today's ferry terminal at St. George. This was a fashionable seaside bathing resort for the wealthy families of New York and many of the southern states until pollution wrecked the beaches and industrial development marred the New Jersey shore. The rest of the island was woods, marshes, and fine stretches of white sand, the haunt of gulls and horseshoe crabs.

The Verrazano Narrows Bridge was opened to traffic in 1964, and since that time the population of the island has tripled. Planners have not had a chance to keep up with the island's growth. Highway engineers have scrambled to provide more and more miles of expressway to cope with the glut of automobiles. If Robert Moses and his like-minded disciples had been given their way, the island would even have lost its few remaining open spaces and sections of its fragile shoreline. However, a great public outcry arose. The citizens demanded a stop to the ticky-tacky suburban sprawl, the highways that inevitably bring more sprawl, the filling-in of the marshes and the kills (streams), the destruction of historic buildings—the mindless pursuit of growth in the name of progress.

It was almost too late. Another decade and the island would have become just another few square miles of homogenized suburbia. As it is, there's been a slowing down, a rethinking of priorities, a redefinition of the concept of community, a new concern about the quality of environment. So, fortunately, there's still much to see and do on the island, and this circular tour includes most of the highlights—an old fort, five museums, nature reserves, woodland walks, a restored early-American village, an old stone house where an attempt was made to end the Revolutionary War, a cottage where Garibaldi rested briefly and made candles for a living, and meanderings among the marshes, along the reed-lined kills. Take your time. Pause occasionally to stroll the uncrowded beaches or explore park trails. Enjoy this island and be thankful that at least a portion has been saved.

Let's begin at the most obvious place—the Staten Island Ferry Terminal at St. George. Pigeons and sparrows chirp and swoop across the vast waiting hall. The smell of fresh pizza and browning frankfurters wafts over the benches, and groups of people wait impatiently for the ferry gates to open. In the corner past the newspaper stand, a small sign denotes the ferry museum (Open Monday–Thursday 8 A.M.–3 P.M. Free)—an excellent place to spend a few minutes before or after the ride to Manhattan. Outside there are displays of ferryboat history and descriptions of their individual fates. The *E. G. Diefenbach,* for example, originally used on the Brooklyn-St. George run, was purchased by the government of Nicaragua and now provides a four-hour trip across the Bay of Fonseca to El Salvador. The *Hamilton* is owned by Costa Rica and makes regular runs out of Punta Arenas. The *Cranford* has now become "the Ferry Boat Restaurant" at Brielle, New Jersey, and the *Miss New York,* decommissioned in 1975, has been sold to the Venezuelan government. There's one of the old ferries, though, that until recently nobody seemed to want. I saw the *Mary Murray* sitting in one of the docks south of the terminal. Her once bright yellow hull was turning brown and some of her windows were smashed. There's talk of turning her into a nautical museum, but funds are scarce and interest seems marginal at best.

Inside the museum, a small white-tiled room, there are models of old ferryboats, ship's bells and wheels, wind-worn and sea-sprayed logbooks, paintings, and odd bits of ferry-related flotsam and jetsam. It's worth a visit, but I hope that one day it may grow into a more significant collection—perhaps on the decks of the old *Mary Murray.*

Up the hill, along the street behind the Borough Hall, is the Staten Island Institute of Arts and Sciences (75 Stuyvesant Place; Tuesday–Saturday 10 A.M.–5 P.M.; Sunday 2–5 P.M.; 718-727-1135. Free). If you come by car, watch the parking meter carefully. The local traffic vultures swoop in quickly and silently. My trip to this free museum cost $20!

Again, like the ferry museum, the Institute has a rather limited display, but the people who run the place, members of the Staten Island Institute of Arts and Sciences, always seem enthusiastic and determined to see the place grow. Downstairs is an odd assortment of fossils, seashells, paintings, Indian artifacts, an old piano, some beautiful examples of eighteenth-century wood carving, and a series of satirical prints reflecting that long and bitter struggle between Horace Greeley and "Boss" Tweed. Along one wall is the museum shop, an even more unusual collection of donated bric-a-brac from Victorian earrings to miniature telescopes and clay pipes. If you know what to look for you might find a few remarkable bargains.

Upstairs is a more spacious display of Staten Island history. Old maps and etchings of the once pastoral landscape indicate the extent of development during the last few decades. Across the landing, in the art gallery, I once enjoyed an exhibition of Barbury Brown's illustrations from John G. Mitchell's excellent book *High Rock.* Mitchell describes the creation of the High Rock Park conservation area in the wooded hills east of Richmondtown, which we visit later in the journey. Call 718-727-1135 for a copy of the Institute's newsletter and calendar of museum and other events on the island. This is a very lively organization!

Leave the museum and travel west along Richmond Terrace following the waterfront. It's all a little run-down today, but try to imagine the scene (described in James McCabe's *Light and Shadows of New York Life*) as it was around 150 years ago:

> No factories marred its shoreline, graceful trees bordered its sides and from New Brighton to St. George the elms arched overhead, completely shading the road. On this drive the rich and great disported themselves of an afternoon and pretty carriages, shiny harness and prancing horses paired to and fro . . . handsome houses with lawns and gardens were on the landward side of the terrace and toward the water green banks sloped to the kills, whose waves lapped up on pebbly beaches. . . . The New Jersey shore was a vast expanse of green salt meadow, shimmering in the sunshine.

Little wonder this became an early seaside resort for the wealthy and later a literary colony—attracting such notables as the humorist Bill Nye, Charles Mackay, George William Curtis, Ralph Waldo

Emerson, and Henry David Thoreau. It was here also that Commodore Cornelius Vanderbilt began to amass his great fortune. Encouraged by his wily mother, he ran a small ferry linking the island with Manhattan. Gradually, using profits and financial leverage in an unusually gifted manner, he acquired more boats, obtained valuable government contracts during the 1812 war, and ultimately had his armada of ships plying transatlantic routes before turning to railroads and building a second transportation empire. When he died he was said to be worth more than a hundred million dollars. His son William took control of his interests and doubled the estate. Both of them lie together in a vast eleven-acre plot in the Moravian cemetery, close to Richmondtown. The great gray basilica-sized mausoleum sits on a terrace overlooking the eastern half of the island. It's an awesome structure. There's a great spirit of peace in the untouched woods that surround the mausoleum—an interesting

Sailors' Snug Harbor

contrast too between the wilderness of nature and the conscious creations of man. Vanderbilt spent over a million dollars to erect his memorial.

Little remains today of the old Richmond Terrace environment. The New Jersey shore is lined with old wharves, petroleum storage tanks, and factory buildings. Large ships move slowly along the narrow channel under the Bayonne Bridge. Up the slope from the shore the old resort mansions are dilapidated, jostled by undignified clapboard structures. The once prominent New Brighton village hall, with its classically austere façade and mansard roof, is now an abandoned wreck. It may soon be lost. Yet there is one glimmering gem here—a remarkable complex set in eighty acres of lawns, gardens, and ponds, known as the Sailors' Snug Harbor (Open Sunday 1–4 P.M.; 718-448-2500. Free). The main buildings, lined along the waterfront like a series of Grecian temples, were once a home for

retired seamen. The central building, approached from Richmond Terrace through a most unusual pedestrian gatehouse, was opened in August 1833, funded by Robert Richard Randall, the son of a wealthy New York shipping merchant and occasional privateer. Many subsequent additions were made until, by the early 1900s, there were almost a thousand "aged, decrepit, and worn-out sailors" living here in a self-contained complex complete with church, theater, recreation hall, two chapels, a fishpond, a gazebo, and a greenhouse. By all accounts the sailors, who always addressed one another as "captain," were not as decrepit as the philanthropic Mr. Randall had supposed. Regular drinking sorties were made by ferry to the pubs and taverns in lower Manhattan, and a nearby watering-hole known as the Old Stone Jug (today the Neville House, at 806 Richmond Terrace) became such a popular rendezvous for the old salts that it was purchased and closed down by the governor of Snug Harbor.

New York is fortunate not to have lost Sailors' Snug Harbor, considered by many architectural historians to be the finest grouping of Greek-Revival buildings in the country. A few years ago, over Landmarks Preservation Commission protests, local courts ruled in favor of replacing the present structure with a more efficiently designed establishment better suited to geriatric care. Fortunately, the city was able to negotiate an amicable settlement. The sailors moved to a new institution in North Carolina (taking with them their collection of hand-crafted model ships, made at Snug Harbor) and the city purchased the buildings and grounds for use as the Staten Island Cultural Center. Although the transformation is still incomplete, it is a milestone example of what can be done with functionally obsolescent but architecturally sound structures, given the enthusiasm of local citizens and generosity from appreciative organizations.

Sailors' Snug Harbor throbs with activity, particularly in the warmer months—free concerts by the Metropolitan Opera and New York Philharmonic, free Joe Papp Shakespeare productions and jazzmobile concerts, art exhibits at the Newhouse and other galleries, outdoor sculpture exhibits sponsored by the Museum of Modern Art, theater, conferences, tours, dance events, fairs and festivals, workshops, art classes, and even a "Children's Harbor" program, which includes an exciting hands-on Staten Island Children's Museum. Also, don't miss out on a visit to a mature Botanical Garden set in part of the eighty-acre estate featuring a Victorian Rose Garden, a "Sensory Garden" for the handicapped, annual flower shows, and a range of nineteenth-century revival buildings, including a church (now a Veterans Memorial Hall Theatre) and a wonderful line of small employees' houses (now being restored) dripping with carpenter-Gothic details and topped off with proud little mansard roofs.

Momentum here is constantly building, new parts of the complex are being renovated, and new activities are planned for an even more spectacular season next year. So, call 718-448-2500 and ask for an events calendar and, while you're at it, also call The Staten Island Council on the Arts at 718-447-4485 for details on activities throughout this amazingly lively borough.

Then continue west along Richmond Terrace. This whole northern shoreline of the island has seen far better days, but if old ships, chubby tugboats, and abandoned ferries are to your liking, you'll find much of interest behind the ramshackle buildings along the street. Past the Bayonne Bridge turn left onto Morningstar Road and continue south along Richmond Avenue. At the junction with Victory Boulevard turn right and then left at Travis Avenue. Here's a glimpse of Staten Island as it once was—views along a winding kill, acres of tall reeds waving in a breeze full of the sea smell, herons standing single-legged in marsh pools, and invisible creatures making rustling sounds in the shallows. Determined individuals can make arrangements for specially organized field trips through the William T. Davis Wildlife Refuge (call 718-727-1135 for details), but for most visitors it's an all too brief experience. Soon one is back among the new houses with their plastic-stone façades and plaster gnomes prancing across Astroturf lawns.

Go south on Richmond Avenue and almost immediately east at Richmond Hill Road. At the top of the hill the highway crosses Latourette Golf Course and then without warning drops sharply down the slope into the Richmondtown restoration, Staten Island's most ambitious preservation project.

Richmondtown Restoration

Much has been written about Richmondtown. There have been controversies over the use of funds, furious debates over the architectural relevance of some of the properties relocated to the site, lawsuits, claims of fiscal corruption, and most frustrating of all, long periods of inaction. But even in its incomplete state, Richmondtown is a charming place to spend a warm afternoon, and will be even better when the traffic is routed completely around the restoration.

Originally known as Cocklestown because of the abundance of shellfish in the nearby kills, the community was established in the late 1600s and later prospered as the county seat. In 1898, however, Staten Island became part of greater New York and the town was largely abandoned as growth centered around the docks and ferries at St. George and New Brighton. Even as far back as 1939, the Staten Island Historical Society recognized the potential value of preserving the village as a showplace of regional architecture and country life during the seventeenth, eighteenth, and nineteenth centuries. Members began by buying and restoring the 1695 Voorlezer's House, the oldest elementary school building in the country. Then, slowly, more properties were acquired and examples of early island dwellings, such as the Guyon-Lake–Tysen House (1740) and the Britton Cottage (1670), were moved to Richmondtown and restored. Today there's almost a complete village here.

Up on the hill, with its sturdy white pediment resting on four fat Doric columns, is the County Courthouse (1837). Across the street is the museum located in the Surrogate's Office, and down the slope of Court Place there's the Stephens-Black House and general store, with a splendidly Rockwellian interior. Then comes the Victorian Edwards-Barton House, a re-created carpenter's shop, a display of dolls and children's toys in the 1839 Bennett house, and the Redware Pottery Works featuring demonstrations of traditional pottery-making in the cellar of the Guyon-Lake-Tyson house.

Between Richmond and Mill Pond (complete with ducks, geese, and turkeys) are restored homes, a basketmaker's shop, a cooper's shop, a sawmill, a blacksmith, a small transportation museum, a printer's shop, a basketmaking workshop, and even an inn at the Guyon Store. And there's more planned for in the future. Visit the museum (Open Wednesday–Friday 10 A.M.–5 P.M.; Saturday–Sunday 1–5 P.M. Fee) and pick up brochures on the restoration—they provide details on each of the buildings, and members of the Historical Society occasionally serve as guides. (Call 718-351-1611 for details and a schedule of events.) Visitors, particularly those who live in New York, are always surprised by the scale of the restoration and sometimes even its existence. "Why, I just had no idea all this was here," an elderly lady told me as she walked along the paths between the old clapboard buildings. "I live just on the other side of the bridge, I've been there all my life, and this is the first time I've ever come. I wish I'd known about this before. It's a lovely, lovely spot."

There are a few other places you should visit while you're in the area—places not well known to outsiders. On the hill overlooking the restoration, for example, is a huge stone lighthouse built in 1912 that still operates in conjunction with the Ambrose Light. It's unusual to find a lighthouse so far inland, but this one is situated on some of the highest land between Maine and Key West. Nearby Todt Hill (409.8 feet) is, in fact, the highest point.

A little farther down the hill, at 340 Lighthouse Avenue, is one of the most unusual museums in the greater New York area, the Jacques Marchais Center of Tibetan Art (call 718-987-3478 for times and special events). Once you enter its silent garden, New York and its trappings are left behind. Bright goldfish move slowly through pools, life-size Buddhas beam from leaf-shrouded glades, carved rabbits, monkeys, and snakes occupy niches in the walls, and sacred mantras are carved on garden stones. The place is a miniature facsimile of a Tibetan lamasery. There's a library here, a small gift shop, and a magnificent Tibetan altar with a central sculpture of Tsong-Kha-Pa, a religious reformer and founder of the Yellow Hat sect of Buddhism. He is surrounded by religious objects—prayer wheels, butter lamps, offering cups, masks, horns, altar tablets, and incense burners. Wall banners (tankas) made in Tibet present teachings of the various deities. The place is a treasure trove of Buddhist art and is said to be the largest private collection in the world.

Leaving the museum, it's hard to return to the hustle-bustle outside—so don't. Instead take Richmond Road east to Rockland

Avenue, turn left, and then after a short distance, turn right along Nevada Avenue. Follow this to a small parking area just inside the lovely High Rock Park Conservation Center (Open daily 9 A.M.–5 P.M.; 718-987-6233. Free). Here you can continue your reveries and contemplation in a seventy-acre woodland complete with ponds, swamps, a visitors' center, a tactile garden of plants for the blind, and four distinct exploratory trails. Watch the toads and turtles around Loosestrife Swamp. Listen for woodpeckers or the rustle of rabbits in the undergrowth. Find your own quiet here in the heart of the island, and listen to life around you. One person I talked to traveled regularly all the way from the Bronx just to sit in this silent place.

When the weather is good a thorough exploration of Richmondtown and other nearby places of interest can take a good part of a day, but if you still have some time left, drive to Tottenville at the southern tip of the island. Here you'll find the ambience of an old country town full of Victorian villas, narrow lanes, and views of the ocean between clusters of large trees. It's a different world, as yet undamaged by the commercialism to the north. At the end of Hylan Boulevard is the Conference (Billopp) House (Open Wednesday–Sunday 1–5 P.M.; 718-984-2086. Fee), dating back to 1680. Here, Lord Howe entertained John Adams, Benjamin Franklin, and Edward Rutledge on September 11, 1776, and endeavored to persuade them to accept British peace terms. The occasion was marked by decorous civility on both sides. Adams was particularly impressed with the setting and noted that Howe "had prepared a large handsome room by spreading a carpet of moss and green sprigs, from bushes and shrubs in the neighborhood . . . and he entertained us with good claret, good bread, cold ham, tongues and mutton!" The conference was, however, a failure and the long Revolutionary War began in earnest shortly thereafter.

On the return journey, explore the lonely Clay Pit Pond Reserve between Arthur Kill Road and the West Shore Expressway. Then, driving up Hylan Boulevard to the Verrazano Bridge or the ferry, there are plenty of delightful parks and beaches to while away a warm afternoon. Wolfe's Pond Park has excellent bathing and boating facilities, and farther to the north Great Kills Park and the adjoining Miller Field reflect another attempt to preserve a segment of island marshlands, while at the same time providing valuable recreational facilities and a fine stretch of bathing beach. Frustrated New York fishermen fed up with grimy catches from the Hudson or East rivers should be relieved to hear that the park authority claims there's an abundance of flounder, bass, porgie, bluefish, and even crabs here.

The start of the Franklin D. Roosevelt boardwalk is at Miller Field, a 7,500-foot-long oceanfront stroll that eventually leads to Fort Wadsworth, under the Narrows Bridge. Here you can explore the intricacies of the Battery Weed, a trapezoidal structure on the water's edge with four levels of gun turrets. The original fort, a diminutive timber blockhouse, was built by the Dutch in 1663 as a defense against local Indians. It was erected, however, somewhat after the fact. During the early skirmishes between settlers and natives variously known as the Pig War, the Peach War, and the Whiskey War, the settlers had been driven off the island on each occasion and eventually ended up buying the land back from the Indians at least five times before peace was finally made. Cornelius Meyer, one of the early settlers, complained: "They [the Indians] supposed that ye island by reason of ye war, by killing, burning and driving us off, was become theirs again." It was also at Fort Wadsworth that the last shot of the Revolutionary War was fired. The British, who captured the island almost as soon as the conflict began, left ignominiously on evacuation day in 1783, jeered by crowds of Americans. The infuriated commander of a British warship fired a cannon shot at the fort. The shot missed—but the jeering echoed halfway across the Atlantic.

A short distance north of the fort, at the end of Hylan Avenue (past the delightfully shady Arthur Von Briesen Park), is the Alice Austen House, one of Staten Island's most charming architectural anomalies. What originally began as a diminutive Dutch farmhouse (1691–1710) was later transformed into a rambling villa trimmed with delicate Gothic-Revival details by John Austen, a prominent New Yorker and grandfather of Alice Austen. In 1868, Alice came to live here and used the house as a base during her remarkable life as a photographer and promoter of the women's liberation movement. For decades her work was unrecognized. Her more than 7,000 photographs and glass negatives were stored away in shabby boxes. A tendency to injudicious spending dissipated her fortune and, in 1945, she had to sell the house and live in a charitable institution for the poor. Then, in 1951, an article in *Life* magazine featuring her photographic work brought belated fame and financial comfort for the remaining months of her life. Today, the house stands as a fitting memorial and museum to this remarkable woman (Open Saturday and Sunday 10 A.M.–4 P.M. Fee).

A few more surprises await before leaving the island. First, take Tompkins Avenue from its junction with Wadsworth Avenue north as far as Chestnut Avenue. In a garden raised above the street is the Garibaldi Memorial, a simple clapboard house with a restrained Victorian-Gothic character (Open Tuesday–Friday, 10 A.M.–5 P.M.; Saturday and Sunday 1–5 P.M. Free). Here the great Italian liberator lived after the fall of the Roman Republic in 1849. In the back garden there's a furnace where he made candles for a living. It was a penurious existence for a man who later went on to lead the legendary One Thousand in the liberation of Sicily and Naples, and saw the unification of all Italy—his life's ambition.

Take time to explore the adjoining community of Stapleton, currently sprucing itself up for when the proposed new Naval base arrives here. New restaurants, antique shops, singles' bars and waterfront apartments are all signs of a healthy renaissance in this pretty (yet in parts pretty-funky) town.

Then, up over the hill behind Stapleton, you'll discover two of Staten Island's many delightful green spaces—the Clove Lakes Park, ideal for jogging and romantic woodland strolls, and Silver Lake Park and golf course, which encloses a large landscaped reservoir. Between Broadway and Clove Road you'll also find the tiny Staten Island Zoo full of children's exhibits (deer, ponies, prairie dogs, etc.), plus one of New York's best reptile collections housed in a dark, spooky setting complete with huge African Rock pythons and clusters of vampire bats!

And there are still more secret places on this relatively undiscovered island—places like the new Blue Heron Park off Hylan Boulevard near Philip Avenue, 20 miles of trailways through the circular "Greenbelt" encompassing Willow Brook and La Tourette parks, and the lovely old-fashioned town of Travis fringed by marshes near the William T. Davis Wildlife Refuge.

Staten Island is full of surprises! Come and see for yourself.

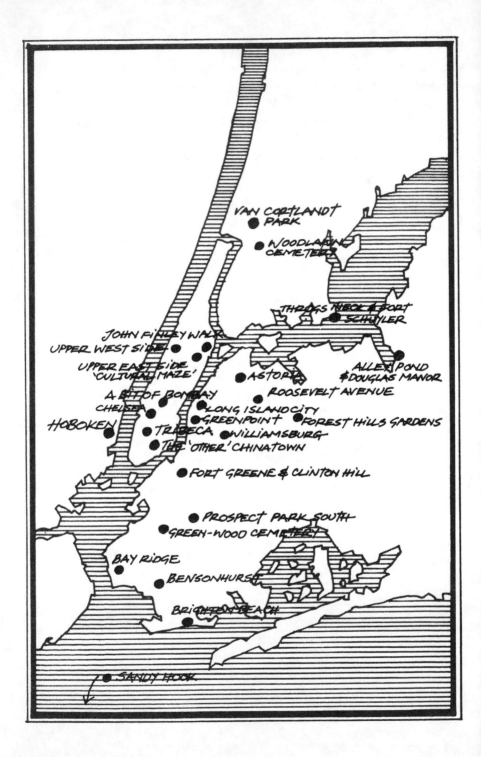

⚎ MINI-TOURS

Well—the big walks are over now and the blisters are healing, but the problem is that there's so much more to explore in the five boroughs.

So, in this final part of the book are a few glimpses, glances, and tempting tantalizers to spark the nook-and-cranny-hunting spirit again. In Manhattan we'll discover a little bit of Bombay, a lovely East River walk near Gracie Mansion, a touch of Williamsburg in the West 20s, and a new neighborhood bursting with swank bars, chic restaurants, and rollicking night life.

Outside Manhattan we'll explore two unusual cemeteries (even one that offers public concerts), delightful enclaves of architectural extravaganzas, little slices of Scandinavia, Italy, Russia, Greece, and Poland, and New York's most intensely Jewish neighborhood.

We'll even cheat a bit and cross the Hudson to wander in the reincarnated "Mile-Square-City," and lose ourselves in reedy creeks and woods deep in Queens.

Finally, we'll round off these short strolls with a visit to an

English village, a handful of little-known manors and forts, and a cultural maze in midtown that will stimulate, once again, even the most weary of urban wanderers.

Enjoy.

MANHATTAN
The "Other" Chinatown

The next time you venture into the aromatic alleys around Mott, Mulberry, and Pell streets in the heart of New York's official Chinatown, cross the Bowery near the curved towers of Confucious Plaza and take a short walk along East Broadway and Division Street. Here you'll discover a compact, congested little neighborhood offering some of the finest—and most unusual—culinary delights in town.

Smoke-smeared tenements huddle together here under the boomings and grumblings of the Manhattan Bridge; delivery vans double-park all along East Broadway, and scores of shoppers (the Chinese always seem to be shopping) nibble gelatinous strips of rice noodle dunked in soy-based sauces bought at street vendor carts scattered along the sidewalk.

You don't come here for the touristy spirit of pagoda-style eaves

Subway: Any subway to Canal Street (preferably Lexington Avenue IRT trains and BMT N, QB, or RR), and walk east to the Bowery and south to Chatham Square
Bus: M1, M6

and telephone kiosks found on the other side of the Bowery (although halfway along East Broadway there's a Buddhist temple complete with offerings of oranges on the altars); instead, you come to visit the excellent stores filled with succulent Peking ducks and ritual displays of barbecued innards, ears, and webbed feet, and to gaze at window-tanks brimming with lethargic carp, wily eels, and sad-eyed turtles. There is also the herbalist's store neatly stocked with jars of dried roots, beans, flower blossoms, bark, spices, and exotic aphrodisiacs, as well as excellent homemade and take-home frozen dim sum at Chow's (49 Division Street).

But everyone really comes here for the restaurants—small, cramped, overlit, underpriced, and with staffs invariably indifferent to the brazen antics of ill-informed customers, who try to pry out the secrets of dishes listed in Chinese characters on colored strips of paper stuck to peeling walls. However, perseverence does finally pay off.

For example, visit Lan Hong Kok Seafood House on Division Street, a typically modest place of wholly unnotable design where you can lose yourself in a welter of new tastes and textures. The menu includes such specialties as fish maw soup with crabmeat, seafood in a bird's nest basket, salted baked squid stuffed with shrimp, sautéed eel balls, blue crab in black bean sauce, and dried oysters with fat choy (a delicious seaweed). And two doors down is the Great Shanghai's excellent and low-priced Peking Duck dinners with all the trimmings, as well as such samples of sweet Soo-Hang cuisine as the wonderful chicken with orange sauce. A few yards in the opposite direction is the new Canton Restaurant, complete with its stained-glass window depicting a school of carp, and filled with an unusually well-dressed clientele.

There are also many places that offer Vietnam, Fukien, and Mongolian cuisine (try the firepot creations at Foo Joy at 13 Division Street), and almost everywhere you'll find such prized delicacies as sliced jellyfish or sea cucumber, fish head casserole, whole ginger carp, hacked chicken, salted duck, pickled Chinese cabbage, pigeon in wine sauce, and some of the most refined Szechuan dishes anywhere at Szechuan Cuisine (30 East Broadway), the nearby Hwa Yuan, and Szechuan State at Chatham Square. For value my favor-

ites are Hoo Lok Fang on East Broadway (with the almost obliga-
tory "Koch Ate Here" photo in the window), and the adjoining Say
Eng Lok with its "special dishes" list usually taped to the front of
the menu—try the fried roll fish with bean curd sheet, black mushroom with puff, lion head (pork balls in dark anise-flavored sauce),
and an unusually rich double-cooked pork.

A few words of advice: Avoid patronizing many of these restaurants on Mondays, which is usually the chef's day off; come with
a group and make a banquet out of the meal (prices are low and
portions large, so go easy on the first round of orders); try one or
two dishes you've never heard of (the worst they can be is mediocre,
but you just might discover a whole new range of tastes); and expect
anywhere from basic drab to distinctly crumby decor in most of the
best places.

Just close your eyes—and eat!

TriBeCa

I tend to be suspicious of new neighborhoods with strange-sounding names. Take TriBeCa for example—"the TRIangle BElow CAnal Street"—one of the more recent additions to the nomenclature game in New York and still in search of its refurbished soul among the beautiful people, gorgeous restaurants, serious galleries, and eerily dark, quiet nighttime streets. It will doubtless find itself one day, but new neighborhoods foster traditions over time—and TriBeCa ain't there yet. However, it's still a fun place to visit.

By day the area booms with true downtown gusto, thronged with delivery trucks, but as the grimy cast-iron-fronted warehouses and workshops close, the streets lose their life and, at first glance, seem far too wide and empty to encourage casual exploration. SoHo, immediately to the north, has overcome the day-end doldrums, and the West Broadway spine is now a chic strip of high-priced bou-

Subway: Seventh Avenue IRT to Canal, Franklin, or Chamber Streets; Sixth and Eighth Avenue IND to Canal or Chambers Streets; BMT City Hall stop at Broadway and Murray
Bus: M6 (downtown on Broadway; uptown on Church)

tiques, lively wine bars, and cavernous white galleries with obliga-
tory white Corinthian columns. But TriBeCa is still taking shape;
for many devotees and resident loft-dwellers, it's the most happening spot in the city.

Architecturally, the neighborhood is a visual and spatial hodgepodge.˙Bounded by Broadway, Canal Street, Chambers Street, and
the Hudson River, it houses a potpourri of Hopper-flavored restaurants (look out for the Market Diner near Laight at the river),
ponderous stone and stucco structures, façades of finely detailed
cast iron, and a few shards of the once-volatile Washington Market
(Manhattan's Les Halles) in the form of dairy wholesalers—all in
a trapezoidal tangle of streets restrained by the white stateliness of
the Federal buildings to the east and the World Trade Center/Bat-
tery City complex to the south.

The old market, removed to Hunt's Point in the Bronx, has been
replaced by the towers of Independence Plaza and the culturally
active Manhattan Community College, with its famous triplex of
theaters catering to all tastes, from the blues to ballet to Brecht.
Huddled below the new brick bastion is a delightful row of restored
eighteenth-century townhouses, complete with cherry trees and
cobbled streets.

Surprises like these make TriBeCa an intriguing place to explore
during the day. You move quickly from sunless streets with their
cobwebs of black fire escapes, to the local "Park Avenue" section
around Hudson and North Moore streets, rapidly filling with palatial lofts. Then, on to the Cheese of All Nations store (153 Chambers
Street), where you'll find some of the best free samples in the city,
to the open–air and breezy urban horticulturalist's Farm and Garden Nursery (Sixth Avenue near White), to the dainty little park at
Duane and Hudson, and to the tiny Thomas Street Inn at 8 Thomas
Street—a jewel of Romanesque-Revival (and easily overlooked).

Although not as flamboyant and commercial as SoHo, the range
of galleries around the Church, White, and Franklin streets block
is remarkable evidence of TriBeCa's importance as yet one more
artists neighborhood. (Ironically, though, when the galleries move
in so do the six-figure salary boys, and the artists are on the road
again seeking out the next niche.) Particularly notable are the exper-

Thomas Street Inn

imental outposts at Franklin Furnace, featuring regular performances by artists using text, image, and other media, and the Alternative Museum and Artists' Space, both of which are operated by artists for nonmainstream artists. Other gallery groups can be found farther south along the lower Hudson Street area and around Chambers Street and West Broadway.

Also, between the northern fringe of the district and the southern reaches of Greenwich Village is a fourth burgeoning gallery, pubs, and loft area around Greenwich Street, with the famous White Columns (325 Spring Street at Greenwich) acting as a focus for more consciousness-expanding art-experiments and performances. (Most galleries are open 10 A.M.–6 P.M., Tuesday–Saturday and some request contributions.)

But the real fun here comes at night when the trucks are gone and the three-piece-suiters have swilled a couple and sailed on home to the suburbs. Then the in-crowd, the artists, the fast-trackers take over. By 8 P.M. you wonder where everyone came from. They're certainly not all locals, they're not your typical trading-floor types, and they don't look like jazzy Jerseyites out for a night of sparkle and glitter in the Big City. I don't have really a clear idea of their origins, but purpose is paramount—and the purpose is food and chat and more chat, and not your predictable how-long-to-bedtime baseline dialogue of singles bars, but intense eye-to-eye, gesture-for-gesture sharing of abstractions and absolutes over warm chèvre-salad, cassoulet, rack of lamb, Wellfleet oysters, and the best crème brulée in town.

The oysters gave it away—right? You've heard of the place—The Odeon, of course—pioneer of the patch and still about the best restaurant, bar, and intellectual hot spot in this active nexus. Housed in an old Art Deco cafeteria at West Broadway and Thomas Street, the place has somehow avoided the vagaries of the in-crowd and maintained its excellent reputation for years, complete with all the "here-but-for-the-money" touches in the form of white tiles, cheap tumblers, toothpicks in shot glasses, and the original cafeteria's help-yourself newspaper rack.

But The Odeon is now only one of TriBeCa's many outstanding wateringholes and gourmet niches. Le Zinc is nearby at 135 Duane

Street, famous for classic and nouvelle French dishes served bistro-style in a red wall and mahogany setting to a truly mixed clientele of monacled male models and "ooh-isn't-this-wonderful" stargazers. Then there is the tiny Montrachet (West Broadway at White Street), where I wonder how they manage to produce such delicate concoctions in such cramped quarters; Belgian delights at the barn-sized Le St. Jean de Pres (112 Duane Street); the even larger Bon Temps Rouler (59 Reade Street), where alligator sausage, love sauce, and voodoo stew are served under the collective title of Cajun/Creole cuisine, and the well-lauded Ecco (124 Chambers Street near West Broadway) in yet another twenty-foot-high space, ornately furnished, and serving some of the best Italian cuisine in town.

For lighter fare, a garish jangle of colors (black and white giraffe spots covering the façade) announces the always-busy El Internacional, famous for its tapas snacks (219 West Broadway). Nearby you'll find the male bastion of The Sporting Club (99 Hudson Street), with its giant televisions and stadium-sized score screens, and the delightfully low-key Riverrun (176 Franklin Street), complete with neighborhood pinboard and excellent brunches. One Hudson Café (1 Hudson Street) features good jazz and satisfactory French cuisine, while the Beach House (399 Greenwich Street), offers the basic booth-and-brick-wall ambience. A handful of pre-loft TriBeCa locals includes the funky Raccoon Lodge (Warren Street between West Broadway and Church), Puffy's Tavern (Hudson Street at Harrison), and McGovern's (Reade Street near Hudson).

For the serious nighttime crowd who regard dinners and pub chat as merely a prelude to a marathon of after-midnight madness, there's the outstanding Area disco at Hudson between Hubert and Laight. Scores of enthusiasts scramble nightly to pass beyond the "rope," pay the ritual $15, and dance till dawn in old Pony Express stables that are transformed, chameleonlike, every five weeks into new theme pleasure-palaces (a clever way to keep the crowds coming). Other nearby night places include S.O.B. (fast South American dance club at 204 Varick Street at West Houston), Heartbreak (good old rock 'n' roll, 179 Varick Street at King Street), Club

Senzala (more salsa disco at 59 Murray Street), and the Reggae Lounge (285 West Broadway)—all high-energy dance spots.

So, watch this new neighborhood. It's still taking shape and the sifting-out process for bars, galleries, restaurants, and discos is far from over. Just like all the other "in" areas of this constantly churning city, the crowds move round and out and on, searching for just the right combination of mood, quality, and attitude— something like the search for a perfect marriage partner. The only danger is that in the search for the ultimate, so much of the good and true can be discarded. TriBeCa has lost many of its old places; we wait to see how long the new will endure, or whether we are now truly in the oft-predicted accelerating age of constant change and casual choices. As TriBeCa goes, so goes the world?

Chelsea

Much of Chelsea's Greek-Revival and Italianate-flavored historic district, which lies along West 20th to 22nd streets between Ninth and Tenth avenues, was part of Clement Clarke Moore's (" 'Twas the night before Christmas . . .") pastoral estate, and thanks to his foresight as an amateur architect and planner we can enjoy its delightful ambience today.

The General Theological Seminary (Chelsea Square) occupies the central portion of the historic district. Visitors are encouraged to stroll through its shady grounds to the accompaniment of bird song, or psalms wafting from behind the ornate doors of the Chapel of the Good Shepherd. Alternatively, browse through the ecclesiastical tomes in St. Mark's Library here.

Although relatively small, the district contains a number of notable features, including Paul Frieberg's children's park at Tenth

Subway: IND AA, CC, E to 23rd Street and Eighth Avenue
Bus: M10

Avenue and West 22nd Street, and the 1831 L and S Dairy building (183 Ninth Avenue at West 21st Street). This Federal-style charmer with its three adjoining wooden houses, brings a little Williamsburg flavor to this corner of the city.

Spend time exploring the area. Admittedly, the streets outside the historic district lack much of its charm, but there's abundant evidence of enthusiastic renewal, and the restaurants and stores along Eighth and Ninth avenues reflect the whims of Chelsea's cosmopolitan population.

And while you're in the neighborhood, step inside the famous Empire Diner (Tenth Avenue and West 22nd Street). It never closes, and always offers a very up-market menu to an up-market clientele in a ritzy setting once described as "the ultimate homage to the American Diner."

Then either stroll north to the Fashion Institute of Technology (West 26th–West 28th streets between Seventh and Eighth avenues. See Chapter 6, The Garment and Fur Districts) for fashion-related exhibits and a glimpse of the mystiques of garment-guru training. Or stroll east to the one-time literary mecca of the Chelsea Hotel (West 23rd Street between Seventh and Eighth avenues), frequented by the likes of O. Henry, Mark Twain, Thomas Wolfe, Brendan Behan, Dylan Thomas, Tennessee Williams, and a host of other boisterous and boozy notables. This matronly red and white Victorian-Gothic creation graces the street and tingles with filigrees of flower-patterned, iron balconies. Today more a rooming house than a hotel, she still deserves respect in spite of her decrepit lobby.

And if you're still strolling east beyond the Chelsea area, why not include a visit to the delightful Little Church around the Corner at Fifth Avenue and East 29th Street? This unexpected masterpiece in the Cottage-Gothic style has been known as the Actors' Church ever since George Holland received burial rites here in 1870 (deceased actors apparently were not welcome at other nearby churches). Come through the unusual lynch-gate, past the Gothic-Revival rectory with mansard roof, and enter the intimate nave. It has all the ambience of a cozy rural church. Note the continued

Chelsea

links with other noted actors—memorial windows dedicated to Richard Mansfield, Joseph Jefferson, Edwin Booth (portrayed as Hamlet), and John Drew, a special chapel in honor of José Maria Muñoz, and the Actors' Memorial Window dedicated to all members of the profession.

A Bit of Bombay

For some reason, Lexington Avenue between East 26th and East 33rd streets is home to half a dozen or more stores selling Indian foods of every description—lentils, dahl, a score of curry powders, ghee, bottles of brown, gold, and ochre spices, flat waferlike papadums (when quickly fried they triple in size and become wonderfully crunchy accompaniments to curry dishes), pickles, sticky desserts, and sacks of the finest long-grain Indian rice. And that's only the beginning. Come browse and sample the aromatic arrays of Tandoori and Tikka specialties: sags, bhagees, kurmas, aloos, biryanis, vindaloos, and sabjees at the Annapurna, Shaheen, Madras Palace (vegetarian), Curry Curry, and the (exactly what it says) Curry in a Hurry. While the choice is not as extensive as the famous 6th Street strip of twenty or so Indian and Pakistani restaurants between First and Second avenues (see Chapter 3, The East Village), here you'll discover a more eclectic range of Middle

Subway: IRT 6 to East 28th Street and Park Avenue South
Bus: M1, M101, M102

263

Eastern and Armenian restaurants, two good French places (La Petite Auberge and La Colombe d'Or), the down-home Italian Francesca's, ruled over by a large lady of the same name, and the lovely Joy's Café, which offers the widest range of budget entrées in the neighborhood.

The Upper East Side Cultural Maze

Did you realize that in addition to such stalwart New York institutions along the Fifth Avenue "Museum Mile" as the Metropolitan Museum of Art and the Guggenheim, the Upper East Side (from East 58th to East 105th Street) is home to more than fifty museums, galleries, libraries, and performing arts centers—all offering free or inexpensive cultural delights and surprises for everyone?

The next time you have a month of free time to fill, why not make the exploration of this magic maze your #1 priority project. In the meantime you can pick and dabble, using these selected brief cameos and tantalizing glimpses as your guide. You may never leave The Big Apple again.

Abigail Adams Smith Museum

421 East 61st Street between First and York Avenues/838-6878
Monday–Friday 10–4 P.M. Admission $2

A real delight and surprise off the First Avenue Singles Strip (see Chapter 8, The United Nations and Vicinity, page . . .).

Alliance Française

22 East 60th Street/355-6100

This school and cultural organization reflects French interests and perspectives and offers various courses to residents of New York. (The theater is currently undergoing renovation.) Low-cost weekly programs include:

- Tuesdays: Lectures (usually in French) on French topics ($1.50)
- Wednesdays: French films with subtitles ($2.50). Call for times
- Fridays: "Teletech"—French video films and documentaries with subtitles 12:30–7:30 P.M.
- Once-a-month story hour for children 3–6 years old ($1)
- Twice-monthly music events on a flexible basis, plus other activities

Call for details and brochure.

American Institute of Graphic Arts

1059 Third Avenue at 63rd Street/752-0813
Monday–Friday 9:30 A.M.–4:30 P.M. Free

Four wide-ranging competition—exhibitions each year of published graphic design—everything from can labels to record sleeves, book jackets to maps. Call for details about the current exhibition. Also an excellent research library.

American-Irish Historical Society

991 Fifth Avenue at 80th Street/288-2263
Free

A library for true patriots, with abundant material on those of Irish descent who made it in the New World. Call first for hours of operation.

Asia House

112 East 64th Street between Park and Lexington Avenues/581-2294
Monday–Saturday 10 A.M.–5 P.M.; Thursday 10 A.M.–8:30 P.M.; Sunday 1–5 P.M., Free

Cofounded by John D. Rockefeller and housed in an understated glass structure designed by Philip Johnson, Asia House offers a wide range of public lectures on Asian affairs, at least three special loan exhibitions yearly, theatrical, music, and film presentations, and an extensive library. Tape-recorded tours of exhibitions are normally available. Members are entitled to exceptional group charter rates to Asia.

Asia Society

725 Park Avenue at 70th Street/288-6400
Tuesday–Saturday 11 A.M.–6 P.M.; Sunday noon–5 P.M. Free

A very active center featuring a permanent exhibition of Asian art from the Mr. & Mrs. John D. Rockefeller III collection, plus a series of regular loan exhibitions, each one focusing on a particular Asian country. Members also enjoy a wide range of cultural events, including lectures, performing arts, classes, and films, many of which are available to the general public free or for a nominal charge (usually $2 for nonmembers; $1 for students and senior citizens).

American Zionist Federation

515 Park Avenue between 59th and 60th Streets/371-7750
Free

Coordinates the American Zionist movement and presents a wide range of forums, fairs, celebrations, and informal programs for the public. Call for details.

American Scandinavian Foundation

127 East 73rd Street off Lexington Avenue/879-9779
Wednesday–Saturday noon–5 P.M.

Free exhibitions throughout the year featuring the work of Scandinavian artists, sculptors, and crafts people.

Center for Inter-American Relations

680 Park Avenue at 68th Street/249-8950

Art gallery is open free to the public Tuesday–Sunday, noon to 6 P.M., with five or six exhibitions a year of Latin American and Canadian artists, pre-Columbian artifacts, Guatemalan textiles, Peruvian ground drawings, and other varied themes. Lectures, films, and children's programs are often included, plus occasional poetry readings and concerts, including the notable free Bosendorfer piano concert series usually held every Saturday between January and April at 6 P.M. (first come, first served). These excellent recitals are broadcast on WNCN-FM 104.3. (Call 581-9420 for details.)

Center for the Study of the Presidency

208 East 75th Street at Third Avenue/249-1200
Free

By appointment. A public policy research center that houses a small library for students and researchers and offers a fall series of popular free lectures at Fordham University (Lincoln Center) on various aspects of the presidency and national policy formation. (Quarterly newsletter available through subscription.)

Central Park Conservatory Gardens

105th Street and Fifth Avenue

Through the elaborate wrought-iron gates we enter a magical (and little-known) world of arbor walks, formal lawns, fountains, bowers of blossoms, and the sweetest-singing birds on the East Side. The Untermeyer Memorial Fountain has three nymphs frolicking around a carved plinth—one of the most delightful creations in the park.

Many park lovers avoid the northern extremities. They shouldn't. This is wonderful territory, full of woodland walks, gorges, rocky bluffs, natural streams, and waterfalls, and a peace rarely found in New York. If you're anxious, come with friends—but *do* come. It's as good as a trip to New England (almost).

China Institute in America (China House Gallery)

125 East 65th Street between Lexington and Park Avenues/744-8181
Monday–Friday 10 A.M.–5 P.M. (Gallery) Free

Offers a wide range of cultural activities for members, plus free public exhibitions on Taiwan and mainland China, calligraphy, art exhibits, and a lecture series (single lectures are usually $5; price for series varies). There are usually only two (small but exquisite) exhibitions here each year, so it's best to call in advance and check the program. Credit courses are also available in Chinese culture, literature, cooking, art, music, and dance, and, as with most New York City institutions of this kind, members are entitled to group rates on charter flights. Don't miss the rear reading room overlooking the garden, which still retains all the flavor of a nineteenth-century townhouse library.

Church of the Resurrection

East 74th Street between Park and Lexington Avenues/879-4320
Saturday and Sunday 2–5 P.M.

A free permanent exhibition of brass rubbings taken mainly from English church brasses, plus a chance to do-it-yourself for a fee ($4–$35). Be warned, however: even a small "rubbing" involves more time than you think. You'll need a rest at the adjoining Kings Angel tearoom where traditional English afternoon and high teas are served by an English woman whose cake and bun recipes are "nonpareil."

Cooper-Hewitt Museum

2 East 91st Street/860-6868
Tuesday 10 A.M.–9 P.M.; Wednesday–Saturday 10 A.M.–5 P.M.; Sunday noon–5 P.M.
Adults $2; seniors and students $1; children under 12 free
Tuesday 5–9 P.M. Free

This branch of the Smithsonian, housed in the old Andrew Carnegie Mansion, has vast permanent collections of decorative arts. Regularly changing exhibitions related to some aspect of design include textiles, glass, wood, ceramics, and metal work, plus one of the largest collections of original design and architectural drawings in the world. Free lectures and symposia plus performing arts events are offered on an intermittent basis. Workshops, weekend seminars, and special tours for young people and adults are also conducted. Scholars and students are invited to use the museum's 35,000-volume library, reference center, and study facilities, by appointment.

El Museo del Barrio

1230 Fifth Avenue between 104th and 105th Streets/831-7272
Tuesday–Friday 10 A.M.–5 P.M.; Saturday and Sunday 11 A.M.–
5 P.M. Contribution

A lively expression of Hispanic culture, including rare pre-Columbian artifacts, sculpture, photography, collections of precious Santos de Palo, and a dynamic program of cultural activities and regularly changing exhibitions. Events include free concerts, lectures, children's activities, films, dance, poetry readings, productions by the resident theater group (Teatro 4), and workshops at the adjoining Escuela de Arte. Call for schedule.

The Explorers Club

46 East 70th Street between Park and Madison Avenues/628-8383
Library open to the public—call for appointment
Free

If you're thinking of making an expedition to some exotic hidden corner of the world, call the club and see if any member can help plan your adventure, or check on the public-lecture schedule (Monday 8 P.M.–10 P.M., September–May, $6). You will also want to make an appointment to use the excellent research library. A stimulating and handsome place.

French Cultural Service

972 Fifth Avenue near 79th Street/570-4400
Monday–Friday 10 A.M.–5 P.M. (Exhibitions)
Free

A McKim, Mead, and White mansion with an elegant lobby often used for exhibitions of French photographers. Also a useful bilingual reference library. Call for details on special cultural and other programs.

The Frick Collection

1 East 70th Street at Fifth Avenue/288-0700
Tuesday–Saturday 10 A.M.–6 P.M.; Sunday 1–6 P.M.
Adults $1; seniors and students 50¢; Sunday $2 (for everyone); children under 10 not admitted; children under 16 admitted with adults Free concerts

Enter the refined world of Manhattan's early money-barons in Henry Clay Frick's mansion filled with masterworks (Rembrandt, Turner, El Greco, etc.), fine furniture, sculpture, porcelain, prints, and silver artifacts. Rest in the pool–court or attend a lecture on the collection (shown at half-hour intervals throughout the day), scholarly lectures on European art (Thursday and Friday at 3 P.M., Saturday at 4 P.M.), or, providing you write in for the tickets, free Sunday chamber concerts in the small concert room (5 P.M. September–May). There's also an excellent art library for scholars and researchers.

Genealogical and Biographical Society

122 East 58th Street between Park and Lexington Avenues/755-8532
Monday–Saturday 9:30 A.M.–5 P.M. (Saturday openings October–May only; closed August)

Reference library open to the public for research forays (with librarian assistance for the serious searcher). $3 contribution: nonmembers; five-lecture series $30 for nonmembers.

Goethe House

1014 Fifth Avenue at 83rd Street/744-8310
Tuesday and Thursday 11 A.M.–7 P.M.; Wednesday, Friday, and
Saturday 12–5 P.M. Free

A German cultural institution offering a wide range of activities
for the public, including a regularly changing series of free art
exhibitions, new German films on Saturday at 2 P.M., and an extensive series of free lectures relating to German history, culture, and
art held intermittently during the week. Also, several annual free
chamber music concerts and a pleasant, well-stocked library.

The Grolier Club of New York

47 East 60th Street between Madison and Park Avenues/838-6690
Monday–Saturday 10 A.M.–5 P.M. (call first to confirm)
Free public exhibitions October–June

There's a leathery, clublike atmosphere in this splendid stone
townhouse with wonderful displays of rare books and manuscripts
celebrating the world of book printing, design, illustration, binding
—even paper manufacturing. Four major annual exhibits centered
around books and original manuscripts from October–June. Even
if books don't excite you, go just for the ambience of the place,
designed by Bertram Grosvenor Goodhue in 1916.

International Center
of Photography

1130 Fifth Avenue at 94th Street/860-1777
Tuesday 12–8 P.M.; Wednesday–Friday 12–5 P.M.; Saturday and
Sunday 11 A.M.–6 P.M.
Adults $2.50; students and seniors $1; children under 12: 50¢
Tuesday 5–8 P.M. Free (courtesy of Chase Manhattan Bank, N.A.)

A comprehensive photographic institution featuring changing exhibitions of photographs, and photographic styles and techniques,

plus a large permanent collection of documentary photographs. Lectures, seminars, workshops, and screening-room events. Lecture fees vary. Museum shop open to the public and resource library by appointment only.

The Jewish Museum

1109 Fifth Avenue at 92nd Street/860-1888
Monday–Thursday noon–5 P.M. (Tuesday to 8 P.M.); Sunday 11 A.M.–6 P.M.
Adults $3; children, seniors, and students $1.75
Tuesday 5–8 P.M. Free

Part of Manhattan's Museum Mile, this is the largest institution in the U.S. dedicated to collecting, preserving, and interpreting the art and artifacts of over forty centuries of Jewish life and tradition. Guided tours, lectures, special exhibitions, films, and concerts are usually free with admission, as are the popular "Family Workshops," which encourage parents and children to learn together about Jewish traditions and culture and to develop their creative skills. Visit the recently opened department—the National Jewish Archives of Broadcasting.

Leo Baeck Institute

129 East 73rd Street between Park and Lexington Avenues/744-6400
Monday–Friday 9 A.M.–5 P.M. (closes at 3 P.M. Friday during winter. Closed August to local residents). Summer hours 9 A.M.–4 P.M. (open to foreigners in August)

This refined townhouse houses an outstanding center for German-Jewish history and culture, with regular free exhibitions of the work of German-Jewish writers and painters, and assorted memorabilia. Extensive range of German publications. Also, free lectures during the academic year and an excellent library with genealogical archives.

Madison Avenue Presbyterian Church

Madison Avenue at 73rd Street/288-8920

A culturally active center offering a regular series of Sunday music recitals (chamber/organ or choir at 4 P.M.—suggested donations $5, $3 for seniors), free films or lectures on spiritual or historical subjects (most Wednesday evenings), and a popular adult swimming program at the pool next door to the church (Tuesday, Wednesday, Thursday 6–9 P.M.; Sunday 4–6 P.M. $15 for five sessions).

Magic Roofscapes

The most neglected art forms in the city are the "castles in the air"—those wonderful disguises designed by architects to shroud rooftop water tanks. Here are a few favorites. Look up and discover your own.

- Sherry-Netherland Hotel at 60th Street and Fifth Avenue
- Pierre Hotel at 61st Street and Fifth Avenue
- 63rd Street at Lexington Avenue
- Park Avenue at 72nd and 73rd Streets
- 76th Street at Madison Avenue
- 80th Street at Lexington Avenue (also note the lovely garden across the avenue at the Unitarian Church of All Souls)
- 84th Street at East End Avenue

Marymount Manhattan College

221 East 71st Street between Second and Third Avenues/517-0400

An independent liberal arts college for women offering a wide range of activities that include free theater workshop productions by students and occasional dance performances (ext. 474); free monthly

"Castles in the Air"—Water Tank Disguises

art exhibitions in the Nugent Gallery, and Mary-MMC Gallery; occasional free lectures (including Lefkowitz on political science) and workshops by the Office of Lifelong Learning (ext. 565).

Metropolitan Museum of Art

Fifth Avenue at 82nd Street/535-7710
Tuesday 9:30 A.M.–8:45 P.M.; Wednesday–Sunday 9:30 A.M.–5:15 P.M.
Suggested admissions: $4.50; children and seniors $2.25

This is Manhattan's best known and most popular museum—a magnificent repository of the world's finest art, sculpture, decorative arts, textiles, and costumes (separate entrance), musical instruments, arms and armor, and religious artifacts, reflecting just about every culture known to man. Particularly important are the exten-

sive collections of Egyptian, Greek, Roman, Far Eastern, Islamic, Medieval, and European works. Recent additions include the refined Robert Lehman wing, a spatial American wing, the Temple of Dendur set in its own glass hall complete with reflecting pool, and the Michael C. Rockefeller Collection of Primitive Art. Regular special events include:

- Free daily gallery talks and/or films
- Free walking tours of individual sections starting at 11 A.M., with special general tours at 11 A.M. and 1 P.M.
- Free Sunday programs including films and special lectures

Many other varied free concerts and events. Pick up a free copy of the museum's Calendar/News for details.

Equally fascinating is the Junior Met Museum (Tuesday–Saturday 10 A.M.–5 P.M.; Sunday 11 A.M.–5 P.M.; 736-2211 or 879-5500. Contribution). Here children and families enjoy more hands-on exhibitions aimed at involving visitors as participants in learning. Regular family events include:

- Free gallery talks and performances Saturday and Sunday 11 A.M.–1:30 P.M.
- Free slide talks, Saturday and Sunday 1–3 P.M.
- Studio Workshops Saturday and Sunday 1:30–3 P.M. ($1.50)
- Free films, Saturday at noon
- Written gallery hunts (free "game" for children)
- Free Tuesday evening gallery talks September–June 7 P.M.
- Free art classes (Tuesday–Friday 3:30 P.M. high school students only)

Also special concerts and performances during the weekends, popular seasonal events, and an imaginative library for youngsters.

Museum of the City of New York

Fifth Avenue at 103rd Street/534-1672
Tuesday–Saturday 10 A.M.–5 P.M.; Sunday 1–5 P.M. Free

A wonderfully rich panorama of New York life and history, including the fifth-floor John D. Rockefeller Rooms (taken from his 54th Street home), old fire engines in the basement, a dollhouse and toy collection, permanent displays of Duncan Phyfe furniture, a fashion exhibition, dioramas of city history, a costume gallery, maritime exhibits, period-furnished rooms, regularly changing exhibitions often reflecting contemporary issues and urban problems, plus a wide range of special activities that include:

- Free Sunday solo or ensemble concerts twice a month, September–May 3 P.M. (and "meet the artist" socials at 4 P.M.)
- Sunday musical extravaganzas and family events at 3 P.M., often with notable artists and musicians ($3)
- Saturday children's puppet shows at 1:30 P.M. ($2.50)
- At least ten different walking tours of New York neighborhoods every Sunday led by knowledgeable guides, 1:30 P.M. April–October ($6)
- "Please Touch" demonstrations for children and families in the seventeenth-century Dutch Room ($1)

An excellent and active institution.

National Academy of Design

1083 Fifth Avenue at 89th Street/369-4880
Tuesday noon–8 P.M.; Wednesday–Sunday noon–5 P.M. $2.50

Founded in 1825 as the American equivalent of London's Royal Academy, this notable institution boasts the finest national artists as members and offers at least ten art exhibitions a year (with introductory seminars) from its own extensive collections of portraits and exhibits gathered from around the world. Also there are the excellent sketching classes with live models ($4), Monday–Friday 4:30–6:30 P.M.; also Thursday and Friday 7–9 P.M.; Saturday 9:30–11:30 A.M., 1:30–3:30 P.M.; plus occasional free lectures and demonstrations by artists. (Other courses are more expensive.)

New York Academy of Medicine

2 East 103rd Street/876–8200
Monday–Saturday 9 A.M.–4:45 P.M.

The library is open to the public and contains just about everything you'll ever need to know about medicine and the medical sciences. There's also a regular series of free lectures open to the medical and allied professions. The cafeteria is available to those using the library and other facilities.

New York Academy of Sciences

2 East 63rd Street at Fifth Avenue/838-0230

Established in 1817 to further communication among scientists, the academy offers a wide range of free nightly lectures (Monday–Friday 8–9:30 P.M.) in environmental sciences, microbiology, anthropology, biochemistry, etc., from September through June. Most lectures are quite technical (word has it that public policy, history, philosophy of science, economics, and psychology are less so). All free—including refreshments after the lecture.

New York Society Library

53 East 79th Street/288-6900
Monday 1–5 P.M.; Thursday 1–8 P.M. Other days 9 A.M.–5 P.M.
Closed Sunday
Closed Saturday mid-May to mid-Sept.

A charming library located in a landmark townhouse designed by Trowbridge and Livingstone in 1854. Nonmembers may use the reference section and the staff is helpful.

Society of Illustrators

128 East 63rd Street near Park Avenue/838-2560
Gallery open 10 A.M.–5 P.M.; Monday–Friday (Tuesday until 8 P.M.); closed August
Research library open by appointment only

Regularly changing exhibitions of excellent illustrations, plus an annual Christmas show and auction in early December, as well as an Illustrator's Annual Exhibition (normally held in February and

March) featuring the best of U.S. illustrators. (There's an excellent buffet lunch served upstairs, but you have to be a member or guest to indulge!)

Solomon R. Guggenheim Museum

1071 Fifth Avenue at 88th Street/360-3500
Wednesday–Sunday 11 A.M.–5 P.M.; Tuesday 11 A.M.–8 P.M.
Adults $3; seniors and students $1.75; children under 7 Free
Tuesday 5–8 P.M. Free

One of Manhattan's best-known landmarks. Frank Lloyd Wright's masterwork contains ever-changing exhibitions of contemporary art, plus large permanent collections of works by Picasso, Klee, Chagall, and Kandinsky. (Hint: Start at the top and work your way down.)

St. Nicholas Russian Orthodox Cathedral (1901–1902)

97th Street (between Fifth and Madison Avenues)

A wonderful edifice tucked away ignominiously on 97th Street, with its five onion domes, ornate terra-cotta details and baroque-flavored columns and trimmings. A creature as magnificent as this needs space. But alas, this is Manhattan, not Moscow. See it if you're doing the museum stroll along the "Gold Coast." Also take a look at the Squadron A Armory (1895) nearby on Madison (94th to 95th streets). Actually, there's only part of it left. The Landmarks Preservation Commission managed to save the western wall and towers. Take a stroll around the back—there you'll find a park!

Sculpture Center Gallery

127 East 69th Street between Lexington and Third Avenues/879-3500
Tuesday–Saturday 11 A.M.–5 P.M. Free

St. Nicholas Cathedral

Located in a charming old carriage house, this one-time bastion of traditional techniques and artwork is moving in more avant-garde directions, both in its sculpture exhibitions and in its lecture series and occasional performances of "new music." Fresh and original ideas are being tested and schedules tend to be flexible. Courses in stone and wood carving, clay modeling, and bronze casting are offered, while the gallery shows work by both established and young emerging artists.

Spanish Institute

684 Park Avenue near East 68th Street/628-0420
Monday–Friday 9:30 A.M.–5:30 P.M. Free

Small gallery of Spanish art and sculpture. Special events include recitals, dance performances, free lectures to the public (a few limited to members only), and special language programs (fee).

Temple Emanu-El

1 East 65th Street at Fifth Avenue/744-1400
Open daily from 10 A.M.

The largest synagogue in the world, the largest Jewish congregation, and a magnificent specimen of bold Byzantine architecture with Romanesque overtones. Free tours are available during non-service hours and organ recitals are held on Sunday afternoons in March.

Ukrainian Institute of America

2 East 79th Street/288-8660
Tuesday–Friday 2–6 P.M.; Saturday and Sunday by arrangement
Contribution

Fascinating exhibitions of contemporary Ukrainian art and sculpture, along with collections of historic religious artifacts, folk crafts, and the contributions of notable Ukrainian–Americans. Also five or six cultural activities each month that include lectures, concerts, films, etc., usually free or of nominal cost to the public.

Whitney Museum

945 Madison Avenue/570-3600
Tuesday 1–8 P.M.; Wednesday–Saturday 11 A.M.–5 P.M.; Sunday 12–6 P.M.
Adults $3; children and seniors $1.50 (Tuesday 6–8 P.M. Free)

Always stimulating exhibitions of contemporary American art in an equally exciting building designed by Marcel Breuer, plus an abundance of free activities that include exhibition lectures, live performances, and experimental films. The downtown Whitney Museum in the Phillip Morris building across from Grand Central Station is also well worth a special visit. A new Downtown Whitney also recently opened at Federal Reserve Plaza (33 Maiden Lane), followed by another Whitney opening at the Equitable Center (Seventh Avenue between 51st and 52nd streets). Watch for a new feature—the free lunchtime performances in each of the branches. Programs are always changing, so it's wise to call first.

Yivo Institute for Jewish Research

1048 Fifth Avenue at 86th Street/535-6700
Monday–Friday 9:30 A.M.–5:30 P.M. Free

This transplant from Lithuania, now relocated in a stately Louis XIII–style house, offers almost half a million books and other documents for research into Jewish/Yiddish history and traditions, and showcases changing exhibitions in the elegant lobby.

YM/YWHA

92nd Street at Lexington Avenue/427-6000

A feast of free or low-cost activities and events every day of the year including concerts, classes, recitals, theater, films, health club, special-interest groups, readings, gymnastic displays, art and photo exhibits, and children's activities. Call for extensive details and listings.

The John Finley Walk and Yorkville

This strip is a jogger's paradise and one of the most delightful riverside walks in the city, situated on a broad pedestrian platform above FDR Drive, with good views of Hell Gate, Wards Island Park, and Roosevelt Island.

Carl Schurz Park, at the northern end of the walk, is an exquisite swathe of lawns, shade, play areas, tunnels, and curving stairs leading to cobbled walkways. The delicate white trimmings of Gracie Mansion peer from behind dense thickets of trees, and across the road at East 86th Street and East End Avenue is Henderson Place, surrounded by towering apartment complexes yet maintaining its classic repose. Lamb and Rich originally designed the thirty-two townhouses as a "single harmonic whole." Today there are only twenty-four remaining, but the subtlety of the architects' intent is still evident.

Between East 81st Street and Carl Schurz Park (East 84th to East 90th streets) along the East River
Subway: IRT 6 to East 77th Street and Lexington Avenue
Bus: M31

Henderson Place

It's possible to continue walking (or jogging) alongside the river in both directions (north from East 90th Street and south from East 81st Street to the 59th Street Bridge), but these routes are far less pleasant than the Finley Walk itself.

And while you're in the neighborhood, take a stroll up and around East 86th Street among the scattered remnants of Yorkville, once the city's German nexus. Here you'll still discover a wonderland of wursts at Schaller and Weber, and Karl Ehmer's Pork Store crammed with prosciutto-like cured hams, even more wursts, kassler ripchen (smoked loin of pork), and the unusual lox-flavored pork creation known as lachs-schinken. Bremen House is a multilevel extravaganza of everything German from beer steins, Bavarian mushrooms, and Düsseldorf mustards, to Westphalian pumpernickel, Hummel porcelains, and Black Forest cuckoo clocks. Then, of course, don't miss Yorkville's fabulous bakeries—"Konditoreis" —Kramer's, Café Geiger, and Kleine Konditorei, and the last stalwart restaurants, the Ideal (excellent potato pancakes), Schaefer's, and the still very Germanic Heidelberg, famous for its inexpensive schnitzels and paprika-laced dishes.

A little farther south along First Avenue around East 75th–72nd streets is the almost solitary souvenir of Little Czechoslovakia—the beloved Vasata restaurant. This cozy, old-country, inn-style favorite of Eastern Europeans offers button-busting platters of roast goose, duck, boiled beef, veal, and pork chops, with glutinous dumplings, sauerkraut, beets, thick gravies, and a hearty, robust staff determined to ensure the total satiation of every guest. It's a welcome remnant but also a sad reminder of days long gone.

Upper West Side Delights

Talk about renaissances and neighborhood renewals—the Upper West Side has soared into the stratosphere, with property prices and rents outstripping its long-time up-market rival neighborhood on the opposite side of Central Park. The once-dowdy Columbus Avenue is now the city's most hectic restaurant/wateringhole row, with a singles scene that rivals the East Side's First Avenue.

Amsterdam Avenue otherwise known as "Cinderella Avenue," is now home for "the young, the rich, and the restless," and so much of this burgeoning neighborhood has become self-consciously hip that it's hardly nook-and-cranny territory anymore. Even Zabar's, once of country-store size, has gobbled up its neighbors and, while still crammed with devotees, now seems as overtly commercial as the scores of other new stores in this amazing part of Manhattan.

However, while explorers of the Upper West Side will be awed and entranced by the changes, they should keep an eye open for the lovely old streets in the West 70s and 80s. On a "façade-finding" tour look out for sections of idiosyncratic-revival townhouses among the apartment monoliths (some of the best examples of fantasy architecture in the city) and don't miss the following:

- West 73rd Street between Columbus Avenue and West End Avenue
- West 74th Street between Central Park West and Columbus Avenue
- West 74th Street west of West End Avenue
- Most of West 75th Street
- West 76th Street west of West End Avenue (76th Street between Central Park West and Columbus is one of the most stately streets in the city and, appropriately, a designated Historic District)
- West 77th Street around West End Avenue—the odd Dutch-style complex of the West End Collegiate Church and School
- West 81st Street between Columbus Avenue and Amsterdam Avenue
- West 83rd Street between Central Park West and Amsterdam Avenue
- West 85th Street between Central Park West and Amsterdam Avenue

Even farther north is Pomander Walk, an intriguing little alley linking West 94th and 95th streets between Broadway and West End Avenue. It says "private" on the sign, but the gate's normally unlocked. Residents don't seem to mind visitors strolling through this unusual replica of a narrow English walk, complete with half-timbered gables, wooden porches, flower boxes and neatly trimmed privet hedges.

Much farther down Broadway at West 65th Street is one of New York's best-loved cultural clusters at Lincoln Center. Facilities here include the Metropolitan Opera House, Avery Fisher Hall, the New

Pomander Walk

York State Theater, Alice Tully Hall, Juilliard School, the New York Public Library and Museum of Performing Arts, and an adjoining Fordham University Campus, all set in plazas and gardens adorned with fountains, trees, and a monolithic *Reclining Figure* by Henry Moore.

While this remarkable nucleus is neither nook nor cranny, the range of free and low-cost activities, fairs, outdoor concerts, and festivals here often amazes even the most knowledgeable New Yorker. Juilliard, for example, has offered free Tuesday and Friday evening concerts for years (call 799-5000 for information on its rather complex procedure for obtaining tickets), and the library has free classical recitals on weekdays at 4 P.M. and Saturdays at 2:30 P.M. (call 870-1630 for details). But there's much, much more, so call the general Lincoln Center information number at 877-2011 and you'll be overwhelmed by the wonderful range of freebies here.

Van Cortlandt Park and Mansion

Here's an opportunity to explore an entrancing part of the Bronx, little known to most residents of the other four boroughs. The park itself is a vast expanse of mature woods, hills, meadows, and quiet places, with abundant outdoor activities in the summer that include free opera and symphony concerts, and even winter skiing. The good old Urban Rangers offer their regular bevy of free walking tours (call 360-8194 for details), and the Van Cortlandt Mansion near Broadway and West 246th Street is an appealing diversion (Tuesday–Saturday 10 A.M.–4:45 P.M.; Sunday noon–4:45 P.M. Fee. Call 543-3344 for details about free lectures and other activities).

This stately stone-built Georgian mansion, set in the rolling parkland, was another of Washington's headquarters during the Revolution and is now decorated in period style using many of the furnishings of the Van Cortlandt family, who occupied the house

Subway: IRT 1 to West 242nd Street, the Bronx
Bus: Bx20 via Kingsbridge Road and Broadway
(Additional attractions if you come by car)

until 1889. My favorites are the Dutch bedroom with cupboard-style bed, and the charming eighteenth-century dollhouse.

If you come by car, then you can maneuver westward to the Henry Hudson Parkway via Manhattan College Parkway, take the service road to Riverdale Avenue and west again on West 254th Street to lovely Wave Hill (entrance at West 249th Street and Independence Avenue. Open daily 10 A.M.–4 P.M. Fee). This splendid 1843 Greek-Revival mansion (with several odd architectural variations) overlooks the Hudson and was once home for such notables as Theodore Roosevelt, Mark Twain, and Arturo Toscanini. It was donated, along with twenty acres of land, to the Parks Department for use as an experimental horticultural center, and there's an interesting range of art exhibits, gardens, greenhouses, outdoor sculptures, and various weekend activities that often feature musical recitals and folk dancing. Call 549-2055 for details.

Also, less than half a mile to the north, off Riverdale Avenue, in the estatelike grounds of the College of Mount St. Vincent, is Edwin Forrest's odd Gothic mansion-castle, Fonthill, complete with tower, turrets, and finely detailed battlements. Forrest was a famous, if idiosyncratic, Shakespearean actor in the mid-1800s who became even more notorious for his feud with William Macready, the noted British actor, which sparked the Astor Place Riot of 1849 (see Chapter 3, The East Village). Hardly known for his modesty, he explained in a speech about his home:

> In building this house, I am impelled by no vain desire to occupy
> a grand mansion for the gratification of self-love . . .

NOTE: You can reach Wave Hill by bus using the Liberty Lines Riverdale express (call 652-8400 for details) to West 252nd Street and walking two long blocks to the entrance on Independence Avenue.

Woodlawn Cemetery

Green-Wood Cemetery (see page 313) has its splendid Gothic entrance, but Woodlawn is, without doubt, the most beautiful cemetery in the metropolitan area, if not the country. It was founded in 1863 as a rural burial ground and has managed to preserve that flavor, although surrounded on all sides by rapid development.

Pick up the map and guidebook at the Jerome Avenue entrance and wander through and around the wooded dells, lakes, and past the incredible mausoleums—an encyclopedia of architectural styles memorializing such notables as Frank Woolworth, Fiorello La Guardia, Jay Gould, George M. Cohan, Herman Melville, Duke Ellington, "Bat" Masterson, Roland Macy, and Joseph Pulitzer.

Ironically, in this resting place for the departed, history comes very much alive. There's abundant activity here, with free monthly concerts and events organized by the cemetery's dynamic public

Southwest entrance: Jerome Avenue at Bainbridge Avenue
Open daily 9 A.M.–4:30 P.M.
Subway: IRT 4 to Jerome Avenue/Woodlawn
Bus: Bx4, Bx16

relations director, Jeanne Capodilupo, plus special holiday theater at Christmas and the New Year in the F.W. Woolworth Chapel. "We go a little crazy every July 4th, too, with an outdoor big band concert featuring all of George M. Cohan's best-known songs," Jeanne told me. "We're a pretty unusual kind of cemetery!" (Call 920-0500 for details on special events.)

A short(ish) walk south down Bainbridge Avenue to West 208th Street brings you to the Museum of Bronx History (Open Saturday 10 A.M.–4 P.M.; Sunday 1–5 P.M. $1 fee) housed in the Valentine-Varian House, a sturdy example of an eighteenth-century fieldstone farmhouse. Here you'll find a wealth of displays, photographs, and relics of local history from Indian days through the Revolutionary War period to the present, plus a small research library. Call 881-8900 for details on special lectures, tours, and recitals.

Throgs Neck
and Fort Schuyler

Standing on the stumpy cliffs at Silver Beach, I gazed into a brilliant scarlet sunset across the broad East River. The piers of the Bronx-Whitestone Bridge seemed to be burning, and I could just hear the grumble of jet engines from La Guardia, three seagull-flying miles to the southwest.

A narrow footpath, "The Trail," meanders along the clifftops past tiny cottages, originally built as summer homes in the 1920s. Barbecues and brightly colored lawn furniture suggest a laid-back, California life-style here; below the cliffs are boat docks, bobbing fiberglass dinghies, and the lapping of little waves. Two pig-tailed girls in party dresses chase one another between the golding trees along the path, and a dog barks in the backyard of a white clapboard

Subway and Bus: Take Lexington Avenue subway, Pelham Bay Local #6 for a fifty-minute trip to Westchester Square; switch to a half-hour bus marked Bx40 Fort Schuyler for a twenty-minute ride to the campus entrance

The Trail—Silver Beach

cottage, with peek-a-boo bay windows, chintz curtains, and a plaster Siamese cat poses primly behind diamond-shaped panes. At the end of the footpath, bounded by a small grassy park, two elderly men in baseball caps sit fishing on rocks at the water's edge as the sun eases down behind the purple pillars of the Manhattan skyline and the lights wink at Mauro's seafood and steak restaurant on the other side of Pennyfield Avenue.

I'd arrived earlier in the day after a rather arduous journey by bus and subway, and spent a few hours exploring the campus of the 1,200-cadet Maritime College of the State University of New York, located in a series of blandly modern buildings on a narrow peninsula under the Throgs Neck Bridge. The highlight of a trip here is the enormous granite bulk of Fort Schuyler at the southern tip of the peninsula, where Long Island Sound joins the East River. Built over a period of twenty-three years (1833–1856) as part of "The

Third System" of seacoast defenses, this sturdy pentagon is considered one of the most impressive examples of a French sea/land type fortification in the U.S. and, at the height of its importance, was armed with more than 450 garrison and heavy guns. (Group tours: 10 A.M. on weekends in October, November, February, March, and April. Free. Call 409-7276 for details. Individuals welcome on a self-conducted tour basis.)

There's a small Marine Transportation Museum inside St. Mary's Pentagon with several exquisitely detailed model ships. The sixteen-foot-long *Bremen* even has a scaled version of a catapult-launched seaplane with every rivet accounted for. A major expansion of the museum is underway. Also, don't miss the adjoining Luce Library, a splendidly masculine restoration of gray-blue granite arches, bronze chandeliers, and brilliantly polished wood furnishings. And, best of all, groups are able to tour the nearby 530-foot-long *Empire*

State training ship usually in port here all year except during the eight-week summer training cruise to the Mediterranean.

Obviously a car is desirable to reach this secluded Bronx niche, but public transportation is available and on a sunny weekend day, it's certainly worth the effort.

Greenpoint

They say the locals call this neat little neighborhood "Greenpernt" in true Archie Bunker fashion, but, strolling down its trim streets and the bustling "Avenue," I never caught more than a clipped "Greenp't." The white pantheon-domed bank at a pivotal location on Manhattan Avenue properly refers to itself as the Green Point Savings Bank, maintaining the area's original name. Henry Dowlowski, one of the many Polish residents I met here, said his dad nicknamed Greenpoint "Pete's Place" after the legendary district leader Peter McGuinness, who loved the community and its people and proclaimed it to be "the garden spot of the world!" True, there's the spacious, tree-filled McCarren Park at the southern end of Manhattan Avenue, dominated by the onion-domed bulk of the Russian Orthodox Cathedral of the Transfiguration (Sunday masses here are a mystical mélange of incense, lights, and somber chants), but, as

Subway: IND GG to Greenpoint Avenue (Brooklyn-Queens Crosstown) BMT
LL to Bedford Avenue
Bus: B24, B61, B62

Milton Street

for gardens, they have been filled up with row after row of Green-point's primped three- and four-story townhouses, primped and pastel-shaded in their new aluminum sidings.

A small historic district has recently been declared here, bounded by Kent, Franklin, Calyer, and Leonard streets, and the view along Milton Street to the red and white Roman Catholic Church of St. Anthony of Padua matches anything to be found in Park Slope or Brooklyn Heights.

A few larger mansions around Noble Street are reminders of the mid-1800s when the East River frontage was crammed with ship-building yards, and wealth was amassed by local entrepreneurs whose most notable creation was John Ericsson's *Monitor,* launched here on January 30, 1862. The ironclad ship's later igno-minious demise off Cape Hatteras in no way diminished the pride of Greenpoint's workers, whose descendants still frisbee and picnic around the Ericsson monument in Monsignor McGoldrick Park at Driggs Avenue and Russell Street.

The Polish spirit still flourishes: on Manhattan Avenue there's a Chopin Theater, polish sausage stores, the Poznanski bakery, and the tiny, simply furnished Baltazar Restaurant featuring an amaz-ingly inexpensive selection of stuffed cabbage, vigos, pig's knuckles, potato pancakes, pirogi, blintzes, sauerkraut and mushrooms, and a rich veal goulash. Looking north back up the avenue is the silver shrinelike Citicorp building, a striking reminder of Greenpoint's proximity to midtown Manhattan in spite of its small-town spirit.

There's nothing dramatic here; Manhattan Avenue stores are a slightly up-market variation on 14th Street, but the people are friendlier, the pace less hectic, and Poznanski's bialys are some of the best this side of the river. Give Greenpoint a try for an hour or two.

Williamsburg

Try to make two visits to this unique New York neighborhood, home of the largest concentration of Hasidic Jews outside Israel. Come first on a weekday. If the weather is pleasant, walk across the Williamsburg Bridge from Delancey Street on Manhattan's Lower East Side instead of taking the subway. Explore the scores of Hebrew-signed shops, small and cramped, many selling exotic arrays of imported foodstuffs and the most truly kosher of all kosher products in the city. Pause and snack at the equally tiny restaurants with their chicken dishes, matzoh-ball soup, and gefilte fish. Marvel at the rich displays of silver ornaments and bowls behind barred windows.

Then, on your second visit, come around dusk on a Friday evening or on a Saturday when all the stores are closed and the Satmar Jews (the most devout of all Jewish sects) celebrate their sabbath.

The heart of the district lies around Bedford Avenue and Keap Street
Subway: BMT J or M to Marcy Avenue and Broadway
Bus: B39, B53, B60, B61

The males dress in traditional black—black fur hats, long black coats gleaming as if polished, black trousers, black boots (and white socks). The regimented streets of brownstones are filled with hundreds of identically dressed Satmar males leading their sons to the synagogues. The females are less evident. A few walk together in groups, their wigs close-cropped and unstyled (according to Hasidic tradition, after marriage wives shave their heads permanently).

The unity, and uniformity, one senses reflects the philosopher Martin Buber's explanation of the messianic ideal that is the foundation of most Hasidim, including the Lubavitchers of Crown Heights and the Belz, Bobor, and Ger Hasidim of Borough Park. "This is the way of redemption: that all souls and all sparks of soul which have sprung from the primeval soul and have sunk and become scattered in all creatures at the time of the original darkening of the world or through the guilt of the ages, should conclude their wandering and return home purified. . . . He who prays and sings in holiness, eats and speaks in holiness . . . and in holiness is mindful of his business, through him the fallen sparks are raised and the fallen worlds redeemed and renewed."

Even after a dozen visits you'll continue to be amazed at the cultural purity of this tiny oasis in the vast polyglot sprawl of Brooklyn.

Fort Greene
and Clinton Hill

This area is what might officially be termed marginal, although such streets as South Portland Avenue and South Oxford Street, immediately south of Fort Greene park, are magnificent material for brownstone buffs. If Park Slope and other Brooklyn neighborhoods are any indication, the renaissance will arrive here soon.

The park itself is a shady mound topped by a monument to the martyrs who died in the British hospital ships during the Revolutionary War. A most impressive flight of stone steps rises to the column-shaped tower from the north side, and views over the city from here or from the delightful Classical-Revival conveniences are delightful. As one might expect, the park was designed by Olmsted and Vaux on the site of Old Fort Greene, a fortified hill in both the Revolutionary and 1812 wars.

Take time to explore the adjoining neighborhood of Clinton Hill,

DeKalb Avenue at Fort Greene Place
Subway: IND GG to Fulton Street and Lafayette Avenue
Bus: B19, B38, B54

Skinner House

particularly the mansion-lined Clinton Street and the Skinner House at Lafayette and Vanderbilt avenues, bedecked with an Italianate cupola and Greek-Revival trimmings on a building of Federal proportions. Also note the extravaganza of styles in the tiny carriage houses along Waverly Avenue between Gates and Myrtle avenues, and the expansive boldness of Charles Millard Pratt's House at St. Joseph's College at 241 Clinton Avenue between De-Kalb and Willoughby avenues (the ornate pergola next door is a lovely idiosyncracy on an otherwise overbearing street).

And of course you've heard of the Pratt Institute a couple of blocks to the east, but have you been there? Not only is the campus known for its public activities and exhibitions (call 718-636-3600 for details), but it is also recognized for the splendor of its Romanesque-Revival library (an 1896 William Tubby creation) and main hall. While I find much of the campus dour and dull (in spite of the architectural notables who created the individual buildings), I love the activity here—in fact this whole neighborhood is a wanderer's delight. Take a camera or sketch pad and enjoy!

Prospect Park South

A total surprise—the kind of nook nook-seekers dream of, hidden away in a largely marginal neighborhood just off Flatbush Avenue in the funky heart of Flatbush. One moment you're strolling by cut-price liquor stores and cheap furniture showrooms and then suddenly East 16th Street changes to Buckingham Road, complete with an Anglophile estate of enormous revival-style mansions set on primped lawns with streets guarded by impressive brick gateposts.

This arcadian niche, lined with maples and poplars, was created by Dean Alvord in the late 1800s, who bestowed such regal titles on the roads as Albemarle, Westminster, Argyle, Rugby, and Marlborough. Bounded by Church Avenue, Beverly Road, Coney Island Avenue, and the BMT/IND cut just south of Prospect Park, this

Subway: IND F to Church Avenue
Bus: B12, B16, B33, B35, B41

The Mansions

tranquil neighborhood is a feast of Palladian windows, Shingle-style eaves, Corinthian and Doric columns (temples galore!), terra-cotta details, Queen Anne façades, and all the wonderful extravagance of what is often known collectively as Carpenter Gothic.

Not a large area—but what a wonderful discovery!

Green-Wood Cemetery

It's worth coming here just to see Richard Upjohn's Gothic-Revival gatehouse, an incredible piece of architecture in an otherwise unimpressive part of Brooklyn. Inside the cemetery (pick up a map at the gate) one enters a bucolic environment of ever-winding roadways (twenty-two miles on 478 acres), lakes, manicured hills, and splendidly ornate mausoleums. The notables among the estimated 500,-000 burials in the cemetery include De Witt Clinton (father of the Erie Canal), Horace Greeley, the Reverend Henry Ward Beecher, Nathaniel Currier and James Ives, "Boss" Tweed, Pierre Lorillard, Duncan Phyfe, and Eliza Gilbert, better known as Lola Montez. Truly "a haven of posthumous Americana."

Green-Wood Cemetery was the precursor of New York's parks. Because of its enormous appeal as a weekend picnic area in the 1850s, William Cullen Bryant and Washington Irving stressed the

Main Entrance: Fifth Avenue at 25th Street/718-768-7300
Open daily 8 A.M.–4 P.M.
Subway: BMT RR, N to 23rd Street and Broadway
Bus: B33, B63

need for similar open areas throughout the burgeoning urban development—hence Central Park and many others.

Green-Wood is somewhat forgotten today. Come and enjoy its tranquillity. Then, by way of contrast, especially if you come around a weekday lunch hour, slip down 25th Street to Third Avenue and experience a true dockland flavor of raunchy restaurants, bars, and boisterous street-corner gatherings of waterfront workers—a bit of real New York.

Green-Wood Cemetery Gatehouse

Bay Ridge

Cut off from the rest of Brooklyn by the moatlike extension of Owls Head Park, Bay Ridge seems a place removed, a serene community of gingerbread mansions (once the homes of the tugboat barons) and quaint Revival-style row houses around Senator Street. The old Irish bars on Third, Fourth, and Fifth avenues have now received a trendy face-lift and appeal to a younger crowd of brownstone renovators—newcomers to the neighborhood. Every week there seems to be a new addition to the strip, particularly along Third Avenue in the 70s and 80s, featuring such notables as Chelsea Station, The Waiting Place, Silver Rail, Hobnails, T.J. Bentley's, Circles Bistro, Nell Flahertey's, the Greenhouse Café, Yesterday's Pub, and the charming Astor House.

Take a stroll west on Bay Ridge Avenue to the tiny pier stuck out in The Narrows. Pause awhile to relish the views of Manhattan, and

Subway: BMT RR to Bay Ridge Avenue/Fourth Avenue or 95th Street
Bus: B37, also B27 Express

then wander south through the shoreline park, admiring the great mansions around 86th Street.

In addition to enjoying the general charms of the neighborhood you can visit two of the most special stores in southern Brooklyn. Lund's (8122 Fifth Avenue) reflects the Scandinavian heritage of the community, with its whole-wheat rugbrød, Swedish limpa (orange-flavored rye bread), sweet yeast coffee breads (Christmas and Easter), a delectable array of puffy Danish pastries, and one of the most popular specialties, a Danish coffee cake laced with sweet butter known as "Seven Sisters." Nearby is Fredericksen and Johannesen at 7719 Fifth Avenue, with its own array of traditional Scandinavian meats and canned imports. Try the homemade sausages (polse or korv), fish-pudding, corned lamb, and rullepølse (a spicy meat roll made from a Danish recipe). At holiday season Kris

Johannesen gets all misty-eyed as he and his partner hang more than 500 legs of his dry-cured lamb (Fenalaar) and hams from the store ceiling. "People cry sometimes when they see the lamb. It's a very traditional dish and we do it better than anyone—or so they tell me." (Kris is a modest gentleman.) "We do a good Norwegian pork pâté too, and Servelatpolse—sort of a Swedish bologna. And we've got a good recipe for Irish black pudding and Lapskaus hash using our salt meat. I tell you—if we haven't got it right after thirty years we don't deserve to be in business!"

A relatively new attraction in Bay Ridge is the Fort Hamilton Harbor Defense Museum (entry on 101st Street at the Fort Hamilton Parkway). Relocated in 1981 from Fort Wadsworth on Staten Island, the museum is housed in the sturdy granite remnant of the 1825 fort (part of which is now an elegant officers club), and the

Bay Ridge Mansion

small collection of uniforms, guns, swords, models, and etchings gives a fascinating glimpse of military life in the nineteenth and early twentieth centuries.

The site itself is significant as the first skirmish location with the British on July 4, 1776, when a small American battery fired at the man-of-war HMS *Asia,* and inflicted damage and casualties before being silenced. Britain's full response on August 22 led to a humiliating defeat of Washington's troops in the famous Battle of Long Island; the Revolution was saved only by the general's brilliant retreat tactics in a timely fog.

The impressive line of modern antitank guns leading to the museum and its delightful hill-top park are matched only by the mammoth Civil War cannons in the park beneath the Verrazano Narrows Bridge (a short stroll along 101st Street at Fifth Avenue). New condominium developments in the area suggest a healthy revival for this prim neighborhood on the western fringe of Brooklyn.

Bensonhurst's "Little Italy"

This place deceives. At first glance Eighteenth Avenue (between 60th–85th streets) looks about the same as a score of other mainstream, middle-income commercial strips in the metropolitan area. But observe a little more closely and you'll discover an aromatic little Italian neighborhood brimming with fruit stands, salumerias, fish stores, a live poultry market, gorgeous pastry shops and bakeries, and a sense of leisurely indulgence without the hyperactivity of Manhattan's Little Italy.

"Most of 'em 'round here are from the south y'know—Puglia, Sicily—the foot-bit of the boot. They don't move so quick like they do 'round Roma and Milano—they take it easy, enjoy life." So said Charlie Gieri on a visit to the Bari Pork Store, where you can barely see the staff behind the cascades of sausages, salamis, provolones, strips of sun-dried tomatoes, and plump little bundles of homemade mozzarellas. Bari seems to be taking over the strip—I counted four different stores here on my last visit.

Subway: BMT B or N to Eighteenth Avenue at 64th Street or 86th Street
Bus: B8

Nearby is the grandly styled Café Mille Luce, serving excellent espresso and cappuccino to wash down John Gentile's delectable brioce, pesche (tiny circular pastries flavored with peach liqueur and topped with dollops of apricot puree), and melt-in-your-mouth cannoli. He also makes some of Brooklyn's best gelati in the summer. For a more substantial snack, try the deep-fried calamari, mussels in marinara sauce, and arincini (tiny deep-fried balls of rice) at the Focacceria snack bar, or indulge in more formal Italian repast at the small and intimate Il Grottino. But always try to keep a little extra room for snacking as you discover Angelo's Salumeria, the Alba Italian Pastry Shoppe, and Bendetto Togati's Eighteenth Avenue Bakery, famous for authentic lard bread, crammed with offcuts of salami and cheese.

Bensonhurst—I'll be back.

Brighton Beach

The signs reads: "Zydyes Gavaryat Parusski" and it's absolutely true. Russian is indeed spoken fluently in more than half the stores down Brighton Beach Avenue, and spoken with such speed, gusto, and grit that most conversations sound like the final volleys of unsuccessful nuclear disarmament negotiations. Auditory counterpoint comes from the subway cars clanging and clattering a few feet above the sidewalks on the ancient el, which keeps the avenue in a perpetual state of murk. So what with the murk, the din, the constant guttural chatter, and the crazy traffic, you may wonder why I bother to visit, and particularly to revisit this Little Odessa-by-the-Sea just down the road from Coney Island, time and time again.

Well, the reasons are simple enough, I suppose. I love the place. I love the large Russian ladies in headscarves with gold teeth and bulging Naugahyde shopping bags; I love the Russian fisherman with a huge moustache who sets up an instant fish market on the

Subway: IND D, BMT QB or M to Brighton Beach or Ocean Parkway
(The bus takes far too long from just about anywhere!)

Under the El

sidewalk and sells out in six minutes; I love Mrs. Stahl's knishes, especially the spinach and the mushroom-potato; I love the fur-swathed old grandmothers sitting on cheap fold-up garden chairs and staring at the ocean for hours on a freezing day when even the seagulls huddle together under the boardwalk; and I love the National Restaurant, where you can cram three hundred overweight, vodka-filled torsos onto the dance floor after a wedding-binge of endless platters of cold meats, pickles, pirogen, kishkes, and varencki.

And if that isn't enough: I love Misha and Luba Fidler's Gastronom Moscow on the boardwalk (end of Brighton 6th Street), where the older emigrees play dominoes and drink kvass, a strange-tasting concoction made from fermented black bread; I love the blue, silver, and red riot of the Primorski Restaurant where servings of Georgian chicken, "chakhombili," mutton soup, and sturgeon steaks are "as big as Buba" Khotovliga, the owner (wonderful appetizers here, too —and it's all so reasonable, including the liter carafes of ice-thickened vodka); and I love Nadler's self-service kosher meat store where everything looks so authentic.

More than 20,000 Russians now live in or around Brighton Beach, and recent waves of immigration have created a few local problems. The Orthodox Jewish population, who frequent their favorite kosher places—Nadler's, Feldman's, and Schechter's—find the pork- and sausage-laden Russian stores offensive; neighborhood Hispanics claim "the visitors" attack them for chatting up the Russian girls and for invading the heart of "New Moscow," around Brighton 6th Street. There have even been police investigations of the "Russian Mafia," and occasional rumors of KGB cadres among the emigrees.

But overall, the place has certainly improved in recent years; the Brighton Beach Baths and Racquet Club is always packed, and the new Seacoast Tower condominium project is a harbinger of a promising future. Even the once-cramped International Food Store has doubled in size, offering dozens of different types of smoked fish, caviars, dried meats, and wizened sausages, along with enormous domes of black bread and a whole upper floor devoted to chocolates, cookies, European preserves, and cakes.

So—go and enjoy Brighton Beach, particularly during weekends when nightclubs rock until the early hours and the glamorous Odessa, Primorski, and Zodiac restaurants glitter. And don't neglect the appetizers of marinated eggplant, plums with walnuts, pickled vegetables, pirogen, smoked sturgeon, Georgian sausage—all washed down with waterfalls of iced vodka. Marvelous!

Astoria

It seems that every time I come to this neighborhood of tidy, tiny homes and clean sidewalks, the old Greek spirit, for which it was once so famous, seems just a little more diminished. But don't be too disheartened—there are still enough coffeehouses (kaffenion), pastry shops, and tavernas along 31st Street from Broadway to Ditmars Boulevard to make exploration worthwhile.

Actually, if you leave the subway at 36th Avenue and 31st Street you can start at one of the neighborhood's newer attractions, the Kaufman Astoria Studios. This fifteen-acre spread of low white-washed buildings (35th Avenue between 34th and 38th streets) was once the hub—"The Big House"—of the New York film industry. Ten years ago the place was a disaster zone; even though the Army used it for scores of propaganda films during World War II, it never recovered from a 1932 bankruptcy. Long gone were the days in the twenties when Famous Players–Lasky (later Paramount Pictures) turned out scores of silent movies, and a respectable number of

Subway: BMT QB or RR to Broadway or Ditmars Boulevard and 31st Street

sound features starring such legends as Rudolf Valentino, Edward G. Robinson, Ginger Rogers, W.C. Fields, the Marx Brothers, and even the extravagant Tallulah Bankhead who, according to Broadway director George Abbott, insisted on daily "milk baths" at the studio. Gloria Swanson loved the place, thriving on "the free spirits, defectors, and refugees who were all trying to get away from Hollywood and its restrictions. There was a wonderful sense of revolution and innovation in the studio in Queens."

But, for over fifty years, Hollywood dominated and Astoria was forgotten. Then, in 1973, the Army donated the property to CUNY who, along with a local city planner, Glenn Ralston, managed to have it classified as a landmark and persuaded Sidney Lumet to make his $24 million musical, *The Wiz*, here in 1978. This was followed by *Hair; Eyewitness; Fort Apache; The Bronx; Arthur;* and *The World According to Garp*. Thanks to the enthusiastic financial support of George Kaufman and his group of well-heeled film-folk investors, the place now appears to have a rosy future. At the moment there's a small museum of posters, film equipment, costumes, set designs, and inexpensive video screenings (call 718-784-4520 for details), but if fund-raising plans are successful, 1987 will see the opening of the ambitious American Museum of the Moving Image (AMMI), and Astoria will once again be on the movie-fans' map.

Until then you can amuse yourself with a stroll up 31st Street past the St. Demetrios Greek Orthodox Church, the Lefkos Pirgos "Kaffenion," the Vedeta restaurant, and numerous psistarias and tavernas (the names keep changing) where you pick and choose aromatic dishes from altarlike steam tables. On Ditmars Boulevard you'll find a couple of excellent Greek food stores and restaurants featuring quail, pheasant, octopus, baby lamb, and pungent goat meat dishes.

Then take an after-dinner stroll down the boulevard to the East River and the verdant Astoria Park, rolling and wooded beneath the enormous piers of the Triboro Bridge, where people enjoy an almost ritual summer evening "passeo" alongside the fast-moving waters of Hell Gate.

An alternative for night-life lovers is the Grecian Cave (31–11 Broadway; 718-545-7373), a lively spot for belly dancing and real

Greek entertainment back down 31st Street. And a final suggestion: for a real introduction to Greek customs and traditions, try to attend Astoria's Greek Festival, usually held in early May. It's a fabulous three-day panorama of dances, weddings, theater, and food galore! Call 718-222-0550 for details.

Long Island City

"A couple of years from now, you won't recognize the old place." That was Long Island City resident Dick Davis speaking five years ago, and I've been back and back and back and—well—I'm still awaiting the transformation. The old warehouses, chemical plants, and factories continue to clutter the East River waterfront; vacant lots speckle the tiny community; and some of the dusty stores along Vernon Boulevard and 21st Street are right out of a Jacob Riis scrapbook.

Yet there are some signs of change. PS1 (Jackson Avenue and 21st Street) has been converted from a school into artists' lofts, and the exhibition space is usually open to the public (Thursday–Sunday 1–6 P.M. Contribution.). The International Design Center opened in October 1985 and will eventually provide over a million square feet of home furnishings showrooms, primarily for the trade. And sculptor Isamu Noguchi, famous for his vermilion cube outside the Ma-

Subway: Flushing #7 train/LIRR to Hunters Point Avenue Station
Bus: X18, X20, X24, X51

rine Midland Bank in downtown Manhattan, invites everyone to his studio and adjoining Oriental gardens on Vernon Boulevard.

According to Linda Henley, director of the Long Island City Business Development Corporation, these are only the first petals of a brilliant flowering: "It's really going to skyrocket here with the Citibank project for a forty-six-story office tower on Jackson Avenue, the Redstone Rocket building next to the Design Center, and the Port Authority's Hunters Point development project. Already we've got two hundred artists living here—not bad in a community of 2,000 families. More galleries are opening, too, and Silver Cup movie studios are starting an Off-Broadway theater here soon and then there's . . ."

Well, okay. But meanwhile there are always the restaurants in the Hunters Point section—the fishnet-adorned Waterfront Crabhouse and Prudenti's across the street from one another at Borden and 2nd Street, Manducati's popular family-style trattoria at Jackson and 47th Street, and The Water's Edge, a refined, up-market establishment on the waterfront at 44th Drive, featuring a chef from La Côte Basque, a marina, and spectacular vistas of midtown.

There's a long way to go yet in Long Island City's renaissance, but if the recent restorations of the little townhouses on 45th Avenue between 21st–23rd streets and the new East River tennis clubs are any indication, this place has an exciting—and intriguing—future. Watch out for it.

Roosevelt Avenue

This began as a short piece on the blarney and Black 'n' Tan traditions of Irish Woodside, all around the Guinness-lovers nexus of 61st Street and Roosevelt Avenue. But then it became very apparent that for every Irish Pony, Blackthorne, and Hanlon's Bar, there were an equal number of Korean and Japanese establishments—I even lunched on tempura in a converted Irish tavern, where pseudo half-timbered walls and stained-glass shamrocks in the window clashed valiantly with paper lanterns and a pristine sushi bar!

Even farther east along Roosevelt Avenue, in the heart of Latino Jackson Heights around 82nd Street, Oriental restaurants, and new Italian places proliferate, along with an Irish nightclub in glaring green and white stucco, The Esmeralda Salon (the word "saloon" still seems taboo in some neighborhoods).

So, forget trying to label neighborhoods—they're changing so fast here that the labels are outdated as soon as they're invented. In-

Subway: IRT 7
Bus: M32, Q18, Q29, Q45, Q53

stead, enjoy the raucous riot of Roosevelt from 56th–86th streets, with the el screeching and clattering an inch or two above your skull and food galore all the way down the strip—Donovan's wonderful beef and kidney pies and roast lamb, excellent Spanish dishes at El Inca and Flamingo, strange Argentinian and Colombian snacks at tiny storefront niches, including chorizos, tamales, pasteles, empanadas, plantanos fritos, and papas rellenas, and a plethora of new Korean, Chinese, and Japanese places. One Irish tavern, The Fiddle and Bow, went topless "to let them know we're still around," but in Gaels and Dillons and Finnegans you can almost feel the stoop-shouldered customers, crouched over their stouts and Murphy's, dreading the day when their beloved shepherd's pie will be transformed into seaweed-bound cylinders of sushi.

Another Guinness, Charlie. Quick.

Forest Hills Gardens

Past the odd towered and turreted Forest Hills Inn, where visiting tennis stars once stayed during tournaments at the nearby Forest Hills Tennis Stadium, is a unique housing development of curving streets and large shade trees—a convincing replica of an English village. Grosvenor Atterbury, the designer, and Frederick Law Olmsted, Jr., the landscape architect, were inspired by the "Garden Cities" movement which, during the twenties, was considered an ideal way to relocate low-income families from the slums of English cities. The philanthropic Mrs. Russell Sage had a similar idea here when she initiated the project, but by 1923 the development had become fashionable, attracting many notable residents.

Stroll down Deepdene, along Beech Knoll and Ivy Close. All that's missing from the picture is a herd of cows on their way to milking and a village pub near the green, although Beefsteak

Enter under LIRR bridge by Forest Hills Station (Seventy-first Avenue and Greenway Terrace)
Subway: IND E, F, GG, N to Forest Hills/Queens Boulevard
Bus: Q23, Q60

Forest Hills Inn

Charlie's in the old Forest Hills Inn is a plausible substitute. The adjoining commercial strip under the railroad bridge (the cobbled plaza here feels like a comic-opera set) is known locally as "the village" (alias Austin Street), and has become quite a sophisticated niche of pretty gift shops, restaurants, boutiques, and fancy-food places in the last few years.

Pause here awhile.

Alley Pond Park and Douglas Manor

What a welcome relief! Way out in Queens, among the seemingly endless tract house blocks of Bayside, Bellerose, and Little Neck, comes this narrow stretch of ponds, reed-forests, creeks, woodlands, and winding pathways.

The main "Environmental Center" on Northern Boulevard (Open Tuesday–Saturday 9 A.M.–5 P.M. Free) is a schoolkid's paradise, full of live snakes and turtles in glass tanks, displays of stuffed birds, and abundant hands-on material. Enthusiastic volunteers offer Sunday nature tours at 1 P.M., plus a wealth of workshops, concerts, botanical safaris, and birdwalks. Pick up a trail guide with a choice of the modest quarter-mile Cattail Pond Trail, the two-mile Pitobik Wetland Trail around Alley Creek, and, for the dedicated, a four-mile odyssey under a tangle of expressways and parkways,

Subway and Bus: IRT #7 Flushing subway to Main Street, Flushing (the last stop); Q12 bus from Main and Roosevelt Avenue along Northern Boulevard to the first stop after the Cross Island Parkway overpass
Rail: LIRR to Douglaston station; walk south to Northern Boulevard and turn right to the Alley Pond center

south through woods, to the Alley Pond Nature Center off Grand Central Parkway.

On a good day you'll see turtles, toads, rabbits, maybe an opossum or two, blue herons, and hundreds of migrating birds during the fall season, and best of all, you'll lose yourself (literally, if you're not a careful trail-spotter) in a slice of old Long Island, the way it looked long before the suburban sprawl. (Call 718-229-4000 for details on weekly activities and special events and festivals.)

You get the same feeling at the nearby Queens County Farm Museum (73–50 Little Neck Parkway in Floral Park—ask directions at the nature center) located on a forty-seven-acre tract of undisturbed farmland adjoining the Creedmoor Psychiatric Center. The main attraction is the restored farmhouse, built around 1770 and expanded in the mid-1800s, and an array of volunteer-run agricultural projects. But a glance at the calendar of events will show you that this is a real community center with a series of fireside concerts in the farmhouse, American Indian dance competitions, craft courses and fairs, concerts, an annual Bluegrass festival, and a full schedule of children's events (call 718-468-4355 for details).

And finally, if you happen to arrive in this part of Queens by car or are returning to the city via the LIRR, take a stroll along the posh streets of secluded Douglas Manor (immediately north of the station). Here's a glimpse of how the other .0001 percent of New Yorkers live, peering out over Little Neck Bay and Long Island Sound from porticoed verandahs and between huge old chestnuts and oak trees shading billiard-table lawns. Wander along Bayshore Boulevard, past enormous Tudor, Victorian, and Colonial mansions, and even several contemporary newcomers, adorned with trellised arbors, perky gazebos, and "Patrolled by Our Own Police" signs. The huge colonnaded Douglaston Club peers pompously down at the bay where residents (only) promenade on the short pier on summer evenings, and seagulls skim the shallows as the sun descends behind La Guardia Airport.

Douglas Manor

Hoboken

Okay—so we're cheating a little here, stretching the boundaries a bit to encompass the tiny "Mile-Square City" of Hoboken, just across the Hudson River, and within shouting distance of the World Trade Center. But here's the reason.

Ten years ago, hardly anyone in Manhattan knew or cared that this dreary, depressed enclave of Italians, Irish, and Germans was once a vibrant port, railhead, and cultural nexus filled with theaters, gardens, amusement parks, and rows of refined neo-Georgian townhouses. They called it the "Seacoast of Bohemia" in its heyday, when P.T. Barnum held his "Buffalo Hunts" in the Elysian Fields, and Cronheim's Theatre, near the Germania Gardens, offered some of the best music hall entertainment in the northeast. But, as New York City became the hub of the region, Hoboken and nearby Jersey City sank into anonymity. Occasionally, the faded little town

PATH Subway from limited stops in Manhattan to Hoboken (West 33rd Street at Herald Square; West 14th Street at Sixth Avenue; West 9th Street at Sixth Avenue; Christopher Street at Hudson, and the World Trade Center)

would be remembered in conversation as "Frank Sinatra's birth-place," or as the home of a famous, if funky, seafood bar and restaurant, The Clam Broth House. Nothing more.

Well—today all that has changed. In the last five years Hoboken has become a vibrant offspring of mother-Manhattan, attracting hundreds of the young and affluent who flow, lemminglike, every evening from the great portals of the Erie-Lackawanna station (still a wonderful extravaganza of ornate green copper façades, stained-glass ceilings, and Art Nouveau signs) and down the tight grid of narrow streets to refurbished brownstones, row houses, and lofts—wave after wave of trenchcoats and slim leather briefcases.

"And you ain't even seen the start yet," one real estate broker told me smugly from behind his new desk, in his new office, in yet one more newly renovated building with highlighted Victorian detail-ing. "Wait till they develop the waterfront proper—Baltimore Har-bor twice over! It's happening all the way along the Hudson from Jersey City to Edgewater—they call it "The Gold Coast"—but Hoboken's your key spot. Places you wouldn't have been seen dead in awhile back, now you've got one-bedrooms going for four times what they were three years ago—$150,000 may get you a small place in a row house with no view and a twenty-minute walk to the PATH. Sometimes I don't believe it myself!" (But the way he chor-tled and played with his gold bracelet, it was obvious he found the suspension of disbelief an easy task.)

Beautiful mansions and Georgian townhouses line sections of Hudson Street and gather in clusters adjoining the Stevens Institute of Technology set on its rocky campus overlooking the Hudson. But the real heart of the neighborhood is around the station, near the Clam Broth House, where new chic bar-restaurants like Riverstreet and the superb Hunan Dynasty meld comfortably with such basic traditional taverns as the Irish House and old worn-out rooming hotels crying out for renovation.

The wide and often imposing Washington Street is the spine of Hoboken, stretching the mile-long length of the city from the station to 14th Street at the northern city limit. Here you see neighborhood history writ-clear in a range of bars and restaurants that would cheer the most jaded of Manhattanites—everything from traditionals like Helmer's, famous for Germanic food and flavor, The Elysian Café, with its authentic 1930s decor, and a scattering of old Italian trattorias, to superb French cuisine at The Brass Rail, poetry, jazz, and films at the artsy Maxwell's, lovely stained-glass ceiling and old saloon charm at the Madison, incredible forty-eight-ounce steaks at Arthur's, music and theater at Beat'n Path, sumptuous Italian dishes at the new DaVinci, Mexican fare at East L.A., New Mexican cuisine at The Gold Coast, and a chic-mod mood at Hudson Stakes. And there are more places opening all the time, along with new boutiques, gourmet stores, excellent bakeries, and an exhilarating spirit of fast-paced renaissance. Even Frank Sinatra's birthplace, just around the corner from Anthony's, another excellent Italian restaurant at 5th Street and Monroe, is at the hub of a surprising renewal of one of Hoboken's most marginal neighborhoods.

But all this change doesn't come without problems; there are unpleasant growing pains in this tight little town. Longtime residents often object vehemently to the rapid influx of the young and affluent, and the numerous suspicious fires are thought by many to be the work of greedy landlords anxious to remove old tenants. Political corruption also plagues local administrations and elections as it has for decades along the Jersey waterfront, and a few of the store owners find themselves disenchanted with the newcomers. "They use the town like a dormitory," one told me. "They don't buy here, they don't eat here. They're still New Yorkers in their heads."

But do come and explore the place. If you're one of those New Yorkers hanging onto the ancient myths about New Jersey, Hoboken may convince you that all the hype about the Hudson River "Gold Coast" isn't so zany after all. They're finding new nuggets here every day!

Sandy Hook

After Hoboken, we're really stretching the limit of our exploration, but this wild promontory of dunes and beach is, after all, part of the Gateway National Recreation Area (and on a clear day you can see the towers of Manhattan). Jamaica Bay is the featured attraction, but Sandy Hook is well worth a visit to enjoy over eight miles of beaches and sheltered bayside coves, hundreds of acres of "ecologically significant" barrier beach vegetation, the oldest operational lighthouse in America, a magnificent holly forest, and, at the northern end, the land, facilities, and fortifications of the Fort Hancock complex.

The "Hook" occupies more than 1,600 acres of barrier peninsula reaching northward from the New Jersey coast into New York Harbor. Sand dunes protect portions of Sandy Hook uplands

Train: NY and Long Branch Railroad to Red Bank, then Boro bus 4 to Highlands
Bus: NY—Keansburg—Long Branch Bus Co. from New York City to Highlands
Car: Garden State Parkway or US 9 and NJ 35 south to NJ 36 to park
(Call 201-872-0092 for details and special events information)

341

against sea winds and enable the growth of plant life, which culminates in a holly forest unsurpassed on the eastern seaboard.

Spermaceti Cove Visitor Center, located two miles inside the park entrance, is open daily from 8 A.M. to 5 P.M., with an exhibit room of photos, paintings, artifacts, live animals, and a regular slide show. Free tours of Fort Hancock and natural areas such as the holly forest are offered daily during the summer, along with puppet shows for the young.

It's a good place to end all of these nook-and-cranny explorations snuggled in the sandy dunes or stretched out on a Caribbean-like strand, with seagulls soaring overhead and all the cacophony and crises of city-life left behind, way over the horizon.

Enjoy.

Index